SHADOW OF
THE STORM

SHADOW OF THE STORM

My Life with
Rubin "Hurricane" Carter

Violet
Rutherford

FCP

Full Court Press
Englewood Cliffs, New Jersey

First Edition

Copyright © 2013 by Violet Ruherford

Published in the United States of America
by Full Court Press, 601 Palisade Avenue
Englewood Cliffs, NJ 07632
www.fullcourtpressnj.com

ISBN 978-1-938812-32-3
Library of Congress Control No. 2015938888

Book Design by Barry Sheinkopf for Bookshapers
(www.bookshapers.com)

Cover Photograph, "Storm, Bovina Center, 2006,"
courtesy Barry Sheinkopf

Colophon by Liz Sedlack

TO MY CHILDREN, DEJA AND RANDOL
for the inspiration they've given me

ACKNOWLEDGMENTS

I want to thank Barry Sheinkopf, of Bookshapers.com, for making this experience of publishing a book memorable. Thanks to all the friends who were supportive, and encouraged me, and were an integral part of my life. Special thanks as well go to Kathy and Paul Kaurtheauser, Barbara Faine, Eugenia Koukounas, and Rubin "Hurricane" Carter. I feel fortunate that I had the chance to know what it means to have a soul mate—spirituality not felt on this Earth by many, a purpose and closeness, a love, the kind that is nearest to God's love. We can all spare ourselves those questions that start with "why"; what we call living is all part of God's plan.

FOREWORD

I OFTEN WONDER IF SOME MYSTICAL force settled around East Rutherford, New Jersey, as a blessing when I came into this world, or the foul swamp fumes that hovered over the town were actually a curse. Either or both could have settled my fate.

My earliest recollection is of a sandy-brown shingled one-family home on Cornelia Street. A four-family dwelling, the homes sat side by side, ours at one of the ends with a large playground on the side. Living on the end made me feel fortunate, because when the two families in the middle did or said anything, everybody else could hear it.

Tall, dark-green stairs led to a small porch with a white-and-green jalousie and aluminum roof covering. A large, sprawling backyard behind the houses stretched from end to end. Tables and chairs, a barbecue grill, and a ping-pong table stood underneath a big oak that always reminded me of Jack and the Beanstalk, it was so huge. (One summer during a terrible rainstorm, that tree was struck by lightning and split in two. It felt to me like an omen.) Red brick ran around the base of the house, enclosing a dusty and dirty basement that was hardly used.

All of the houses perched high; rumor had it the stairs had been built that way for when the swamp rose. It was in that worn-out two-bedroom building we would now call a townhouse that my life began.

When you entered the house, brown stairs led you to the upstairs rooms. There, a narrow door put you in the first bedroom: two twin beds, one in front of a window, the other up against a small closet that had been built and attached to the wall, poorly painted with a sliding yellow latch door and lime green borders. Over each window, thin white curtains hung all year round.

The linoleum floor covering featured game boards: checkers, chess,

Chinese checkers, nursery rhymes, things like that.

Near the closet, a square had been cut into the floor to capture the heat that rose from the stove below, to heat all rooms upstairs. Another doorway led to a second room that took you around to a large open closet, clothes, and a small mattress on the floor; from there you could walk through to a hallway that had a handmade coat rack of unpainted plywood with nails used for hooks with dangling coats, and that led you back to the brown stairs.

Our bathroom was downstairs and reminded me of a large outhouse attached to the main building. Before entering it, you passed a pantry where pots, pans, and canned or boxed groceries were kept. Anything that needed to stay cold went into the pantry, especially during the winter months, because if the temperature fell below 30°, things would freeze, including the pipes in the bathtub and toilet, guaranteed.

The living room consisted of mix-and-match furniture—two full-size sofa beds side by side, one gold, with red-and-orange stitched lines, the other covered with a dark brown couch cover. Long heavy gold drapes hung over the windows each winter, and, in the spring, thin blue or green ones.

In my community, fidelity was an intensely promoted attribute, though it harbored its share of failures; and I dreamed of growing up to pledge my love to someone who did the same. As children we sat around fantasizing about what we wanted to be when we grew up. Communities of families encouraged, and reared, their children to abide by certain acceptable norms.

I monitored the relationships of people around me, fighting to find and develop the perfect model for myself, then begin the long search for an equitable love.

The climate of the times when I grew up, in the early sixties, was explosive. Integration laws had just started to be put into force, school systems had to be integrated, white neighborhoods had to fill a quota with people of color, and the job market had to open opportunities as well. And parents disciplined their children with whatever method they felt necessary.

Like most families, mine had been raised in the Church. Everyone, with the exception of my grandmother and mother, went to church each Sunday. Those two would attend on holidays and on special occasions. In church we were taught values and morals. From childhood, I sought to exemplify those lessons and qualities that became personal to me.

As my little life was being shaped, President John F. Kennedy was shot. I was in grammar school, feeling the nation's sorrow in my heart, as well as an unnerving sense of insecurity. The sun was shining brightly that day. Suddenly, fast gray clouds appeared in the sky, out of nowhere; at that moment, we were told of his death. It was a profound betrayal for a nation that had promoted such high standards of trust and anticipation. What a broken promise, I thought.

It was the era of Martin Luther King and his followers, the freedom fighters who marched for justice. James Brown was singing, "Say It Loud, I'm Black and I'm Proud." Spirituality soared in the air, creating funk music, tunes that turned images into sounds that spoke of the times. I was thrilled by all of it.

EAST RUTHERFORD WAS SEVERAL MILES long; as children, we walked from one end of it to the other. On the east end lay the swamps, where I lived; on the west end, the Polish community, where there was no one of color.

Growing up in a predominately white environment in the sixties was difficult, since I couldn't escape feeling uncomfortable because of the racial attitudes. We were fortunate to share the same equal education as white children, along with having the best supermarkets and malls at our disposal.

Environmentally, we lived around toxic fumes and mosquito spray. Each summer the children in our neighborhood jumped for joy seeing clouds approaching in the distance as the mosquito truck drove down the street, spraying thick clouds.

"Hey, here comes the truck!" we yelled.

"Yeah!" We all would run from all directions toward the street.

"Here it comes! Here it comes!"

We ran out behind the mosquito truck as it sprayed fumes and passed. White clouds rising everywhere made us feel as if we were walking in the clouds. We didn't realize how harmful this was to our health until years later.

Sometimes, on very hot summer nights, the smell of the swamp, which would exude for hours, crept into your home as well. We weren't fortunate enough to have an air conditioner, only screened windows that stayed open. Even if you could close them, the smell was overbearing; the odor crept in through the cracks.

The borough, part of Bergen County, indeed made local and national headlines several times. Its high school, Becton Regional, took up an entire block, acres of school built on top of the swamp that sat across the street from my house. I could roll out of bed and land onto the large, long green field.

Becton's championship basketball team was led by Dick Vitale, the famous basketball sports commentator. Our basketball team was led by the late star of the team, Leslie Cason, who I believe also had some type of evil spell cast on him growing up there. A documentary was done about him and his career after a troubled life that led to his death.

The school, also known for being one of the first in the state that drug-tested its students, made headlines for that. Later the town became nationally known for its sports complex, which houses the Giant Stadium, the race track, and the Continental Arena that houses the New Jersey Nets.

LIFE ISN'T ALWAYS GOING TO turn out the way you, or those with whom you exchange the most intimate trust, have imagined. Destiny appears to be altered when free will is imposed upon it. Our hopes and dreams for the future are often shattered by our inability to be faithful, though in the midst of the despair that surrounds broken dreams lurks a very quiet lesson.

The benefits I've gained from what I've gone through have helped me grow spiritually, and my womanhood has become more centered. This book is a true account of a series of startling realizations about personal experiences that resemble a hurricane. Beginning, as a hurricane does, in warm tropical waters, often with wind factors escalating to 150 miles an hour or more, its calm eye is surrounded by high whirling winds. It builds up and heads towards land, destroying anything in its path, accompanied by heavy gales and high tides. This is a pretty good metaphor for my relationship with Rubin Hurricane Carter.

Some people view him as a symbol of justice and a martyr for righteousness. He's a man, certainly, with a gift for crafting words, and readers' thoughts, with great precision—possessing the potential to direct masses of people. His life was turned upside down by an injustice perpetrated on our legal system that accused him of a triple murder. (Justice frequently appears to be manufactured and distributed, intentionally or not, for the occasion, leaving you to wade through an ocean of sorrow, often without a life vest.)

The younger generation may look at Rubin Carter as a leader for justice, a true black man, and an African American hero. They picture his torture and injustice as they reflect on their community and recognize how fortunate they are to have escaped that kind of treatment.

Rubin and I shared a different sort of justice—a relationship that was inevitable, formed as in the calm of the hurricane's eye. As I seek to catalog and coin the experience, it assumes the proportions of a real melodrama.

It was certainly nothing unique; millions have crossed the same threshold in their lives. I've found encouragement in the testimonies of the sisterhood who paint vivid portraits of how they have shared my experience. I've discovered that I'm not alone in this way by listening to them. I had a fairly typical extended affair.

Though I've survived, believing anything is possible, I still feel compelled to share my story with others who may be groping about in the darkness of their own pain, encouraging those who're maybe traveling on the same road. Hopefully, a small lesson from my story will brighten your path.

My intentions are open: I'm not seeking to destroy anyone, only to realize this is how my destiny was shaped for me. I hold only myself and Providence accountable. Nor do I lack a conscience, prepared to sacrifice anything for its brilliance—I'm merely a woman who has gone through a mythic moment on the threshold of the new millennium.

It's hardly my desire either to paint a despicable portrait of a man who may have willfully designed and plotted my pain, and who was more than capable of doing so if he so desired. On the contrary; I want to focus on the quality of what we shared, which has had a great impact on my life, and on the man behind the Hurricane Carter image.

I

THE EARLY YEARS

FELT ALL MY GRANDMOTHER EVER did when I grew up was humiliate, defame, or complain about me, especially when she come in from the bar on weekends, around three in the morning, with bags full of White Castle burgers.

Nana yelled up the stairs, her voice alluring, "Kids, come downstairs! slamming the front door behind her.

"What does she want now?" I asked my sister as I looked at the clock. "She's crazy waking us up at this time!"

In her flowered night gown, my sister ran over to the square hole in the floor and looked down. "She has White Castles." We thought that was great, and we'd jump out of our beds as the aroma rose from below.

". . .Oh!" I danced on top of the bed as my sister watched with a wide grin on her face. Our brother would run into the room and join us.

"Okay!" we yelled.

We ran downstairs in our pajamas and took our places around the kitchen table that sat six, reaching for burgers, onion rings, milk shakes, sodas, and French fries. The kitchen was painted a lime green; in a corner, on my right, was a yellow-and-lime-green-framed dish cabinet built into the side of the wall, with a deep shelf on the bottom, and next to it a white refrigerator.

On the opposite side, where my sister and brother sat, was an old double steel sink where we took baths as smaller children, until they were able to afford a regular sink and fix the bathroom. Next to that were the hot water heater and a stove. The floors were covered with blue indoor-outdoor carpeting, and a ceiling light hung in the center of the table. There we sat, eating our burgers.

"Thanks, Nana," we said, my sister, brother, and I.

"You're welcome," she said as her alcohol breath perfumed the air.

Aunt Judy, a plump but shapely five-footer in her early fifties with a golden brown complexion and black shoulder-length hair, climbed out of her sofa bed in a long flannel nightgown and took a seat on the edge, slipping her feet into a pair of slippers. Standing five feet tall she reached over in the corner for a TV tray, set it up, and scurried into the kitchen, snatching some burgers and a drink. Whenever she ate, she'd shake her left leg and have a smile on her face.

Because Nana was drunk, she expressed herself more freely about what we children hadn't done around the place. She lifted her eyes towards me. "You better get your ass up tomorrow morning and do those dishes."

The alcohol stench overwhelmed me as her breath passed by my nose. I looked over at the sink full of tableware. We always had loads of dishes, because eight people ate there twice a day. The women in that house waited on my uncles hand and foot, as if they were kings.

I stuffed French fries in my mouth. "I did them yesterday."

"I don't give a damn when you did them. You better have them done in the morning."

"It's not my week to do dishes. It's your daughter's turn."

"You kids don't do a damn thing around here but get on my damn nerves," she said.

"Yeah," my mother added with a grin on her face.

"What do you do?" I said to her in a snotty voice.

She jumped up from her chair. "I'll smack the shit out of you."

"Yeah? I don't think so. You don't even work, so why don't you do them like you're supposed to?" I asked. I had no respect for my mother because of the way she treated me.

"You better do those fuckin' dishes!" my grandmother shouted.

Tears ran down my face. "I'm not a slave."

My mother stood over me, looking down over my shoulder. "I'll slap the shit out of you, girl, if you don't shut up!"

I got up from the table and stomped up the stairs to my room, shouting, "One day I'm going to get away from here and never come back."

"Good! You can leave now!" my grandmother shouted.

Sometimes I felt as if I was just a house girl they kept around for the express purpose of serving those queens who'd passed the age of twenty-one; they rang, and I went.

THAT WAS THE FEMALE TRIO of my childhood—Nana, my grandmother; Marilyn, my mother; and Great-Aunt Judy. (My mother was an only child, though we were told to call a number of people "aunt" and "uncle".)

Most of us can understand the pitfalls of abiding in a home full with women—especially for me, the oldest female child as I was. I'd only spoken to my father once because I thought I wanted to meet him, but I had never met or spoken to my own father, Alfred Boswell, again. Apparently, before my birth, both my mother and father felt it would be to their advantage to dissolve their relationship, a decision evidently made without considering its impact upon my life. It inaugurated a pattern of neglect and ungraciousness that has followed me through my life. I've often wondered whether, in doing what they did, they cast an evil spell on my entire future.

Alfred had relationships with both my mother and her cousin. Not only did he date both, but both of them became pregnant by him around the same time, which left me with a cousin who is also my brother. While I was attending college, this young man, who'd played with me all my life, told me all about it. When conversations come up about him, I'd see the family cringe when I called him my cousin-brother; they'd flip.

From that moment on, in any case, other people's decisions have poorly influenced my life and future. A mere sentence to a future in a broken home can be disastrous, topped by a mother who cares very little about her own child.

At the age of seventeen I got pregnant—I hadn't wanted to follow in my mother's footsteps, but it happened; she'd had me around the age of twenty-one. Living at home at eighteen was difficult, of course, especially with a child, but I didn't have much of a choice. It enabled me to go on with my own life as I wanted, have tutors and the opportunity to finish high school, which I did three months after my son was born.

WHEN MY MOTHER FOUND OUT I was with child, she freaked. The night before she heard the news, I'd been over a friend's house discussing it. One of our cousins, a sister to the one who had been pregnant with my brother-cousin, was there. Bookie, a light-skinned, shapely, attractive woman of mixed Italian and black blood—as many of the women in the family were—had long, shiny brown hair, but she was an alcoholic, over-heard my conversation.

The next morning, as I lay in bed, the phone rang around 8:00 AM. I heard it because our rooms were close, and I knew it was big-mouth Bookie. My mother said, "Hello? . . . What? Uh-huh." She hung up and yelled, "Jan, come here now!" She knew. I jumped up and slipped through the narrow doorway. She was sitting up in the bed, her black framed glasses hung from her nose, and the covers were thrown over her legs. Giving me her evil look she asked. "Are you pregnant?

I hesitated. ". . . Yeah." Why lie? She knew already.

Frowning, she said, "When were you going to say something?"

"I don't know. You were my age when you had me. What's the big deal? I made a mistake."

Her eyes got wide. "You better keep quiet," she said. I turned away to return to my bed. She yelled, "You're going to get a tutor for school while you're home, too!"

That day she called one of her male friends and asked him if he'd drive us to White Plains, New York, to the Berkley School of Business, sometime that week. I didn't understand why there, except that she did-n't want people to know I was pregnant. They couldn't tell yet, though I was five months gone. Besides, I always wore a big army jacket, so you couldn't tell.

Several weeks later, one sunny spring day in 1971, she had me take a bus with her into Hackensack to an adoption agency. I didn't realize she was familiar with the place until we arrived. We walked up to a large gray house with white shutters on each window, and entered through wood-framed glass doors that sparkled like crystal, white lace drapes hung with ties on each side. A thin white woman of medium height with long black hair, dressed in a dark business suit, approached. She shook my mother's hand. "Hello, Marilyn."

"Hi. How are you?" she replied posing in a mannish manner.

"Fine, and yourself? It's nice to see you again," the woman said. "Is this your daughter?"

"Yes." We turned into the corridor.

The woman looked me over. "Hello. Have a seat here while I speak with your mother."

"Okay," I said, sitting down reluctantly on one of the three red-cushioned wooden armchairs as I silently glanced at landscapes on the walls. The sun poured in; the floors looked like mirrors, as if they had just been buffed—I couldn't see a single scuff mark. I wondered what they could possibly be talking about and tried hard to listen but couldn't hear a thing.

They were inside for twenty minutes; finally, the door swung open and my mother came towards me with a smirk on her face, one she always had when she thought she was being smart and wanted to annoy me.

"You can go inside," she said.

I said sarcastically, "For what?"

She clenched her purse strap against her bony frame and sneered at me. "Go inside and stop playing with me."

"I told you I didn't want to come here." I got up and dragged myself towards the spacious office, entered it, looked around at more paintings and the high windows framed by lace drapes. A big red oak desk and matching chairs sat in the center of a floor that was mostly hidden by an oriental rug. The sun shone brightly in that room, too; I felt as if I needed sunglasses. I looked down at her desk. It was spotless, and there were thick gold handles on the drawers. I was a shy, quiet person who observed everything around me.

"Have a seat," she said in a smooth calm voice.

I didn't utter a single word and sat.

"Your mother told me you're expecting the baby sometime in February."

"Yes," I said, stroking the arm of the chair.

"She's put up several children for adoption, here at the agency, herself."

I looked at her in surprise. My mouth must have hung open, because she quickly changed the subject, appearing uncomfortable herself, knowing she'd said something she wasn't supposed to. I, of course, still in total shock, could do nothing but stare.

"You know you will not be able to see your baby after it's born."

My leg shook and began to shake uncontrollably. "W-Why not?" I replied.

"It's better that way. You won't have the chance to bond with the child."

". . .Oh," I said, thinking, I'm not giving my baby up anyway. This isn't going to happen. They must think I'm stupid because I'm seventeen and don't know the law or my rights. I'm going to be eighteen in May and considered an adult, so I won't have to sign anything in February. I'm not giving my baby up for adoption; that's what they think. I shrugged and sat up straight.

"I will come to the hospital with the paperwork, when the baby's born, for you to sign the papers at that time."

Still in shock and puzzled by what she'd said about my mother, I just gazed on at her.

"Any questions?"

"No." I stood up quickly, and she walked me out to the hallway where my mother was waiting. They shook hands again.

She smiled at me. "I'll see you in February."

I walked out, leaving them both behind, not responding.

When my mother got to the porch, I turned to her and said, "I'm not giving my baby up for adoption. No way."

"Yes you are, if you plan on living in that house."

Walking ahead of her, I shouted, "That's not your house! Nana pays all the bills there. You don't."

"Put it this way. You won't be bringing a baby there."

"I'm not giving my baby up. Nope, I'm not. Watch me——I'll go live on the streets first."

Never once did I mention to her what I had learned in that office that day.

I GREW UP IN A BROADLY dysfunctional family that had originated in Northern New Jersey, descended from the Ramapo Mountains, Jackson Whites or Ramapo Mountain People, descendants of the Mann clan, a family that later migrated to Hackensack, Newark, then finally into East Rutherford.

Stories were always told to me by my late great-aunt Judy about our ancestors, descendants of the Mann clan, Hessian, American Indian, and West Indian. She would talk openly about our German aunts, uncles, the Manns, and how they owned property in town that we should've had.

Tri-racial we are, and in the 18th century were called "Jacks," a word for freed slaves or blacks, American Indian, mountain people——and the whites (that is, Hessians) who mixed together with them became known as Jackson Whites. My own family heritage thus possessed Italian, American Indian, Asian, and Latin blood.

Back then, the Jackson Whites were known for their incest, closely interrelated families, and intermarriages, which caused genetic abnormalities such as fusion (webbing fingers and toes), retardation——generations down the blood line——albinism (I can remember, as a child, seeing albino cousins (with blue and green eyes), and people with extra fingers and toes in town. My family is, though, an intelligent and good-looking group of people.

When I was a child the family spoke highly of Grandpa Lake, who was an Indian leader. I was told he was one of the first street-cleaner people in the town of East Rutherford.

This is not a myth, legend, folklore, as some claim but an actual population——my heritage and ancestors, who chose to be closely interrelated. I have seen them and heard the stories. I've always been fascinated by my heritage, though many of my relatives would like to keep it under a rug: Jackson Whites are generally damned for their mixed descent.

The United States built itself on the foundation of the European cultures; many colonists during the period (seventeenth and eighteenth centuries), behaved in the same manner as the Jackson-Whites but were not considered "an immoral clan of people."

But their history can be found in various registries throughout New Jersey and New York; they're even on the web. One of the sites mentions one Mozelle Van Dunk, who tried to petition the Bureau of Indian Affairs, with the support of the attorneys general of New Jersey and New York, to recognize the Jackson Whites as a "true Indian tribe," but the states only wanted to classify them as black, not Indian.

MY IMMEDIATE FAMILY CONSISTED OF five elder brothers and sisters: my grandmother, Dee Dee or Nana, and her daughter, Marilyn, Great-Uncle Harry, Great-Uncle Jack, Great-Aunt Lil, and Great-Aunt Judy. All the elders are deceased with the exception of my mother.

Their parents (Mabel and Fred) died when they were young, at ages ranging from eight to thirteen, while living in Hackensack, New Jersey. After their death, the survivors took care of each other, moving to Newark, then East Rutherford. My grandmother had my mother at the age of thirteen shortly after their parents died, and they dragged her along with them, bonding these siblings together even more. Each of them had the opportunity to graduate high school, with the exception of Nana and my mother, who chose not to.

Nana was a very dark-skinned woman, with short gray hair in her sixties and slightly plump around the waist, and she had long fingernails that would grow so long they'd curl. She stood five feet one inches tall, was the oldest of the siblings and head of the household, never missing a day's work, rising at four each morning. She'd put on her lime green hospital dress and white shoes to go off to the Hackensack Hospital (now the Hackensack Medical Center) laundry room. Nana was known by family and friends for her sense of humor and wit.

Uncle Harry was next in age, of medium build, with a golden-brown complexion, a beer belly, a cigar stuck in his mouth or in his hand most of the time, and he worked at a chemical company in town. He had a deep voice that projected loudly when he spoke, and a stubby beard he'd rub against our cheeks each time he hugged us. I'd break out in tiny red pimples and welts from it.

Uncle Jack, dark-skinned like Nana and about two inches shorter than his brother but a good-looking man with wavy, shiny black hair, worked as a long-distance tractor-trailer driver. He, along with Aunt Judy, didn't drink, curse, or smoke cigarettes. They said he was the lover in the family because, even at the age of seventy, he kept two girlfriends—one whom he lived with, and the other whom he visited on weekends and took vacations with. I always got a kick out of that. Jack was intelligent and seemed to be a reasonable man with a personality similar to Aunt Judy's; they both were kind to others and loved to help people.

Both uncles stopped by the house each day—for breakfast, especially coffee, as they read the newspaper, and the dinner that one of their sisters or my mother (their niece) would prepare. Uncle Harry arrived after work or after he'd stopped by the American Legion (VFW) or Frank's Tavern. Uncle Jack had no set time and sometimes didn't show up at all.

Marilyn (my mother) lived in the same household—thin and shapely, very light-skinned ,almost white, attractive, Sicilian or Latin looking— definitely of mixed blood, was twenty years older than me. She had worked sporadically because she quit high school at sixteen. I remember her partying and always having boyfriends, addicted to nightlife. My great-aunt Judy had the responsibility of raising me and assumed her role as my mother, thank God.

Somehow, as I grew into adulthood, I began to understand that my mother was searching for something she couldn't find in the midnight minefields. Her quest to be fulfilled and satisfied only led to more and more misery for me. Her heavy schedule of carousing from early evening to early morning, of course, left her days full of weariness, as her night activity was so overwhelming. Besides, she'd held a grudge against me since my conception because of my father.

I'd wondered for years why her skin was so white when both my grandmother and the so-called grandfather's skin were extremely dark brown. In my late thirties I'd been told a version of the true story behind her color by a cousin on my father's side I'd met. A light-skinned man who lived in Rutherford and looked Sicilian, Latin, or mixed with Jackson White was supposed to be her father. Now, her skin color would make more sense. This cousin on the father's side had also shown me a picture of my dad, whom I've never met.

Harry, Jack, Judy, and Lillian attended church regularly each Sunday, whereas my grandmother and mother went on holidays or special occasions. All of the siblings had been married, separated, or divorced, with the exception of Aunt Judy, who never married. She had a true devotion to her family, especial to late Great-Aunt Lil. Aunt Lil married into a religious family and moved out of state to Philadelphia, Pennsylvania.

Judy and Lil were not just sisters but best friends, and apparently Aunt Judy had chosen family, and her sister, over the man she was supposed to marry. Aunt Lil told me the story when I was an adult, how she made Aunt Judy feel guilty about leaving her behind because Judy's fiancé was in the air force, which meant she would've had to travel with him. Later in life, Lil said, she was so apologetic about doing that to her. Those two were closer than any of the siblings, though Harry, Jack, and Dee Dee had their bond with each other, too.

My uncles were the only two who possessed driver's licenses, and they drove my grandmother anywhere she needed to go. The siblings used a slang, a sort of Pig Latin, when they didn't want people, or you, to know what they were saying to each other. For the most part, they were an intelligent, articulate, close knit group of siblings.

I witnessed the great precision Aunt Judy employed in caring for herself, with her coordinated wardrobe, careful grooming, and eloquent speech. Whenever she went out in public, she had to match her accessories and wore red lipstick. Each week she'd go to the hair salon to have her hair conditioned and curled, and she'd get it dyed monthly. She was the caretaker of the family and the neighborhood; also, on election days, she'd work at the voting booths. Whenever Aunt Judy was disciplining you, she'd grab a part of your skin and pinch it, put her tongue to the side of her mouth, then speak some type of German or Indian language.

Each summer Aunt Judy would manage the playground that sat

alongside our house. She'd supervise a staff, children would make arts and crafts, play all types of games, and go on field trips, to baseball games, to the zoo, etc. Her profession was babysitting; children were always around her, and parents and children loved her.

She was the calmest and the most sensitive of my immediate elders, and provided for me the best role model my family could afford, though she had her share of shortcomings, as did the rest of the family. Even so, her love and compassion minimized her weaknesses, in my view.

Soon, being with them nevertheless became unbearable: I couldn't be all things to everyone, and I grew resentful and retaliatory. My new attitude caused me to back even further away from the family. It was as if, since I had failed to pay, I was being denied an opportunity to play in the family game. While I lived in the house, my address became Loneliness Lane. From childhood, I had known I was different from the rest of my immediate family, especially Nana and Marilyn.

The family was secretive and closed-mouthed about everything related to our history. You couldn't ask how certain people were connected to others without getting snapped at—with the exception of Aunt Judy. There were times she'd tell family secrets, events of our families past history. I can clearly understand now, through the years, I've gathered pieces of family history from cousins who are my mother's age.

As I've said, my child-rearing days were delegated to my very concerned late great-aunt Judy, who served as a surrogate mother in light of my mother's inability to. I often thank God for placing Aunt Judy in my family—a wonderful spirit of a person. Had it not been for her sacrifice, I, along with my sister and brother, would surely have joined the ranks of that secret society of siblings exiled to the adoption agency. Instead, God's grace, and my aunt's love, awarded me the opportunity to feel a measure of love from my blood relatives.

For years Aunt Judy lay on the gold couch each night, until the day Nana passed. The impact of that death was devastating for both my aunt and mother. Thereafter, Aunt Judy left Cornelia Street and went to live in the East Rutherford Senior Citizen apartments. My mother, Marlene, on the other hand, who at the age of forty-two had never left home, finally had to move out on her own and find a place. The thought of living with her and dealing with the craziness and chaos she squawked made me sick. I left home at the age of eighteen, three months after my son was born. Traces of bitterness I acquired in my youth remain even today, whenever I ponder my past and my mother's part in it.

WHEN I TURNED SIXTEEN, AUNT Judy gave me a sweet-sixteen party at the American Legion in Rutherford. I liked a guy from Passaic, New Jersey, and asked him to escort me to my party. We'd met when I went to the movies there, but I only had his first name. I'd never asked him what his last name was.

That Saturday night in May 1970, Nana, Marilyn, and Aunt Judy huddled in a corner until the party was over. They approached me after everyone had left.

"You know we're related to the Manns, don't you?" my mother asked. I said nothing as I listened on in my flowered tee-strapped dress.

"I've told her about them," Aunt Judy said.

"That boy is a Mann," Nana said and walked away.

I said, "He's a Mann? What are you talking about?" I rolled my eyes. "What does that mean?"

Marilyn replied. "You need to stop seeing him. He's your cousin," she added with a smirk before marching off.

I'd had no idea his last name was Mann. That was upsetting to me, because I liked him. Besides, he was good-looking—with green eyes and curly black hair.

Manns and Jackson-Whites—the family links crept into my spirit, soul, and besides it's in my blood stream, I figured, but I never saw him again.

Aunt Judy had told me family stories about the Manns. We even visited some sides of that family in Passaic after church services many times with her and Aunt Lil. She also told me of the Jackson-Whites who lived in the Ramapo Mountains.

I ATTENDED GRAD SCHOOL AT Seton Hall, in the eighties, the stories Aunt Judy had told me about our Jackson Whites ancestors were confirmed. I sat in the second row of a dimly lit classroom with oak floors and dark brown wooden trim, listening to Professor Father Grady. The windows were big, hung with long, wide, heavy shades that had once been white but had faded gray through the years.

The topic that evening was New Jersey history. I raised my hand, and he pointed to me. "Yes?"

"Professor, is it true that there's a group of people in New Jersey called the 'Jackson Whites'?"

Excitement and passion flowed in his voice. "Why, yes, there is!"

"Oh." I sat, listening intently. Oh, my, I thought, Aunt Judy wasn't making that up.

"I know quite a bit about them. I did missionary work there in the Ramapo Mountains. Yes."

Holy shit, I said to myself. "Are they still living there?"

"Some are." He sat on the edge of the desk while my classmates listened.

"I've only heard stories of people riding up there and getting shot at because they weren't one of them."

"Yes," he said, and then went on with their history. "They were known to have intermarriages among themselves, and they're of different mixed races, especially American Indian and German Hessian.

So I hadn't imagined what I had seen as a child. Our family is surely full of mixed races. The family tree I know goes only as far as my great aunts, great-uncles, grandmother, mother, and the siblings parents—it ends there.

THE WOMEN IN THE FAMILY were paranoid and frightened—true to the alleged nature of the Jackson Whites. Surely they had endured much as they grew up back in the seventeenth and eighteenth centuries—just the fact of being who they were trying to survive as a group in America, must have been devastating. My aunts and uncles definitely resemble the pictures of Jackson-Whites found online and in the surviving literature.

And as I have mentioned, I can remember seeing albino people at many family functions. My grandmother said they were relatives. I've seen people with extra fingers and toes in town. We were poor but at the same time fortunate because of where we lived. At parties sometimes, we'd have our own private magician because he lived in the third house down. Our house would be full of wall-to-wall people, music-playing, dancing, talking loud, laughing—close family and friends, smoking cigarettes and drinking alcohol. Men would let their alcohol speak for their actions, making them courageous enough to seek out some children to molest. I despised those parties because of the drunkenness that went on.

The house became an after-hours resort with alcohol supplanting Lysol. No chairs were available for the inhabitants while that collection of family and visitors dominated our home under the authority of my intoxicated superiors.

"Yeah!" The living room was full, because that was where everyone danced.

"Ah, yeah!" someone shouted.

"Shack it!" another would say.

"Shack the piss down!" Nana shouted as she danced around shaking her rump like Beyoncé's (before of course Beyoncé was born) . People would be seated at the kitchen table, drinking, smoking, and laughing; others looked on, blaring comments.

My siblings lived in the same household but were treated specially by my mother, who took them under her wing, a strange setup for a family that lived in the same place but was divided. The youngest is my brother. My sister is the middle child, who followed in my mom's footsteps, quitting high school at sixteen—certainly not because she couldn't make the grades. As children, my sister was the only one who had the opportunity to visit with her father and his family each weekend. My brother and I didn't know our fathers—all of us have a different one.

My late, great-aunt Lil—Big Mommy, a woman of elegant, elitist flair, also contributed a great deal to my childhood development. She extended her home, resources, and a constant effort to provide whatever she could so that my life might be richer. Aunt Lil—"Big Mommy," I called her. Her involvement and presence in religious circles brought her to her husband. A minister's wife—faith had a phenomenal impact on my spiritual life as well. She had a deep devotion and commitment to the church, spent all of her life worshiping and serving God.

Big Mommy married now to Big Daddy, Uncle Marshal, lived in a single-family home in Philadelphia decorated with English furniture. They had five children together—John; Mickey; a set of twins, Jean and Joan; and the youngest child, Marsha. Their children—my second cousins, who are all around my mother's age—I had the chance to grow up with. I've spent more time with them than my own brother and sister; they felt more like siblings. We shared an uncanny relationship. People mistook me for a younger sister until my aunt explained I was Marlene's daughter. Rubin Carter was my great-aunt Lil's children's first cousin, because Lil had married into his family.

I spent each summer month with the Carters along with Aunt Judy, and shared glorious experiences as my great-aunts introduced me to travel, to Wildwood or Atlantic City. Before or after we headed to the shore, we'd always stop at Aunt Lil's in Philadelphia, Pennsylvania.

Aunt Lil's son, John, had married into a family from Wildwood, and my aunts adopted his in-laws as close friends, almost as family. Her daughter Mickey, along with her husband, brought a piece of property, a small motel in Atlantic City, during the '70s. Periodically, we'd stop in South Jersey at Aunt Lil's sister-in-laws. Each aunt provided opportunities for me to see what the world was really like.

Uncle Marshal was a tall, lanky, brown-skinned man with a deep-base voice, and a reverend. I only came into contact with him when we went to church or he came in late, early mornings, from a day's worth of activities—church business, I assumed; Big Daddy was a mystery to me. The late Reverend Marshal Carter, Rubin Carter's uncle, the brother of Lloyd Carter—would play a great role in my future though I didn't know it then. Life is interesting, how it weaves its way as through a maze, finally dumping you ashore not far from where you began.

Aunt Lil's selflessness and love had been so clearly demonstrated that Big Daddy seemed to take it all for granted. I recall her waking up in the middle of the night—early mornings, really—to make a meal from scratch for him, even down to the eggnog, in an effort to fulfill her wifely obligations, even after his unexplained absences. She never questioned him, just did what a wife was expected to. I will forever respect her humility, rare in our family, and the kind of love and patience she sought to demonstrate in my presence as I grew into womanhood.

Through this preacher, Marshal Carter, providence ultimately thrust Rubin and me together, and it intrigues me, Big Daddy played such a positive role in my life while his nephew drained so much from me. Curse or blessing, though, the combination of these forces constituted an important lesson I've learned from them all about love. It could be why I'm composing this book, as I seek to emulate the lessons Lil taught, as I consider my relationship with the reverend's nephew only to realize I became the same kind of victim she was. Being such a truly great woman, she somehow managed to look beyond Marshal's abuse and continued to share all she had; I couldn't.

EVENTUALLY, I LOST THE DESIRE to even interact with those women I lived with, with the exception of Aunt Judy. I guess my withdrawal was insured by their lack of support. Though I felt something powerful and promising within me, I was continually debased and challenged. Life with them became a battle for me; I knew that, soon, I would have to leave. Then came the calm after the storm.

2

A RELATIONSHIP BEGINS

A FTER A SWELTERINGLY HOT, HUMID summer in 1976, at the beginning of autumn, when the trees began to turn, something amazing happened to me. It couldn't have come at a better time, because I'd pulled myself out of a bad live-in relationship with a man who'd started to hit me. It happened twice after I enrolled in college. I'd left my apartment, along with the furniture and other belongings I'd had in it, and him; I knew I could replace those things, but not my life.

That entire summer had been full of trips to Sandy Hook—for me, one of the nicest beaches on the Jersey shore. The sun blazed brightly, and I strolled around in shorts or bathing suits with a sharp, professionally done short hair. I abandoned myself to my summer break without the pressure of having to study in order to make the grade, compounded by single parenthood and work. Music was a big part of my world—and the voice of Stevie Wonder, whose new album, *Songs in the Key of Life*, was being played all over the radio.

When the sun sets there, you can have dinner on a large covered deck area and listen to live music. People stand around chatting in summer outfits, some in bathing suits, some sitting on stools at high tables, eating and drinking at the uncovered section, interacting with the musicians and their music.

That summer, I fondly recalled the press and commentary that surrounded Rubin "Hurricane" Carter's release from a New Jersey penitentiary, though preparations were underway for a second trial on the triple murder he had allegedly committed. As a child, I'd listened to the Carter family whisper bits and pieces about this man. He was an image in my mind, someone I didn't remember seeing at all and wouldn't have recognized if I' had without being introduced.

I was a sophomore in college. My plate was full; I was raising a four-year-old son, attending Fairleigh Dickinson University full-time, and working to pay the rent. I wasn't your typical eighteen-year-old college coed. My tour of scholarship had begun later than that of most of my peers. On the other hand, starting college a few years after graduating high school gave me an advantage in maturity and a start on being independent. I had thoroughly lacked an appetite for the regimentation of the educational curriculum and the years you had to put in.

The true motivation for my change of heart, my willingness to submit to that discipline, came on the heels of a swift blow of reality. I'd worked at a pharmaceutical company right after high school, as a file clerk in the basement of one of many buildings. I quit because of how I was being spoken to. I was going to prevent anyone in a workplace from talking to me in that manner ever again.

Finances were critical, and the Educational Opportunity Fund (EOF) program helped me with that, and I had thus altered the course of my life. Because I had a son, I was prohibited from living in a dorm, since families were not entitled to housing. So I had to commute and find childcare. I will forever be grateful to Aunt Judy, who sacrificed her time and openly offered her hospitality, so that my son would be safe while I pursued my studies.

Aunt Judy had somehow recognized my potential for success in the arts at a very early age. That rigorous and consistent physical exercise up through college provided me with an enormous asset as I grew older. By the time I reached twenty-one, I was astounded each time I looked in the mirror. The results of my aunt's investment showed up in the definitive sculpturing of my body: proportionately feminine curves and muscle tone from head to toe. I knew I was blessed with a beautiful body, and there was nothing that I could do about it or would I have desired to. It served me in many positive ways, though it also had a negative impact on my life.

ONE OF AUNT LIL'S TWIN daughters, Joan, and I were close, and I would spend holidays, all occasions, at her house celebrating. I'd pop over there at any time unannounced. One warm summer evening in 1976, I had an oddly uncontrollable desire to stop by on my way to a store in the area. I'd had no intention of doing so, because I had to study. But a weird feeling came over me all of a sudden, out of the blue.

My son was strapped in the back seat, eating a hamburger from Burger King. I was traveling, thinking about a conversation I'd had with my sister that week, standing outside on Cornelia Street in front of our house. "Jan, did you know Rubin's at Joan's house?" She was playing tag with my son.

I was on the bottom step. "Rubin . . .oh, you mean Joan's cousin? A Carter?"

She'd stopped playing, turned away from him, looked at me, and said, "Yeah."

I had shaken my car keys. ". . .Oh. I knew he was released from prison awhile ago. How long has he been there?"

"Beats me. Maybe since he got out of jail. I don't really know." I came down to the sidewalk. "Bubby's his bodyguard," she'd said with a sinister smile.

"Get the fuck out of here! Bubby? What's Rubin thinking? Someone needs to warn him." We had burst out laughing.

"I've seen him. Matter of fact, I've rode over to New York several times with the two."

"You did?" I had made my way to the car. "Come on, RJ," I said to my son. "If I find time, I'll go visit, but knowing me, by the time I get there, he'll be gone." We'd giggled as I opened the car door.

"Yeah, knowing you, the things you get into."

"I don't know him."

I'd heard the Carters talking about him, and had seen him on television and in the newspaper articles that streamed from the press. I chuckled to myself about Joan's house guest. He must be okay, I figured, because he's over her place. I knew little about him, and maybe I'd get the chance to see what he was like.

I drove off in my olive-green Toronado, which had a light green glow-stripe on each side. Owning a car at twenty-one was something special; besides, though I was a poor college student, I worked to pay the rent, which actually impressed many people.

Peeking up into the rear-view mirror at my four-year-old, I turned right, going over railroad tracks and driving for several more blocks, until I pulled into Bubby and Joan's two-car garage. Both of them were home, because they'd left the garage door up, and their cars were inside. I lifted RJ out of his seat and turned towards the light-green house trimmed in white, in that middle-class section of Paterson filled with quiet blocks and trees.

I opened the gate to the white picket fence that stretched across the front lawn, climbed the flight of stairs to the porch, holding RJ in my arms, and let him ring the bell. I reached down and checked to see if the door was unlocked. It was. I entered the foyer; a large white sliding closet was to my right. Facing the living room and kitchen, two white columns separated me from the family room and the sweeping oak staircase that curved to the second floor.

Bubby—Joan's husband—at five-six, a medium built man, was sitting in gray pants and a white T-shirt on a long, curved sectional couch that extended around in the living room. He'd always be in and out of work for some physical injury; in addition, he had an egotistical personality and a loud boastful voice, a person who has to be the center of attention at all times.

Joan was sitting at the kitchen table; dark skinned, extremely skinny, with short black hair, she yelled, "Hey, you! Where are you coming from, fool?" She had a cigarette in one hand, and, in other, her long fingernails wrapped around a cup of coffee.

I stood in the center, and glanced back and forth at them. "I was going to Corrado's but decided to stop by here first."

Bubby barked, "What's going on, Jan?"

I looked in at him and said, "Nothing much." I entered the kitchen with my son glued at my side.

"Hey, boy," Joan said as she reached out to grab my son's arm and pulled him closer to her.

He bent his head over, acting shy. "Hi," he said shyly. I sat in a chair across from her.

"Don't make believe you're shy. I know better," she said. He giggled and jumped onto my lap.

Joan stood up, dressed in casual clothing, most likely what she wore to work—slacks with a blouse. She turned, reached behind her into one of the brown cabinets trimmed in white, and pulled out a bag of cookies. As she slid over to the sink, she tapped RJ on his shoulder. "Want some?"

His entire body perked up. "Yes!" he said, sitting straight, waiting for her to place them on the table.

"Come sit over here." He got down off me and jumped onto a white wooden chair opposite me, beside her. Joan placed three cookies on a stylish napkin in front of him.

"Do you want some milk with them?"

"Mm-*hmm*." He smiled and watched her open the mustard-colored refrigerator as he bit into a cookie. Joan grabbed the milk and poured some into the cup.

"Thank you," he said.

Joan sat back down. I looked beyond her at the dining room, where a polished table that seated eight sat and, in the distance, plants hung from the windows. She had a great sense of humor and a heart full of compassion for people. Snatching the cigarette that was burning in the ashtray, she said, "Where are you coming from? I know you could've been anywhere. I haven't seen you around."

I watched my son bite into a cookie. "I was home, but I've been busy with school."

"Uh-huh. I know you have some funny stories to tell me."

"You know I do. I'll catch you up on some on the weekend."

She took a drag off the cigarette and said, "Rubin's here."

". . . Oh?" I was glad she mentioned him, because I wasn't sure how I was going to ask to see him.

Tucking my hands under my bare legs I said, "He's upstairs?"

She picked up the cup of coffee took a sip. "Yep."

I crossed my legs and positioned my purse on my lap. "I can go see him?"

She swallowed more coffee. ". . . Sure you can."

"I don't remember ever seeing him."

"You don't?"

I shook my head. "Nope."

"He's seen you many times when you were a little girl. Your yellow behind with that blond hair."

"Oh, yeah" I fumbled about with the napkin holder. "Joan, I can hardly remember my childhood beyond second grade. You know, I don't remember him."

She laughed. "Oh, damn, Jan."

"I remember my mother taking me to spend the night at Tee's—their house—one time when she went out. I didn't really know Tee."

Rubin grew up around my great-aunt Lil's children, too. Joan was one of his favorite cousins, and they were around the same age.

"Go on upstairs and meet that fool." She giggled. "He's in the middle bedroom."

I leaned forward. "He won't mind?"

"Go upstairs." Joan was tapping her long nails on the table.

Bubby yelled from the living room. "Jan, go on." He laughed loudly. He'd been listening to our conversation the entire time I thought he was watching television.

I stood up and grabbed my son. "I'll take him with me."

"Boy, you can stay with me," she said. He shook his head back and forth.

"I'm going to have to leave after that, when I come back down."

"That's fine with me. I'm tired anyway—a rough day on the job—

spent all day in court, placing another child."

"I'll come back on the weekend. Which room?"

"The middle one, silly girl." She said as her frames hung from her nose.

"Come on," I said to my son. I want you to meet someone. Then you can go play. Where's Melvin?

"He's in there with Bubby."

"I didn't see him." RJ jumped from the chair and ran towards the stairs, peeking in the leaving room. I entered the foyer, grabbed his hand, and we went up to the second floor. My stride slowed when I reached the top, because I began to feel reluctant about seeing Rubin. All the doors were closed except for the middle one, which was ajar.

I stepped up, knocked on it, and a deep, confident voice called out, "Come in."

When I opened the door, the sun was peeking through thin pleated curtains, making flickering and sparkling shadows that appeared to dance on the wooden fixtures and two twin beds, covered with green spreads, that sat in the center of the room. A man with a shiny bald head, bent over in a black pinstriped suit that emphasized his curved spine, was sitting close to the edge of one of the beds. A gold tie clip was snapped tightly to his tie, the attached chain suspended in mid air.

I moved closer to him as his head rose. He looked at me in surprise; I believe he thought he was going to see someone else. But when he saw me a beautiful smile emerged on his face. Our eyes met, and I felt sadness radiate through the room, merging into the gloom of the dark wood, but his face lit up. Through the eye-trance we entered, I felt our spirits connect—love at first sight, the strangest experience I've ever felt in my life. I wanted instantly to hold and caress him, seeing his pain and, at the same time, feeling the love in his heart.

Rubin's need for love was palpable; never had I ever felt such unsolicited desire. It made me want to cradle him out of a strong compulsion emanating from deep within to extend all the love I had if it would bring him a measure of happiness. I had no idea what was in store for me.

"Hello," I said. What a shiny head, I thought.

He said, "Hello to you but . . . who are you?"

"The family calls me Jan. Janet? I'm a Jackson." He still looked puzzled. "Aunt Lil's niece. How about Dee Dee, my grandmother? Her daughter Marlene? I'm Marlene's daughter."

". . . Oh, *now* I remember you. You were the little girl always with Aunt Judy!"

"Yep, that was me. This is my son, RJ."

"Hey there, boy."

He smiled, said, "Hi," and looked up at me. "Mommy, can I go play now?"

"Yes." He ran out, slamming the door behind him.

I turned to Rubin and replied, "He went to play with Melvin."

Rubin scratched his forehead. "Oh."

"They play together all the time."

"Where?"

"Over here." I leaned against the wall.

He had a sensual grin as he stared. "I haven't seen you around here."

"I know. Usually I am, really, but I've been busy with finals."

He brought his head straight up. "You're in school?"

"Yes, college, and I work."

"What school do you attend?"

I stared into his eyes. "Fairleigh Dickinson."

"Oh! I'm speaking there in a couple weeks!"

"What campus?"

"The Teaneck campus." He rubbed both of his large hands together; one had a gold nugget ring on it with a jade stone.

"Wow, what a coincidence. I'm on the Rutherford campus, but I take a few courses on the Teaneck side."

"How's your family doing? Dee Dee's a mess. And your mother, how's she?"

I told him flatly, "They're all fine,"

"Why'd you say it like that?"

"Oh, I guess because they consider me the black sheep in the family, 'the strange one.'" I pushed myself away from the wall and switched my shoulder bag to the other side.

With his eyes fixed on me, he said, "Hah. Join the club. My family feels the same way about me." We snickered.

"What's your sign, Jan?"

"I'm a Taurus. What's yours?"

"I'm a Taurus, too."

"Oh . . . ." What compatibility, I was thinking.

With a sexy smile, he looked me up and down, and I nearly blushed. "You've grown up and turned into a beautiful young lady, Jan."

I said shyly, "Thank you. What organization are you speaking for at the University, Rubin?"

"Jan, those I feel are close to me, call me Rube. You can call me that . . . . It's the black group on campus. I can't recall the name."

I was captivated by the magic. "Let me know the day and time—I'll come listen to you."

He smiled. "I'll do that." What a sexy smile he had, and it was nice watching it, because I got the impression he was laughing from his heart. "I know you have a boyfriend, as gorgeous as you are, girl."

"Believe it or not, I don't. I just got out of an abusive relationship. I've moved back home for a little while, until I can save to move out again. I left home at eighteen."

"You did? What happened?"

"He slapped me once and choked me twice after I started attending school. I left my apartment and everything I owned—let him pay the rent."

"He sounds like a punk."

"Yeah, you can say that." We laughed.

I stood in front of Rubin in a pair of cut-off jeans with small slits on each side, a thin colorful quarter-sleeve shirt, a size seven, with a tan, physically fit, well-developed, toned from head to toe; I was a twenty-one-year-old and blessed with a set of legs like Tina Turner's and a body fit for a boxer.

Not once did he move from the bed, nor did I, for one second, think about who he was, a middleweight contender jailed for an alleged triple murder in Paterson—but he was certainly a man who knew what he wanted and seemed straightforward. I like that in a person.

He asked, "What do you have to do tomorrow? Do you have school?"

"Nope. I have off from work, too. I'm free for a day."

"I want you to come back tomorrow. Would you?"

I was only able to stare at him and feel the magical tug that was pulling me toward him. "Come see you?"

Oh, what a smile he gave me. "Yes."

I wanted to say no—I didn't even know him—but I couldn't. "What time tomorrow?"

"In the morning."

"Morning?" I smiled; the chemistry was uncanny.

His eyes pierced through me. "Come see me."

"I'll have my son tomorrow."

"Bring him with you."

"Okay. What time?"

"Around eight-thirty? After Joan and Bubby leave."

"Eight-thirty? That's mighty early, Rubin."

He looked absolutely serious as I stood directly in his face and said, "We'll have the entire day to spend together."

I was set back somewhat, because I didn't quite understand what he was saying. ". . .Okay." The room felt steamy.

"Give me your phone number. I'll call you after they're gone."

"I have my own line, Rubin."

He reached over and picked up a black leather case. "Good, that's even better."

I looked down at my watch. "Oh, I have to go. I'll see you tomorrow." He rose up from the bed and wasn't that tall—five-eight and skinny. He grabbed the door knob, looked directly in my eyes, and whispered. "Make sure you come back."

"I will. I promise."

He opened the door. "You're sure?"

"Yes, I'm sure." I squeezed by, our hips barely touching, holding the strap of my purse so that it wouldn't hit him.

I skipped downstairs wound up, but knew I had to control myself because Bubby and Joan would be sitting on the couch, facing me, when I reached the bottom.

I stood on the stair. "I have to get out of here. I stayed up there longer than I was supposed to. I'll see you on the weekend."

"Alright," Joan said.

My son, who'd fallen asleep, had to be carried to the car. As I laid him down in the back seat of the car, I wanted to shout, *Rubin Carter asked me to come back and see him.* I couldn't believe he was interested in me. I was in shock, flabbergasted.

Approaching Route 80, my mind began to wonder about all the complications Rubin and I had. Our families were stupid, because they'd believed we were related. We had no blood line. My late great-aunt Lil had married Marshal Carter—Rubin's uncle, brother to his father, the late Lloyd Carter. They'd chosen to pretend they were as close as family, Carters and Jacksons.

Also, I recalled the night I'd spent the night at his house with Mae Thelma when I was a little girl. I'd felt uncomfortable and afraid then for some reason, even as a child, and couldn't figure out why. Besides, Mae Thelma was a stranger to me. She was best friends with my mother and Joan. And that called to mind that either Joan or Mickey had told me Rubin had divorced Tee (Mae Thelma), or was in the process of divorcing her.

Rubin's mother, Bert, and Aunt Lil were best-friend sisters-in-law, those two who'd adopted each other and believed we were all family; personally, I found it a bit sick.

That evening, after I got home and put my son to bed, I picked out clothes for the morning: a denim skirt with a tee-strapped top, and a pair of ankle-strapped sandals. What a crystal clear vision of what true love was to be did I have. Spiritually, I knew what was meant by loving mankind—it brought me closer to God. Life was much richer and brighter; nothing bothered me. I knew it was love. Rubin made me feel like no other man ever had before—like a woman.

That next morning, having risen early, I was feeding and dressing my son when Rubin called. I soon headed for Paterson, taking the local route through the streets. My stomach filled with butterflies when I approached the driveway, parked in back, walked to the back door, and knocked once. Rubin opened it; I squeezed by and stood near the sink. "Hi," he said.

"Good morning." He'd been at the table, drinking coffee and smoking a cigarette.

Rube locked the door, turned around, smiled at me in his slacks and t-shirt, and asked, "Would you like a cup of coffee?

"No, thanks, I don't drink much of that." My son stayed close to my side.

". . .Good morning, RJ." Rubin rubbed his head. "Oh, you look good. Have a seat."

"Thank you." I took the chair at the far end of the table near the basement door, and lifted my son onto my lap.

Rubin sat down in front of his cup and ashtray. He picked up the cup, took a sip of coffee, and yelled, "Johnny, come here! . . . Would you mind if he watches RJ for a little while? . . . Are you okay with that?"

"I'm fine with it. I know he knows how to watch kids. He's always looking after his brother and sister." He clumped up the stairs from the basement. "Hi, Johnny."

"Hey, Jan."

"Take RJ downstairs with you," Rubin told him. "Let him watch those cartoons. Look after him, you hear?"

"Uh-hmm," Johnny said as he picked RJ from my lap and carried him down. Rubin sat looking over his cup at me.

"You drink your coffee black?"

"Yep. . . . You look good, girl. Want to go upstairs when I'm finished?"

"Okay." The chemistry and magic had us both. He finished and stood up; I looked him up down while he set the cup in the sink. I rose, he slid up behind me, then I froze as I waited for him to pass.

He pecked my neck. "I like that perfume you have on. What is it?"

"Oh, I don't wear perfumes, only oils. This one's opium oil."

"It smells good, girl. Good enough to eat." He snickered and gave me that sexy smile of his that flipped me, grabbed my hand, and led me up to his room. He immediately closed the door, took me in his arms, and kissed me passionately. For the first time, I was breathing his air. "What are you majoring in?" he asked as he fell on the bed.

"Fine arts theater-speech, with a concentration in dance."

"All that?" he asked. "What are you going to do with it?"

"Well, I'm not sure. I've been thinking about playwriting."

"Oh." He pulled me closer to him. "You're doing a lot for your age. How old are you?"

"I'm twenty-one."

"And you're doing an excellent job with your son."

"Thanks. Do you know my mother wanted me to give him up for adoption?"

"She did what?" He slid over kissed me, and began to undo my blouse. I stopped him.

"What's wrong?" he said.

"I'm not sure about this."

He pecked on my neck. "Why aren't you sure?"

My desire was too strong—I wanted to hold and love him, and an arousal surged through my body. His large hand slid across my chest, then went down to my legs—his feelings rolled from his fingertips into my body. Something real had opened up in that room, and we both felt it.

When he pulled me close, chills ran up and down my spine. I tried to fight the feelings, but he controlled each movement of my body with the touch of his hand, and passion overcame us. He whispered in my ear, "Thank you for coming." He kissed my earlobe, and a mystical pulse began to heat up in that room. I trusted him, feeling naturally comfortable, and had no inhibitions.

We lay side by side. "Do you believe in soul mates?" Rubin asked.

"Yes, I feel that's what we are." I looked him in the eyes.

"We are," he said. I lost all control at that moment. "And we're not strange, thinking that either, girl."

"We're not?" I'd given into the passion.

"No, my love—it's something that's very real. There's magic in it, too. I'd never think you were strange. Believe that, Jan. Have you ever read Plato's *Symposium*?"

"No, but I know of him from school."

"Socrates says, 'In love lies the art of prophecy and the craft of priesthood and rite and sacrifice and enchantment and all magics and witchcrafts.'"

"Wow, Rube. How did you remember that?"

"I have a photogenic memory, baby."

"Interesting! I wish I had one. Not only that but you have an insight to things and an intellect that's phenomenal. I have to be careful with you." I laughed.

"I want you to go to the library and read that, hear me? You're a very intelligent young lady yourself," he said, and tapped my nose. "That's what attracts me to you."

"Oh, thank you."

He ran his tongue across my lips which took me to another dimension, sinking me into him, melting me into a puddle as the tips of his fingers touched ever curve of my body. He made me know what it felt like to love someone unconditionally. We'd let our guard down.

"THANK YOU FOR THAT," RUBE said as we remained snuggled in each others arms.

"You're welcome, crazy man." We both burst out laughing.

"You do something to me, girl. You got me."

I glanced at him laughed. He looked at me strangely. "I'm sorry, Rube, but I was thinking about what just happened, and you're funny."

He wrapped his arms around me. "I am. That was beautiful."

"Beautiful? Yeah, it was nice."

"Yes. You're beautiful—and strong, too." He rubbed his fingers down the side of my cheek and across my lips. "That was absolutely beautiful." Rubin glanced over at the clock. "We have to get back downstairs, my love. You're going to have to leave soon, one of them might stop by on their break."

"I know. They usually do. I sure don't want to be sitting here if that happens. I feel funny already."

"Why? Everything's fine, Jan."

"What about Johnnie? Won't he say something to them?"

He smirked. "No. I've taken care of that already."

"Oh, I see."

Once again we sat down at the kitchen table. Rubin lit a cigarette, and we chatted for ten minutes. He yelled, "John, bring RJ up. His mother's ready to leave."

Johnnie shouted back, "Okay."

We heard their footsteps banging up the stairs. When my son reached the top, I asked, "Did you have fun?"

"Uh-huh."

We all walked to the back door. "I'm going to call you early in the week. I have to go into New York, and I want you to go with me." He kissed me on the cheek.

"Okay," I said and lifted up my son.

"Stay sweet. I'll talk to you real soon, I promise."

I carried RJ to the car, thinking about what Rubin just said. He stood in the door waving good bye. "I'll talk with you." I drove off. What intenseness we'd had. We were forever soul mates, I thought. It gave me a heavenly feeling of completeness and a sense of trust. I trusted the man and felt safe—what an accomplishment for me. I hadn't thought it possible or had it been that I wasn't capable of doing so, certainly one of life's complete fulfillments?

Several days later, Rubin called as he promised. "Hi, Jan want to ride with me to the city tomorrow evening?"

"Yeah, I'd love to go with you."

"Can you get a babysitter?"

"Yes, that's not a problem."

I'd asked my aunt to babysit after he mentioned taking me to the city with him. "Yes. Aunt Judy said she'll watch my son for me. I have to let her know it's tomorrow. Where in the city are we going?"

"Manhattan. I have to see my attorney, Myron Beldock. We're having difficulty getting the trial heard in Hudson County. I have an attorney in Jersey City, William Perkins. We really need to get the case the hell out of Passaic County. They're nothing but a bunch of snakes who're trying to kill me for their own political gain."

"What do you mean? I don't know a thing about your case, or the criminal justice system."

He laughed. "Be glad you don't, baby. Each one of those prosecutors has gotten a promotion since my conviction."

"Oh. This is a learning experience for me. What time are we going to leave tomorrow?"

"Around eight."

"That's fine. It's perfect for me, actually."

"Good. I'll see you tomorrow, then. Be ready, I will be there exactly at eight."

"I will." I hung up and ran downstairs to remind my aunt about baby-sitting for me. There she sat on the couch in her usual spot, wearing a flowered muu-muu house dress with slippers.

"Auntie? Are you still going to be able to watch RJ for me tomorrow evening?"

"Yes. What time are you leaving?" she asked as she jumped from the scene of a mystery movie she was watching.

"Around eight."

"You have to make sure he's fed, bathed, and in his pj's."

"Okay. Thanks!" I began to tickle her. She was silly and would laugh uncontrollably.

EACH TIME I GOT TOGETHER with Rubin, I wanted to have a womanly appearance. He made me feel sexy and sensual inside. I'd wear clothing appealing to his eye, knowing his favorite materials were things that clung to my body and felt silky.

The next day I went to class then went to work about four hours, wishing the evening would come. When I got home that August night, I fed my son, cleaned him up, and got him ready for bed. I groomed myself and put on a short-sleeve tight fitting mini-dress with a pair of heels. I placed the last of my accessories on, scented Lancôme lotion with a dab of perfumed oil, then sat on the couch near the window; only minutes later, a horn blew outside. I pulled back the laced curtain that lay against the wooden panel and peeked out. A long stretch limo-style car was double-parked with Bubby in the driver's seat. I said, "Aunt Judy, my ride is here."

"Alright." I grabbed my sweater and purse, walked over to her and my son, who sat beside her, and kissed them both good night.

I scurried to the hallway and opened the front door, knowing my mother was most likely, sitting at her bedroom window, watching. When I approached the car, Carter jumped out from the back seat. I slid beside him, and he ran his hand up and down my arm. "Your skin feels so soft and smooth, like a baby's."

Bubby was playing chauffeur behind the wheel, looking at us in the rear view mirror. "Hi, Jan," he said.

"Hi."

He looked at us as if he wished it was him in the back seat. If Rubin only knew what kind of punk he really was. I did plan on telling him, too.

Rubin leaned over and whispered in my ear, "You don't like him that much, do you?"

Music played in the background. I whispered back, "No, I don't, but that's a long story that can be told at another time, when we're alone."

He nodded. "Okay." He adjusted his suit jacket and asked, "How are you doing, my love?"

"I'm good. You?"

"I'm fine. You look good."

I blushed, even with a look of passion in my eyes, feeling that strong chemistry between us. It was the most different feeling; our souls seemed to be dancing with each other, spiritually bonding. The entire ride we sat whispering to each other so as not to let Bubby hear. He whispered, "Do you see Bubby looking at us in the mirror?" Rubin would kiss me and smile, knowing Bubby was glancing, taking quick peeks in the rear view mirror.

"Yeah, I see him. What is his problem?"

"Forget him. Let him look." We giggled. He took my face, turned it toward his. Bubby was able to see that, too, until he finally decided to drive and keep his eyes on the road.

"You're crazy, Rubin," I smirked. He reached for my hand. We chatted and laughed. By the time we looked up and out the windows, we'd arrived in Manhattan. It felt good making Rubin laugh and smile. It appeared to be genuine.

We pulled up in front of Myron Beldock's office somewhere on the west side of Park Avenue. Bubby had a hard time finding a spot, so he let us out in front and drove around to find a space.

Rubin and I took the elevator up several floors to a small, dimly lit office; chairs were spread around the room up against the walls. He escorted me to one, approached another door, and knocked. When he opened the door, I could see a man sitting there in a gray suit, holding a phone in his hand. All I could hear was a murmur. Rubin nodded his head, closed the door, escorted me to a chair, and sat next to me. We waited quietly for the lawyer to end his phone conversation. It wasn't long; before I knew it, he'd come out. He nodded in my direction. "Hello," he said. He was about Rubin's height.

I said, "Hello."

"Hey there, Rubin." Rubin rose and they embraced as men do. "Who's this young lady?"

"Myron, this is Jan."

"Nice to meet you," the attorney said. "Excuse us, but we have some brief business to discuss." They both entered his office.

Rubin turned back and said, "I'll be out soon." I gestured back that it was okay. "Bubby will be up in a minute." I'd forgotten about him for a second.

Several minutes later, Bubby came through the door and took a seat across from me. He began small talk, then realized I wasn't interested in his conversation and picked up a magazine.

Thank God they weren't inside long. When Myron and Rubin opened the door, they were still chatting. "Hi, Bubby," Myron called out. "How are you?"

Bubby stayed seated. Myron came over and shook his hand. We both rose. Myron looked over at me and said, "It was nice meeting you."

"Nice meeting you, too." Bubby stood at the door, opened it, and I walked through while Rubin and Myron shook hands and embraced again.

Rubin walked, talking side by side with Bubby, down the hall; I wasn't listening, because we were moving so quickly. When we reached the elevator doors, they automatically flew open, as if they'd known we were coming. All of us got on; Rubin asked, "Could you go to Wildwood with me?"

"When are you talking about?"

He put his arm through mine. "Tonight."

I smiled. "Tonight?"

"Yes. Would your aunt watch your son for you?"

"Yes. . .but I have to call her."

"We can do that. I'll find a pay phone on the way to the car." Strolling along, he pointed as we were coming upon one. "There's one," he said and reached into his pocket, pulled out a quarter, and placed it in my hand. I dialed my house, Aunt Judy picked up, and our conversation was short.

I hung up. Rubin said, "Is it alright?"

"Yep. It's fine." Bubby was leaning on the car about ten feet away from us.

Carter hugged me. "I'm taking you to Wildwood with me, baby, right now," then grabbed my hand and placed me in the car. "Bubby, we're going to South Jersey. He gazed at me. 'Let's go, Jan!" We headed for the Jersey shore.

Suddenly, I wasn't going to get home until the next day. From the time we left New York and entered the New Jersey Turnpike, Rubin sat deep in thought. I said, "You look as if you have so much on your mind."

Rubbing my hand, he said, "You can tell? Huh. You see that on my face? Yes, there is."

I said, "Uh-hmm."

"You know me, girl don't you?" He smiled.

"I don't know about that, but I saw that."

"You sure did. . . . My attorneys are still working hard to get the trial heard in Hudson County, but it's not going too well, especially now that that woman said those things about me."

I sat with my legs crossed. "What type of things?"

"She said I beat her up." I thought, My goodness, what's going on here? And I'm heading to Wildwood with this man. He doesn't seem like he has a violent bone in his body.

". . .Did you?"

"No, I didn't do that. I'd never raise my hand to a woman, I'd walk away first. She was telling me she was going to tell Mae Thelma about our relationship."

"What? You were messing with her while you were married?"

"I'm divorced, remember?"

"Oh, yeah," I said, but sequences in his version of the story made absolutely no sense to me. He was probably married at the time.

"That didn't help me at all. The case really needs to get out and away from those prosecutors in Passaic. Each one of them has gained from it, at my expense."

"How's that, Rube?"

He had a sincere look on his face. "It's all for political gain. They've decided to play with my life. That's what they do to black men in America, Jan, that's exactly what they've done to me. The majority of men in prison are African American and Latinos. Well, enough about that." He pulled me to him and kissed me.

We arrived in Wildwood; it was September, the shore was cool with the atmosphere of motionlessness, and the people were gone for the summer, but we stayed at a hotel all the same. I sympathized with him, because it's the truth. In my heart, I'd felt Rubin Hurricane Carter was an innocent man.

RUBIN HAD PROBLEMS AGAIN THE following month. A judge in Jersey City had disqualified himself from presiding at the second murder trial.

The day came for Rube to speak at the university. He had also been promoting his book, *The Sixteenth Round,* that Fairleigh Dickinson University kept a copy in its Teaneck campus library.

That evening, I walked into the Student Union building in a lime-green dress with matching material wrapped around my head. Rubin was into that Afrocentric look; he himself always wore a dashiki. I opened one of the doors to the large conference room; Hurricane was standing at the podium, talking. He looked up, saw me coming in; I felt that electricity we had, scurried to the center of the room, and took a seat. I wasn't looking like your typical college student that night.

I glanced at my watch and realized I'd missed forty minutes of his lecture and only had another twenty minutes left before it was over. As I listened intently, peripherally, on my left, I noticed someone staring at me. I felt uncomfortable and turned toward the left. I scanned around to look. It was my college friend—a light-complexioned twenty-three-year-old, about five-foot and thin, dressed in college attire, blue jeans and a blouse. She leaned forward; her long brown hair with blond streaks hung over half her face, she whispered, "Jan?"

I turned further around until I was sideways, "Yeah."

She was shocked, placing her hand over her mouth, and giggled softly. "I didn't recognize you. I thought you were some woman that knew Hurricane. What are you doing here?"

"Well, I do know him, and he invited me."

". . .What? You know Hurricane Carter? When this is over, we're having a talk." She sat back in her chair, and we listened to the rest of his speech.

When he finished, students gathered around him for autographs and asked questions. My friend and I stood back, talking. When the crowd left and the room emptied out, Rubin came towards us. I said, "Hi, Rube."

"Hey there, girl. I'm glad you could make it."

"Me, too. Rubin this is my girlfriend, Dee."

"Nice meeting you." He shook her hand. "Jan, I have to get out of here, but I'll talk with you soon."

"Alright." He rushed out with Bubby at his side.

Dee said, "Jan, isn't that Bubba whatever-his-name-is with Hurricane?"

"Yeah, they call him Bubby."

"Get out. Yeah, him. What's he doing with Rubin?"

"That's his chauffeur and bodyguard." We both burst out laughing until tears rolled down our faces. "I'll have to tell you the story."

"We can go to the diner and have some coffee. You can tell me about it there. Can you stay for awhile?"

"Yes." We strolled through the building and headed to the diner near a corner at the edge of the campus.

TIME FLEW BETWEEN US, AND Rubin's court date grew close. One evening in late October, he called and asked me to met him in Paterson. When I got there and walked in, I could see he'd been sitting at the dining room table—papers were scattered all over it as he led me into the living room to the couch. "Jan, have you read my book yet?"

". . .No, I haven't, but I'll buy a copy."

"You don't have to buy one. I'll give you a book, and I'll autograph it for you, too." He walked off into a bedroom and came back carrying a copy in his hand. "Don't you want to know about the man you're with?"

Never having looked at it that way, I said, "Yeah."

He smiled like a Siamese cat. "Here. Read it." He handed it to me, snatched his pen off the table, sat alongside me, and wrote: *October 21st 1976–90. To: One of the Most Important People In My Life. . .Janet. My life would not be as rich as it is today had you not been apart of it! Thank you for that. May you live for ever. Your friend and brother Rubin Hurricane Carter.*

DURING HIS SECOND TRIAL, WE spent almost every day with each other and communicated a great deal by phone. Hurricane took me with him as often as possible—traveling in an underground fashion, without the press or our families getting involved.

The night before the trial, he'd called. "Hi there, baby."

"Hey, how are you?"

"I'd be much better if you'd come see me."

"See you? Where are you?"

"I'm at my brother's house. In Paterson, Floyd, you remember him?"

"Vaguely," I'd said, trying to envision him but couldn't. Floyd was much older then the both of us.

"You've been here. You don't remember?"

"Yeah, I certainly can't. Not really. . . . You sound tired, Rube."

"I've been up all night preparing for the trial tomorrow."

"Oh . . . ." When he said that I'd wanted to reach out and hold him. "I can be there in an hour. You'll have to give me directions again."

He'd perked up. "Good. I'll see you then."

I'd asked my aunt to watch my son, rushed around, and taken care of my motherly responsibilities before leaving the house. While driving—wondering what Hurricane could possibly be feeling, though I couldn't imagine it because I wasn't going through it, nor could I relate to that situation. It was a cold wintry night in 1976.

I pulled up alongside of the small red-brick steel fenced-in home (I had a faint memory or moment of *deja vu*). There weren't any parking spots in front; the closest available one was several houses down. The wind was high, the air brisk and frigid. My silly self, wanted to convey the image of a woman Rubin liked to see, was in heels in that weather with my thin outfit. When I reached the steep stairs, they were covered with ice, even up on the porch. I climbed up slowly, clutching the banister, and reached the porch with ice underneath my feet, and reached and stretched for the bell, feeling as if I was going to fall at any moment.

I could see his shadow rushing toward the door. It opened, but I had to let go of the banister and step slightly to the side—hoping not to fall, to get inside. "Hi, my love," Rubin said, and pecked me on the cheek. He quickly whispered. "My daughter's here." I froze; my feet felt like ice already, and my body still shivering from the brisk and fringed winds. "But she's about to leave," he added and gazed into my eyes. We entered the living room, and there she stood with her coat on, adjusting her shoulder bag—Theodora, 'Poop,' we called her.

I'd been frozen and shocked when he told me she was there. For some reason it made me feel uncomfortable. She said, "Hi, Jan," as she passed to leave.

"Hello," I replied.

She turned back, and a strange expression spread across her face when I sat down on the chair. Rubin quickly grabbed her arm and walked with her to the front door. I waited for his return. I heard him lock the door and shuffle back. He paused in the archway before entering the living room. "Hi again."

"Hi," I replied.

He came in, sat next to me, sliding his finger tips back and forth across my hand. Sadly he said, "The time has come, my love. My fate is in their hands once again," and then he pressed his back up against the couch, crossing his legs.

I didn't know the details of his case, only the fact he had been convicted in 1967, nor did I understand criminal law. I asked, "You can't go back to jail, right?"

Wrinkles spread across his forehead. "Yes. Yes, I can go back to that place."

I was shocked hearing that: Somehow I knew I'd never see him again. ". . .Oh. I didn't know that could happen." His sadness transferred to me.

"I'm being tried a second time for the same crime. I can get life again, and never get out. And now I have this new situation with Carolyn Kelly to worry about. It's her word against mine. There was so much publicity about what happened. The press took her version and ran that story but never ran mine. That's hurting my case."

"Who's Carolyn Kelly? How do you know her, Rube?"

"She was head of my defense fund. One night we met, and she started going off, threatening me about telling Mae Thelma about our affair."

"You had an affair with her?"

"Unfortunately I did."

I knew there was more to that story but he'd chosen to leave some out, because I didn't understand what he meant. What was this woman to him? It made no sense to me. "I see," I said. I didn't want him to return to prison. We had such a special relationship, and I felt he was being sincere about his innocence. "Hum. I guess she can hurt you." So many thoughts ran through my head.

"Yep, she's making it look like I'm a violent person. That's exactly what they want to portray me as."

Now all I could think of was how to take his mind off this for a little while. I was glad he'd called me that evening—I was sure he could've called any other woman.

"Enough of that—how are you doing, Jan?" A wide smile broke out on his face. "No matter what happens in that courtroom, I'm coming back to you. Do you hear that?"

"Yes." A smile emerged, but great sadness was hidden behind it.

"Believe that, too my love."

For forty-five minutes we sat conversing, until Hurricane glanced at his watch. "Oh, shit, where'd the time go?" He leaned forward. "I have to shave. Would you mind if I do that?"

"No, go ahead. I'll get ready to leave."

"Oh, no, baby," he said, kissing me on the cheek. "I want you to spend the night."

"I didn't bring an overnight bag."

"So what? I have to get up around five to do some preparations for court. Will that be alright with you?"

"Five? That'll be fine. I'll get up and go home." I knew I'd be sleepy as hell driving home in the dark; besides, I hadn't a change of warm clothing. At that time of the morning, it would be freezing cold outside. I dreaded the thought.

"Jan, the shaving product I use has a strong and unpleasant odor." He chuckled, as he rose from the couch, pulling me up with him, and we marched off to the bedroom. I plopped on the bed, and he went to the bathroom.

"What type do you use?"

He stood at the doorway of the bathroom. "Magic Shave." I didn't recognize the name of that brand at all. "The one with the blue label, it's the only brand that works for me. I'll be out shortly, my love. Make yourself comfortable. The television remote is on the dresser." He went inside and closed the door behind him.

I went over to the dresser set up with male colognes, picked up the remote, and turned on the TV. It was very chilly in the room, like the heat wasn't on. I draped my clothes over the back of the chair that sat alongside the bed, and jumped in. I decided to get out of my clothes and hope under the covers. All of a sudden a stink floated through the air like rotten eggs. What an awful smell it was; it stank up the entire room.

Rubin cracked the door and peeked out. "You got under the blankets, huh? You're cold?"

"Yes, I stay cold. I'm freezing." I think my lips looked purple.

"I'll turn the heat up." He rushed out and over to the wall by the thermostat and raised the heat.

"Thank you, Rube." He rushed back to the bathroom. I turned to watch the movie that was showing, holding my nose the entire time.

Then Rubin yelled from the bathroom, "Jan, would you please bring me my bathrobe? It's hanging over the back of the chair?"

I looked over to locate it because my clothes were on it and before getting out of the warm covers. "Okay, I see it." I jumped from underneath them, shivering (the room was getting fractionally warmer), snatched the robe from the chair, and scurried towards the bathroom. "Here, Rube," I said and slid my hand through the door, handing it to him. The smell was awful. "Here, Rube." He peeked out again—his face had a white mask spread across it—and mumbled, "Thank you. I can't talk. Don't want to crack this mask."

"Alright," I said, shivering in the doorway. As I ran back to the bed, all I could think about was getting up early in the morning fighting the glacial wind gusts.

EARLY THE NEXT MORNING WE got up, showered, and dressed in the bathroom—that's how cold it was. I asked, "Rube, will the trial go on for weeks?"

"No. It won't be that long, especially with the fact they want me back in jail."

I looked over at him sorrowfully. "I have a few finals this week, but I'll make it to the courthouse every day."

"I understand, Jan, if you can't, but I'd sure like to see your face in that room. When you come, always sit to my left. Then I'll be able to see you." He smiled. "We have to hurry, because I have to get to work. I'm going to miss you, Jan. I won't be able to see you much, but I'll call, and I promise I'll get to you when it's over."

"I'll miss you, too." I stayed silent while I finished dressing. He opened the door and walked out.

When I was done, I grabbed my coat off the couch. Rubin stopped me in the center of the room and passionately kissed me. "I'll see you later."

"Okay." We held hands and strolled to the front door. I had to tackle the icy stairs again, knowing that going down was going to be worse than coming up them in heels. I must have been nuts wearing those clothes and shoes in that weather.

Hurricane hugged me tightly and slid his tongue across my lips, and opened the front door; the freezing, whirling wind caught us off guard. "I'll see you later, girl," he said. "It's cold out there. I'll be waiting for you."

"Okay." I leaned over and kissed him, and let go of his hand. I held the banister tightly, hoping not to fall down the stairs, and shivered all the way to the car, even as I waited for it to warm up.

The minute I finished my exams, I left Teaneck and sped down Route 4 into Paterson that week. When I arrived, I seated myself to the left of Rubin so that he could see I was there. He glanced over and smiled. I listened intently to the testimony of Alfred Bello and evidence the prosecutors had on Rubin, even his affair with Caroline Kelly and the violent attack on her. A lot of their evidence sounded questionable to me. Some of it didn't make sense, and this was my first time hearing his case—but was I being biased? I wondered.

The trial lasted a week; before I knew it, we were all waiting for the jury to come back with a verdict. When they returned and seated themselves, the courtroom became absolutely silent. The foreman, a white juror, rose holding a piece of paper, and handed it it to the guard, who passed it on to the judge, who read the verdict, "Rubin Carter, you have been found guilty of three counts of murder, with three consecutive life sentences."

It was all mumbo-jumbo to me, but I knew it was a conviction, he'd been sent back to jail again, and life with him had just ended; all the things he'd planned to do with me had been taken away and placed in someone else's hands.

In the silence I saw Rubin glance over at me, and felt what he felt; a sharp pain shot through our bodies. I could see it come through his face as no one else in that court room could. Hurricane stood with his head high, shaking it back and forth in disgust. All I could do was stand there and watch the guards come over, handcuff him, and lead him away.

I walked out devastated, almost lost, not knowing if I should cry or not. We'll never see each other again, I thought, because I'm not going to go to that prison. That's something I'm just not going to do. I felt very strongly about it. All of our dreams had been shattered.

ALMOST A MONTH AND A HALF HAD GONE—it was February, when out of nowhere, I received a letter from Rubin asking me to come visit him at Trenton State Prison. At first I was reluctant, but I loved him so, I wrote back and told him I'd come in two weeks. After he received my letter he wrote back asking me to a wear a special costume—a skirt without stockings or panties. That request threw me; I wondered why I should do that for him. I never in my life visited a person in jail, never mind prison, and he wanted me to do that. Neither had I done that before for anyone—but he was my soul mate whom I'd loved and shared wonderful times with. I'd never felt that before.

Before I knew it, two weeks flew by. Even though, I was nervous, I found myself still traveling down the Jersey Turnpike south to Trenton State prison in my Ford Toronado that wasn't in great condition, but I knew it could make the trip. I prayed all the way I'd make it back home safely, to my son.

Never had I seen a prison before nor had an idea of what to do when I got there. I was afraid as hell, but knew I had to keep calm, following his instructions, wearing a long, flared heavy tan wool skirt as Rubin had requested. There were no panties or stockings, only a pair of high brown leather boots underneath.

I came up alongside the high brownstone walls that stretched for blocks; chills ran through my body. Besides, it was one of the coldest days in February and no parking close to the guest building. When I found something, it was at least a long block away from the main entrance. I grabbed my purse off the seat and walked quickly, shaking in my high boots, heading to the visitor's building with cold wind whipping around my bare ass. I crossed over because the building sat on the other side of the street from the main gate to the prison. I entered it, noticing bars over each window, in front of me a bullet-proof window with a husky guard behind it, and another husky one walked around in the visitor's area.

I took my place on line, and carefully watched what the other people were doing when they got up to the window—handing the guard their IDs and stating their names and visitee names. Then I hurried to search around in my purse for my ID before reaching the top. I got to the front of the line, and the guard called me. I slid my identification to him, and he looked at it with absolutely no expression on his face whatsoever. He asked, "Who are you here to see?"

"Rubin Carter."

He scanned a list that hung from a clipboard on the side of the wall next to him. Once again he looked at my identification, then shoved it back under the glass to me. "Sign here," he said. "Have a seat, and the guard will call you, to escort you across to the prison."

"Thank you," I said, turning away quickly. He still had no expression. All I was thinking about what he'd said—escort me across the street. I had to go back out in that brutal cold weather again. I looked around for an empty seat but there were none, so I leaned against a wall with a few others who had to do the same.

All of a sudden the husky guard signaled the tall built one who guarded the floor. I thought it was time to go across, but all they did was chat. Nothing happened. We stood some more; finally, the marbled-faced guard behind the window signaled to the other guard on the floor again. The husky guard shouted, "Line up. I'm ready to take you across."

I froze, wanting to turn away and drive back north. I placed myself at the end of the line, in hope no one would see under my skirt. He led us through the doors, out into the cold, across the street, and through the huge gates. Being at the end, I was able to see everything that went on in front of me, and I needed to imitate those who were familiar with the visiting routine there. Constant fear ran through me of someone seeing through my skirt—paranoid you might say, because the skirt was wool, but I was uncomfortable about the whole script and costume, walking into that prison. What if I got caught?

Once we got in, we stopped in front of a set of steep green steel stairs. We had to climb them. I agonized over the possibility of a guard walking beneath, looking up, and noticing I had no underwear on. But I knew I couldn't show panic, nor could I not believe what I was doing in that prison was because of love. I said to myself, love or no love, I'm not doing this ever again for anybody. I'd begun to think I'd lost my mind. It just wasn't me.

We began to walk up the steps, marching in single file—as we'd done from the beginning, like preschoolers—until we reached the top. Cells ran alongside a wall, in front of us and a big object sat in the center of the floor with a cover over it. A pudgy-looking guard stood holding a list in his hand calling out each prisoner's last name, and pointed to a cell where the inmate was sitting for the visitor to go to. Last of all, he called, "Carter," and pointed to a cell in the center. I strolled over slowly to the middle of the room, entered, Rubin's face lit up, and we embraced.

We sat down on wooden benches that were attached to the cement walls. I'd realized we were in a holding cell of some sort, which afforded some sense of privacy for us, which in turn explained Rubin's strange request regarding my costume. He slid closer to me and gave me another hug, tighter than the other. "Hi, Jan. How are you doing, baby?"

"I'm fine and you? It was scary coming in this place with my outfit."

He smiled. "I can imagine so."

"I'm a little shaken, you can say and very nervous about wearing this skirt with nothing underneath. I thought a guard was going to catch me, especially when I was climbing up those stairs."

He laughed. "Don't worry; no one knew you're dressed that way but me. You can't see through your skirt. It's wool."

"Yeah. You're right, it's just me." I smiled back at him. "How are you holding up, Rube?"

"As well as one can be expected in this place. You look good, Jan. I know you don't know where you are, do you?"

"Nope, you got that right. Where are we?" I said looking around the place.

He reached for my hand. "We're sitting in death row."

"Death row? That's where we are?"

He smiled teasingly. "Yes," he said. "You mean you didn't notice the electric chair sitting in the center of the floor? I was supposed to die in that chair if the death row law was in place—for a crime I didn't commit."

"Where is it?" I stood up, and he followed. We approached the bars, and Hurricane pointed towards the stairs.

"Over there. It's that badly covered mass in the center of the floor. You passed it."

"I noticed a strap hanging below the cover but didn't put it together." It was a frightening thing for me, knowing people had died in that chair.

Rubin pulled me to him and rubbed his hands up and down my sides. "Thanks for wearing the skirt."

"You're welcome. What did you ask me to wear this for, anyway, Rube?"

He chuckled, "You don't know?"

"No. That's why I'm asking."

With a wide grin he said, "I'm going to make love to you right here."

"Here? How are you going to do that? There's a guard walking back and forth every few minutes! In an instant I'd become terrified and awfully uncomfortable about the visit. How dizzy and naive could I have been? I asked myself. I walked back over to the bench. I stared up at Carter, wide-eyed.

He smiled and sat, sliding his body close into mine. "Come here," he said hungrily, kissing me, and stroked my body softly with his hands. He looked up. "Sit up. The guard's getting ready to pass." We straightened up quickly and sat as if we'd been talking the entire time.

I whispered in his ear, "How'd you know that guard was coming?" He laughed. "That's why you asked me to wear this skirt. Rube, this isn't funny. I'm freaking out here."

"I'm not laughing at you, baby. I'm laughing because I can see where the guard is at all times."

"You can? How?"

"Relax, my love, its fine. I'm not going to do anything to hurt you. Do you believe that?"

"Yes." Trusting his word as I'd always done, I began to relax slightly.

"I'm blind in my right eye," he said as he crouched over.

"Oh. . . . I didn't know that."

"I can see that guard through the mirror up there." He looked up and pointed to it. "I see him. He's right down there." He pointed again, and I looked up but couldn't see a thing.

"I can't see him."

"He's there, and he'll pass by right now," Rubin said. I looked and there he was, getting ready to pass us.

"How can you see that far, Rubin?" The guard passed, he snatched me, and began where he'd left off.

"Stand up. The guard's down the other end right now." I glanced at the mirror again but couldn't see him.

"Okay." We engaged in our physical passion.

Rubin looked and whispered in my ear, "He's coming back this way." We sat and talked as if nothing happened, both of us wanting to burst inside. A second later, the guard appeared.

"You have excellent vision, Rube, in that eye."

"My blindness, baby, in one eye has strengthened the other."

"That's phenomenal. That's what they say happens if a person loses one of their senses."

"It's true. You have living proof." He couldn't keep his hands still. I was nervous as hell the entire time but knew it would make him happy; that was the unconditional love I felt for Rubin.

Those round mirrors that hung from the cells, which the guards used to monitor the prisoners, had become a valuable instrument for him to use and monitor the guards instead. He's a different kind of man, I thought. Once the guard passed to go in the other direction, Rubin lifted his dashiki and reached in his pants for the last time.

We had fifteen minutes left before the visitor hour was up. We sat talked and laughed together as I caught him up on my life. "I'm coming back to you, Jan. I promise you I am. Thank you for what you did for me, my love. I love you."

"You're welcome." I sat shivering in my boots, wondering what the hell I was doing there in that cell.

He said, rubbing my hand, "I know you did that for me, and I genuinely appreciate it."

I pulled on my skirt, straightening it out, because I knew we only had minutes left. "I'm so nervous."

"I know, baby." He rubbed his finger across my lips, and I melted inside once again. I hope I don't have a wet spot behind me." I kept placing my hand underneath me.

"Stand up. Let me see." I stood and swung around. "You don't have anything on you. You're fine, girl."

"No?"

"You don't." Rubin took both my hands, held them, and said, "I love you, and I'm going to see you again."

"I love you, too." He overpowered me when he touched me. Before we knew it, our time had ended. A guard shouted, "All visitors must re-port to the stairs." I had to leave him as tears welled up in my eyes. We hugged the other tightly, not wanting to let go; I waved and walked away.

A guard stood stoically while another counted us like cattle before we were all led down and outside the prison gates. All I did was wonder if I had spots on my skirt. On the way back to the car, the wind picked up; it seemed to be brisker than before—whirling winds rolled around underneath my skirt, making the walk feel as if icicles had formed on my ass with each step. I was glad to reach the car, because I'd packed a duffel bag, and slid into underwear and a pair of jeans as I waited for the car to warm up.

A week later I wrote Rubin a letter. He wrote back, correcting the grammar and spelling on it, and that made me furious. I was a college student; the nerve, I thought. I didn't like visiting the prison anyway and vowed never to go there again— which meant I'd have no contact with Rubin Hurricane Carter for years.

3

THE SILENT YEARS

N THE INTERIM, HE WAS moved into solitary at Rahway State Prison. A lot of water had passed under the bridge for Rubin and me. I'd accepted the idea that he wouldn't be part of my life, and didn't yearn for him because I wasn't going back to the prison to see him, and moved on.

In the early eighties, I attend graduate school part-time—three times a week in the evening—worked, and took care of my son.

Aunt Judy watched after RJ for me, as she had when I attended undergrad which was a peace of mind for me, knowing he was safe and always at home, that enabled me to concentrate more easily on my studies. At the end of 1984 I meet my ex-husband, from Oklahoma, five-foot-eight, with a brown complexion and a mustache, who always dressed well, neatly pressed even down to his jeans.

I'd graduated from school in 1986 and married in April of 1988. He had a child, too, than we had one together. After four and a half years of marriage, my husband had decided he wanted to leave. Honestly, we weren't compatible anyway and couldn't live together; trying to had soured our relationship.

Each day I'd stop at my aunt's place, she lived in a senior citizen complex in East Rutherford, and drop my son off for school before I went to work. He was a senior in high school. I'd relax there before work once I left home in the morning, because I wasn't getting much rest at home.

Her large studio apartment contained two sofa-beds, a lounge chair with end tables, a television, walk-in sliding closets in the foyer, a kitchen, and a nice-sized bathroom. A small wooden table set sat up against the wall as you left the kitchen.

One morning as she stood in the kitchen, I walked in yelling, "Aunt Judy?" She peeked her head out from the kitchen doorway, holding an empty cup in her hand. "What are you calling me for?" I came near the entrance; she put the cup on the counter and poured coffee in it.

"I wanted to know where you were, that's all. Can you pour me a cup too, please?" I asked, dropping my bags on the sofa.

"You dropped RJ at school?"

"Yeah."

"The word is *yes*, not *yeah*," she replied, pouring my cup. She was always correcting our English and grammar. I must say, my family was an articulate group of people, Jackson Whites, who drank from mayo or empty jelly jars.

"Have you heard from Mickey lately?"

"I was down there two weeks ago with Aunt Lil." She opened the refrigerator and took out the canned milk.

I stood in the entrance watching. ". . .Oh. When you went to Philly?"

"Uh-hmm. We went down to Bert's place and had a good old time there in South Jersey—Monroeville. And my boy slipped each of us a few dollars. He always does that when he sees me."

I poured some canned milk in my cup and went to sit at the table, blowing on the coffee, and sipped it slowly. "Which boy is that? You call everybody your boy."

"Bert's son."

"Who's that? I don't know who her kids are, really."

"My boy Rubin."

". . .Oh. That's one of her sons?" I'd never put it together until that moment that Rubin was Aunt Bert's son. We'd been told since we were young to call her aunt, but I didn't know why. She wasn't related to us only to the Carter family, and was late Great-Aunt Lil's sister-in-law.

Judy giggled; I guess she could tell from my facial expression I hadn't known. "I really like that fellow." She stood sipping her coffee, in a flowered muu-muu and pink slippers, chatting away.

I finished my cup, got up, and placed it in the sink, then stretched out on the couch. Aunt Judy, seventy-two then and in good health—never heard her complain about anything but back pain—scatted over to the lounge chair. "Rubin's staying at Mickey's."

"Oh. No wonder I haven't heard from her lately—that's why I asked if you've heard from her."

She sat shaking her leg; it was something she'd did, especially when she was eating. "Micky lives around the corner from Bert. . . . I have to go to the bathroom," she said and jumped up.

I lay, thinking about what she'd said. I couldn't believe it, I'd found Rubin again. I knew he'd been released from prison in 1985, but I wasn't looking for him. I remembered the year I graduated and happened to be at Joan's house one evening when Rubin called. I'd asked if I could say hello, grabbed the phone, but he'd talked unenthusiastically. Maybe I could call Mickey's house and ask for him, I thought.

Both my aunts—Lil and Judy, had been to South Jersey and knew he was there. I wondered how long he'd been around. This was the first time Aunt Judy mentioned him to me. I wondered if that was because she knew of our relationship. He picked me up from Cornelia Street in 1976. She didn't know who I was going out with that night I went to New York. Oh, Hurricane Carter was back.

I remembered, when I was younger, going to Carter family reunions with my aunts at his mother and father's house, in South Jersey, a three-bed-room ranch surrounded by acres of land with woods behind it that extended for miles. Aunt Judy had told me they sold vegetables to Campbell Soup.

For days after Judy mentioned Rubin to me, all I could do was think about him. I found it strange the way she'd brought him up anyway, out of the clear blue sky. He sure was the last person I'd expected to hear about—especially with my husband leaving.

I was drained, weak, after the failure of my marriage; Rubin could have been set in my path to help me with what I was going through. It had to be God. It would be our second time of coming together out of nowhere. Was it a spiritual thing, free will, or sheer coincidence? I could call Micky's house, I told myself, because I did that anyway, and speak to him. . .but I wasn't sure he wanted to speak with me. I'll wait until to-morrow, when Aunt Judy's out; hopefully Rubin will pick up the phone. It was as if God had said, Here's another opportunity for you to see him again. I wanted to talk with Carter.

The next day, on pins and needles, I went to my aunt's, who'd left early for a senior citizen affair. I picked up her phone, sat at the small mahogany table, punching in Mickey's number on the tan portable phone, dialed, and hoped he'd answer. I stared out the window as my heart raced and I grew nervous; all of a sudden a deep voice said, "Hello."

Oh, my God, it's him, I said to myself. "Hi, Rube."

"Hello—who's this I'm speaking with?"

I rubbed my hand across the back of the chair. "Jan."

I heard a moment of silence. "Jan?"

I watched an airplane's contrail from the window. "Yes. Do you re-member me?"

"Of *course* I remember you, Jan. How could I forget you?"

"How are you? I wasn't sure you wanted to speak to me—after the last time we spoke at Joan's."

I went over to the sofa. "Oh girl, that had nothing to do with you. It was the people I was around. They were listening in, being nosy."

"You sounded so stand-offish. I didn't know what to think. And I thought you didn't want to speak to me after all those years I hadn't bothered to visit or write you."

"No, it wasn't any of that. How have you been, my love?"

"I'm fine. Who was listening?" I plopped down to listen intently, trying to feel him out.

"The Canadians."

I frowned. "Who are they?"

"The people I lived with, my wife. They were always listening in on another line to my conversation."

"What? You're *married?*"

"Yes." My heart stopped. "You?" he asked.

"Yeah, but I'm getting ready to go through a separation."

"That's what I'm going through, too. I can't take being with them anymore."

My head fell against the couch. "I'm sorry to hear that." I was disappointed he'd married. "You're okay, Rube?"

"I'm fine. That's one of the reasons I'm in New Jersey—I left that place."

"I found out you were here accidentally, from Aunt Judy. She told me she was at your mom's and saw you there. She likes you."

"I really like her, too."

"She said you're a good boy because you're always slipping a few dollars in her hand when you see her." He laughed. "How long have you lived in Canada, Rube?"

"Since I was released in 1985, I went from one prison to another."

I rose and paced the floor. "Why do you say that?"

"I can't go anyplace by myself. They're with me everywhere I go—even if I want to go to the store and buy a pack of cigarettes, one of them has to be with me."

"Wow. I see what you mean."

"Yeah, they're controlling. My wife controls everything, my money, even the remote control for the television. We watch what she wants to watch. At one time there were fourteen people living in that house."

"*What?* That many people? I'm sure you bring in a lot of money."

"Yeah, but I have no control over it. They give me an allowance, like I'm a child."

"Get out of here, Rube."

"They'd go to the bathroom with me if they could." We laughed. "Enough of them. What about you, Jan, are you alright?

"Yes, I'm hanging in there."

"I remember you so vividly, girl. I see you so clearly, especially that day you walked into that room in 1976. It's like yesterday."

"You remember that?"

"I sure do, could never forget it."

Actually, I didn't know Rubin, except for those few short months we'd had the opportunity to share together in 1976. I don't remember seeing him at any time as a child. A man eighteen years older than I, he was still a stranger to me.

"I've been raising children. I have a daughter now who's going on one." I walked in the bathroom.

"Oh! . . . I'd sure like to see you, Jan, if I could. Is that possible?"

I turned on the light. "Maybe. I can probably arrange that. I'm off right now for the summer."

"Um-hmm. Are you leaving your husband, or is he leaving you?"

"He's leaving me. Matter of fact, he just brought new furniture that he couldn't wait for me to see, and had it delivered to the house, and placed it in the garage. He just wanted to hurt me more." I stood in front of the mirror.

"He sounds like an asshole."

"Um-hmm. That he is. But he's a good provider and responsible."

"Be glad he's leaving you."

"I guess," I said sadly and turned out the light that was next to me.

"It could be a blessing in disguise for you, too. Look at it that way."

"It was hard at first accepting the fact my marriage was ending, but I'm getting stronger each day."

"He sounds like a projectionist. But you'll be alright, girl. I'll help you through it. Come see me."

"I don't know about that."

"Come on."

"I'm not sure."

". . .Think about it."

Seconds of silene went by before I replied, "Okay, I'll see what I can do. I have all three of the kids."

"Three? I thought you said two."

"He has a son he'd got custody of from his second marriage. I'm his third wife."

"Oh, Lord. His third wife. Yes, that man has problems. I see, married three times. Bring the kids with you, that'll be fine. They can play with Curtis. He's here."

"RJ would love that. He and Curt are best cousins."

"Sounds good. See what you can do, and call me back."

"Okay."

"It was good hearing from you, girl. I'm sure you're still as beautiful as ever."

"I don't know. I'm older, that's for sure. I'll call you back around Tuesday and let you know if I can get down there or not."

"Okay, try. Take care of yourself, my love."

I'D DECIDED TO GO ON Friday, but had to think about how to approach my husband and tell him the kids were going with me to South Jersey, because I'd be using one of the cars. When I did—that evening, after dinner, he sat on the coach with an attitude. I said, "Hello?" in a soft but clear voice.

He looked over at me with his neatly trimmed, thick black mustache and beard, still dressed in his work clothes, wearing an Yves St. Laurent suit, a silk tie, socks that matched his outfit, and spit-shined shoes, but he had attitude spread all over his face. "What?" He said, nastily.

"Friday, I'm taking the kids with me to my cousin's, Micky's."

"Where's that?" he said, rolling his eyes at me.

"She lives in south Jersey, off of Exit 2."

"I don't give a fuck what you do," he said. "You're never home any-way, always have your ass out in the streets."

"I'm out, yeah, but with all three children. You don't take them any-where, except we all go to the movies once a week. You don't take them places by yourself."

"Yeah, I bring in the money." He jumped up from the couch, ran into the bedroom, slammed the door, and began doing the same to the dresser drawers, mumbling loudly.

He acted as if he didn't care, but if I'd taken off without letting him know, that would've caused an argument. It didn't matter at that point in our relationship because he'd put into motion steps to move. He was leaving me, teaching me a lesson, he had told me. I couldn't wait to call Hurricane and tell him that I was coming.

The next morning, I called Rubin after feeding the children their breakfast. The boys went to their room to play, and I placed the baby, who had fallen asleep, in her crib. He answered the phone.

"Hi, Rube."

"Hey there, baby."

"Did I wake you?"

"No, I was up bright and early. Is everything alright with you at home?"

"Yeah, why are you asking?

"Because I can feel you, girl," he said.

It's tense around here. He's leaving us this weekend."

"That man doesn't know what he's doing."

"I'm coming down Friday."

"Okay, in two weeks."

"No, actually *this* Friday, if that's alright with you. *Is* it alright with you, Rubin?"

I could feel the smile form across his face through the phone. Bubbling with excitement, he said, "That's great. Oh, that's good, girl. I can't wait to see you."

"It'll be nice to see you, too," I said, but had doubts about going. "You'll have to give me directions once I get off Exit 2. I could never find the house on those winding roads."

In his sexy bass voice that hypnotized me each time he spoke, he said, "I'll meet you near the exit when you get off. All you have to do is call me in the morning before you leave, and we'll time it from there. It takes two hours to get down here."

"That sounds good," I said.

"It's been a long time, Jan."

"I know." I sat at the dinning room table in silence, counting the pastel-colored cloth mats as the sun poured through the windows.

"It'll be nice to see you," he said. "Thirteen long years have gone by."

"It's been that long?" Squinting in the glaring sun, I said, "Yep, that is a long time, isn't it?"

"You're right. I went back to prison in '76, and now it's 1990. It feels like yesterday—but you know how we are, we just pick up from where we left off. I tried calling you back at Joan's after we spoke, but she told me you'd moved and she didn't have your phone number."

"Yeah, she told me you called only a day after, when I called to give her my number. I was hoping you'd call back, but you didn't. I got married shortly after that. You could've saved me, Rube," I giggled.

"When did you get married?"

I sat stone-faced. "In April of 1987."

"I got married the same year, in November. Who knows—maybe we could've both saved each other if we'd talked that day in 1984."

"Isn't that strange, how we married other people around the same year, now we're going through separations at the same time, too?"

"Yeah, it's ironic. I should've been married to you, Jan. Be careful with that guy."

I replied in a daze, "Who?"

"Your husband—you don't know what he's capable of doing. Do you hear me, Jan?"

"Yes. I'll be careful. I'll see you at the end of the week, Rube."

"Get here early."

"There you go with that 'early' stuff. I'll try to get out as soon as I can, especially that I have to get the three kids together—not my son so much, but the two younger ones. I can probably get there around nine."

"That'll be fine."

It was my first marriage but Rubin's second. Who knew? When he made the call, if we'd talked at Joan's in 1987, things might have turned out very differently for me. Rubin had gotten married only several months before me.

Friday came quickly, and the excitement was overwhelming. I felt nervous and began feeling doubtful about going to see him. I was faulting myself over my marriage, but my husband *was* leaving *me*. And I again felt the guilt of not visiting Rubin in prison after 1976. I wondered why a man like him would want to see me after I'd demonstrated such a lack of interest and communication. I was no longer the twenty-one-year-old he'd met; I was thirty-four, a mature woman.

I filled up a cooler with sandwiches, snacks, and drinks for the children, after feeding them; I made sure the eight-year-old was dressed, and knew my sixteen-year-old son was able to handle himself. I slipped bottles, diapers, and baby food into the diaper bag. The baby had been busy playing in her playpen. I picked up the portable phone and walked into the bedroom. "Hey, Rube, I'm getting ready to leave."

I could sense his luminous smile as he spoke. "Great. I'll leave out ten minutes before you get to the exit. Jan, after the toll booth there's an empty parking lot on your right. I'll meet you there."

"Oh, okay." I looked around to make sure I hadn't left anything.

"Then you can follow me in. When you go back, I'll lead you out to the Turnpike."

"Thanks, Rube," I said with a sigh of relief.

"Come on, girl." He laughed. "Take your time and drive safely, but come to me."

"Alright, I'll see you in two hours."

I gathered the children, we went down to the garage, and I placed my daughter in the car seat, then walked around to strap my stepson in. My son rode with me in the front of the four-door gray Renault. Away we went to the Garden State Parkway South towards the Turnpike. I knew the kids wouldn't stay awake any longer then thirty minutes before they'd commence to dozing off.

The sun shone brightly in the August heat that shimmered on the horizon. I wore a pair of thin, gold-framed, dark brown shades with a short denim skirt and a sleeveless print top, listening to favorite R&B tapes as my mind wandered freely, no longer feeling controlled by my soon-to-be ex-husband.

The two hours flew by; before I knew it, I was pulling off the highway at Exit 2, heading to Monroeville. I paid the toll, road a short distance down the road, and pulled into the empty parking lot, where a yellow Chrysler was sitting.

I pulled up alongside him, glanced in the rear-view mirror, and noticed everyone was still asleep. He had his window down, looked at me, and said, "Jan?"

I smiled. "Yes, it's me."

For some unknown reason, I wasn't expecting to see an older man, but a very healthy, good-looking one sitting behind the wheel. He had hair and was no longer bald.

We looked at each other, smiling from ear to ear. "Step out real quick, so I can see what you look like," he said.

I opened the door quietly, not to wake anyone, and stepped out. Rubin gave me his gleaming TV smile, showing all his white teeth. "Look at you," he said.

I said shyly, "What?"

"You're beautiful. You've grown into a gorgeous woman."

"Thank you," I said as I slipped back into the car.

"Come on. Follow me, Jan."

"Okay." The two boys then began to move and awaken, but my daughter was still asleep. Before pulling out, all I could do was blush and grin; never since I'd married had a man given me such compliments.

"Come on girl, follow me."

We drove off, and I stayed close, not to get lost on those winding rural roads and passed the nudist camp, which was fenced off. We entered the horseshoe driveway of my cousins' newly built home. I stopped and, immediately, the boys jumped out. "Hey, you two—don't you speak?" I shouted as Rubin stepped out of his car.

RJ halted in his tracks, turned back, and said, "Hi, Rube."

"Hey there, boy. You remember me?"

"I sure do," he said, smiling.

I said, "The little one is my stepson."

"Hi," Rubin said.

"Hi," he said bashfully.

Curt stood on the front porch, looking on. Rubin yelled over to him, "Curt, take the boys and go play. You can go in the back."

"Can we go down by the lake?"

"Yes, but be careful."

I shouted, "RJ, make sure you watch after him."

"Okay, Mom." They ran inside.

My son and Curtis were best cousins—late Great-Aunt Lil's daughter—Micky's son. Acres of land stretched behind the house where Mickey and her husband had built a man-made fishing pond that a rowboat sat in.

I stood stretching while my daughter lay asleep in the car seat. Rubin came towards me and looked me up and down from head to toe. "Look at you. You're absolutely beautiful." He grabbed me and hugged me gently.

"Thank you."

Whispering in my ear, he added, "Oh, you feel good. Do you want me to take your daughter in?"

"Nah, I'll get her." I opened the back door and pulled her out slowly, so as not to waken her. Rubin reached for the diaper bag, and we walked into the living room. I laid her down on the couch. He watched every move I made, electricity flew ubiquitously, making me feel uncomfortable because I wasn't sure what was going to happen between us; I felt as I had when we first met in 1976. Rubin and I were together once again; it appeared to be we had begun where we had once left off; mystery, magic, and providence had been at work.

"Now, tell me, Jan ,why would your husband be leaving such a tantalizing woman like you?"

"That's a long story. My spirit feels as if it's slowly perishing from this marriage, being around all the verbal abuse, Rube. It's too much for me."

"You're here with me today. I'm going to help you relax, and to forget about all that negativity going on in your life with him. We have all day." He laughed.

I stood in front of my daughter after laying her on the couch. "I want to leave before the traffic begins. I guess around three."

"Okay. Do you want some coffee?" he asked.

"Yes, that sounds good. I'll take a cup."

"Let's put a few pillows on the floor in case the baby rolls off."

"Alright." Rubin placed them in front of the couch, and we walked back to the kitchen.

"I'm surprised you want coffee. I can remember you wouldn't touch the stuff."

"Yeah. It started once I attended grad school, that all changed."

He pulled two cups from the cabinet and the canned milk from the refrigerator. "This is the only kind of milk I use in my coffee."

"That's fine, that's all I use, too."

He pulled out the sugar bowl. "How many sugars, Jan?"

"Two. I see you don't use sugar at all."

"Nope."

He fixed our cups, and we strolled back to the living room. I sat on the other side of my daughter while he plopped down in the love seat. The cushion hung on the edge of it.

"Where'd you and your husband meet?"

"At a girlfriend's wedding, the one you met in '76 at Fairleigh?"

"Oh. How's she doing?" he asked, looking at me devilishly.

I took a sip of coffee. "She's fine but got divorced a year ago. It's been quit a messy one and is still going on. Where'd you meet your wife, Rube?"

"We met while I was in prison," he said, staring at me.

I became uncomfortable. "Why are you looking at me that way?"

"You're beautiful, absolutely beautiful." He smirked and leaned over to grab his pack of cigarettes from the end table next to him.

I fanned my hand. "Could you smoke that in another room, please?"

"Sure." He took a lighter and the cup out with him to the pantry. I looked at my daughter, picked my cup off the floor, and followed him. He stood near a window; I slid beside him and noticed the boys playing out back.

"They're fine," he said as he blew smoke out the window. "I see. Your stepson's having fun with them. I forgot how you were with cigarettes, baby." He bent down and kissed my neck. I tried fighting my feelings, but it was hard. "Umm, you smell good."

Staring out the window, I said, "Thank you. How long have you've been in Jersey?"

"A few months. I was tired of being with the Canadians and with her." He peeked out the window, slid behind me, and nibbled on my ear.

Feeling awkward, I slid out from him and said, "I need to go look at my daughter in case she rolls off the sofa." He grabbed my hand and pulled me into him, stopped me, and passionately kissed me.

"I love you." I looked at him bizarrely. "Come on, let's go check on her," he said.

He held my hand while we walked; we stopped at the entrance to the living room, peeked in, and I noticed she was in the same spot on the sofa as before. "Oh, she's fine."

"Told you she'd be okay," he said as he placed more pillows from the love seat on the floor next to where she lay.

I asked, "Rube, that time you called Joan's you were in Canada?"

"Yep, that's why I couldn't talk to you—they were listening in on the phone. It wasn't that I didn't want to talk. I always want to talk with you, Jan."

What a fantastic reunion we shared, beginning from where we left off, a bond that was inevitable.

4

DISCOVERING A REAL HURRICANE

ONTHS FLEW, TURNED INTO YEARS; Rubin and I became closer than ever before, growing spiritually, sharing some form of mental telepathy—and we finally had our chance to be a couple, growing as best friends.

Hurricane's strength helped me return to myself and gain renewed confidence. Our weekly talks provided me with his wisdom and knowledge, along with his hypnotic voice that, in itself, became a kind of therapy for me.

Within a year, by 1990, I'd legally separated, but Rubin remained separated, for business purposes he claimed, and we went on that way for ten unbroken years, becoming best friends, so I thought.

IN 1991 I'D INTRODUCED RUBIN to my favorite relatives Jean and Ken. They'd come up from Virginia to spend the weekend, in Vailsburg; we chit-chatted and listened to music. Jean, my cousin, a light-skinned woman of mixed blood with short, shiny black hair, medium built, and five foot five, danced by herself— in the middle of the living room, near her husband, six-two with similar skin, curly black hair, and slender, who wore wire-framed glasses who sat quietly on the couch.

"You know what, you's guys?" I stood at the dining room table pouring a blush Zinfandel.

Jean said, "Listen to her. You can tell she grew up in East Rutherford, using 'you's guys.'" They laughed.

I picked up two glasses, walked them into the living room, and handed one to each. "Remember I told you, back in 1976, I was dating Rubin Carter?"

"Yeah," Jean said as she grabbed hold of a glass, shaking and gliding.

I smiled mischievously. "I'm seeing him again."

"What?" Ken said as I handed him his glass. "You mean the boxer, Hurricane?"

I looked somberly at him. "Uh-hmm."

Jean said, "I remember you telling me about him when you were in college."

I scooted back to the table, poured myself a glass, and took a sip. "Yeah, that's him." The sun poured through the bamboo shade, temporarily blinding me, as I sat opposite them on the sectional.

"How'd you catch up with him again?" she asked.

"It was purely accidental. Aunt Judy told me he was staying at Mickey's a few weeks before she died."

Jean said, wide-eyed, "Oh, she did."

"I wonder if she mentioned it intentionally because she knew she was dying. But anyway, I called Mickey's house, and he answered."

"You mean Aunt Lil's daughter, right?"

"Yeah. She lives in South Jersey."

Ken sat back and listened intently, sipping his wine.

Jean stopped dancing. "That's where he is now?"

"Yeah, South Jersey."

A big grin ran across Jean's face. "This girl is always dating men like that."

"I want both of you to meet him the next time I come down."

Ken said, "Sure, bring him with you. I'd love to meet Hurricane."

"I have to talk it over with him first, of course, because he's pretty private."

Ken nodded. "That's understandable. You know, we're the same way. I remember seeing a few of his boxing matches on television when I was young boy."

"You saw some? Wow," I said. "Rubin doesn't have male friends that I know of. He's like you, and he's a Taurus. I'm sure the two of you will get along just fine."

The phone rang; I hurried to the dining room and picked it up. "Hello?"

A deep sexy voice responded, "Hey, there, baby. What are you doing?"

I peeked over at them. "Hi, Rube." They looked at me in surprise as I leaned on the archway wall. "I'm here with my cousins. They're up from Virginia for the weekend."

"Which cousins are they? Do I know them?"

"I'm not sure. Jean, she's related to me, on the Jackson side."

"Oh. I'm sure I don't know her, then."

I said spryly, placing my hand on my hip, "No, I'm sure you don't, but I'd like for you to meet her and her husband. You'd really like them. They're my best friends and family. Jean's more like a sister to me than my own sister."

"You seem to be excited about them visiting."

"I am. When we get together, we have such a good time. You have to meet them, Rube." I slid down the side of the wall onto the floor. "They're really cool people, and you'd get along great. They're loners like us."

"Alright, my love, you know what I like, you know me better than most people."

I smiled. "Would you say hello to them?"

"Yeah, I'll do that."

"Let me get the other phone so they can both talk to you at the same time." I got up, went to the bedroom, and came back, handing one cordless to Ken and the other to Jean. "Rubin wants to say hello."

They both beamed. Ken placed his glass on the floor beside him on a hand-made coaster from Africa. He said, "Hi, Rubin." I paced around then took a seat at the dining-room table. The archway separated the two rooms.

Jean said next in a soft voice, "Hi. Should I call you Rubin, or Rube, like Jan?" She chuckled and showed her pearly white teeth that sparkled in the sunshine pouring through the bamboo shade. "I've heard so many things about you."

"*Good* things, I hope," Rubin replied.

Ken added, "I hope we get the opportunity to meet."

Rubin asked, "You live in Virginia?"

"Yes. I grew up there," Ken said and leaned forward.

"Oh."

Jean listened in as she puffed on a cigarette. Ken continued. "Rubin, Jan's coming down in a few weeks. I hope you can come with her!"

"I'll do that, my brother."

Ken rose, smiled, and began walking from room to room. "You will. Oh, man. We'll be glad to have you. I look forward to seeing you, then."

"It was nice talking to you, Rube," said Jean. "I'll see you in a couple of weeks. Bye." She placed her cordless on the end table near her.

"Okay, Rubin, here's Jan," Ken said, and handed me the phone.

I lifted the smoke-colored receiver to my ear. "Hey, Rube."

"I told them I'll come with you when you go down."

I was ecstatic. "You *will?*"

"Yes. They sound like great people. I trust you and your judgment. Your family and friends are mine, baby."

That was the beginning of a long friendship among us all. Hurricane and I traveled many weekends and holidays down the turnpike to Virginia in rented cars to see them, or they came to visit us, until his return to Canada.

IN THE SUMMER OF '91 Hurricane had gone to Canada on a business trip. That afternoon, I received a call from an unfamiliar female voice. "Hello?"

"Hello. Do you know Rubin Carter?"

"Who's this?" I responded. "Who is this? And why do you want to know?"

"I'm calling you because your name has been appearing on my phone bill."

In an agitated voice, I said, "My name? I don't even know who you are."

"Yes, your name."

I stood in the center of the bedroom floor, glaring sun poured through the windows, and shadows of tree branches stitched the wood floors. I snapped back. "Why would my name show up on your bill? Who is this? And what's your name?"

"Don't worry about it. I'm a Newark police officer," she said.

I began to shake uncontrollably. "Why would my name show up on your bill?"

She asked again, "Do you know Rubin Carter?"

"Yes, I know him. But what business is it of yours, anyway?"

"It's my business because Rubin's been using my calling card."

". . .Oh—but what does that have to do with me? You allowed him to use it. That's between you and him." I couldn't wait until I spoke to Carter. He'd been using her card, and now I was involved in his bullshit? "What do you want *me* to do?" I shouted.

"Tell me, what does Rubin call you for? Is it for business or is it personal?"

I said, boiling as I paced the floor, *"What?"*

"I asked you if it's business or personal."

I started to hang up on her at that moment but decided to answer. "It's business. Why?" She tried scaring me by telling me again she was a police officer but didn't know how close I was to telling her to fuck off.

She asked, in a curious tone, "It's business?"

I said with a smile, "Yes, that's what I said, didn't I?"

"Oh," she said as if she didn't believe it but had no choice but to accept it.

"Is there anything else you want to know?"

"No." I could hear the puzzlement in her voice.

"Good-bye, then," I said and hung up.

Several hours later, the phone rang. It was Rubin. "Hey, baby," he said cheerfully. "What's going on?

I controlled my anger. "I should be asking you that," I said, crumpling a piece of paper in my hand.

"I'll be home tomorrow around six o'clock."

I stared out the window while sitting at the pine colored computer desk. "Okay."

"What's the matter, Jan? I can hear it in your voice. Something's wrong."

I glanced down at the pile of paper on the floor. "You can detect something's wrong, huh?"

"Yes. What is it?"

"Some woman called here today asking me questions about you." I stared at the paper, thinking of how I had to shred the pile.

He got excited. "Some woman? . . . What kind of questions? Did she say what her name was?"

"She didn't say, but told me she was a Newark police officer."

"What? . . . I know exactly who that was."

"I'm sure you do. She told me my name kept appearing on her phone bill because you use her calling card."

". . .Oh. That's all she told you?"

I picked up a few papers and began looking them over. "You have her calling card, Rube?"

"Yes. She's one of our business associates."

"Uh-hmm. One who allows you to use her calling card?"

"Yes," he said. I could hear him lighting a cigarette in the background.

"Then she had the nerve to ask me if you called for business or was it a personal. What would a business associate be asking that for?"

There was a long pause. ". . .What did you say?"

"I told her it was business." I knew then he was full of it. Why would he care what I said?

He responded with a sigh of relief, "Good, baby. That's exactly what you were supposed to tell her."

SEPTEMBER OF THAT YEAR, MY suspicions about Rubin came full circle. It was a fall day that felt like one in July, hot and humid. My son and his friends, along with Elaine, Hurricane, and I, were moving me from Vailsburg, in Newark, to Plainfield, New Jersey. The guys—with the exception of Rubin, decided to go ahead with the moving truck to unload the heavy items. Elaine and I were loading small odds and ends into the trunk of the mid-size Ford parked several houses down the street, a quiet one with little traffic.

We gathered the last of the small boxes and miscellaneous items and took them to the car, leaving Rubin behind for a final look around and to lock up. We chatted as Elaine's large-framed body, with the broad shoulders of an athlete and straight, shiny hair cut close to her scalp, strolled up alongside me. Both of us were tired from running up and down the stairs. I turned to her and said, "I'm going to back down the street and pick Rubin up."

Elaine huffed and puffed. "That'll be nice. He's probably as tired as we are. You have the poor man working his ass off!"

"Elaine, he practically lives there, too. He can help out." We reached the car.

I unlocked the trunk, shoved everything in, and we hopped in the vehicle. I backed slowly down the street, looking in all the mirrors. No cars approached. I pulled up to the driveway and parked in front of the red brick house, then looked to my left. Rubin was standing by the garbage can at the side of the house. He hadn't noticed us because his back was turned toward the car. His body language seemed strange to me.

"Lannie, look at him. What's he doing over there?"

"I don't know. Watch."

All of a sudden, to our surprise, his head tilted back. In his hand was a twisted brown paper bag molded in the shape of a bottle, which he brought to his mouth. It had to have been a fifth of Smirnoff. And in the other hand he held the lid to the garbage can while he gulped down the last sip of vodka at seven o'clock in the morning.

I turned toward Elaine, perplexed. "What's wrong with that picture?" I asked as she gazed out the window but had no response.

Rubin threw the empty bottle into the can. He replaced the lid and turned sideways toward the door. The keys were dangling from his hand when he happened to glance over his left shoulder and saw the car parked out front; we were looking straight at him. Boy, what shock scrambled across his face. He'd been busted, and there wasn't a thing he could do to get out of it.

Fuming, I slid the window down. My rage stemmed from my childhood experiences with my grandmother, who had thrown weekend or holiday alcohol-infested parties that included drunken perverts who lurked for prey in the shadows of our house.

Elaine said, "I can see it in your face, he's in trouble. Leave him alone, Janetta." That was a nickname she used for me.

"I'll leave him alone, alright. He's standing there having a drink at seven o'clock in the fuckin' morning!" I said as I looked over at him locking the door. ". . .Yeah, I'll leave him alone."

She laughed. "You're crazy. You better stop before he knocks your lights out."

"Uh-huh. You're going to see me get real crazy on his ass in a minute. Wait until he gets over to this car."

He pulled out the keys, slipped them in his blue jeans pocket, and turned around slowly, making his way down the driveway.

I looked at Elaine with a devilish smile. "Uh-huh, here he comes."

"He's going to smack the shit out of you. That's what's going to happen to you."

I rolled my eyes at her. "I wish he would."

He walked around the back of the car, opened the door on the passenger's side, and climbed in behind Elaine without saying a word.

I immediately turned around and looked him directly in the face. "What the hell were you doing over there?"

He looked up at me with sad puppy eyes. " . . .I—"

"I nothing. You were having a drink at seven o'clock in the morning. That's what you were doing, Rube. You're a fuckin' alcoholic, that's what you are."

He leaned forward, placing his arms over the seat. "I am."

I shifted into drive but kept my foot on the brake, turned around once more, looked at him, then drove off. I had been steaming so badly, my sunglasses had fogged up. He leaned back in the chair and didn't utter a single word.

I kept my head forward. Elaine glanced at me as if to say, Have you lost your mind talking to him that way?

Rubin said, "Elaine, you know she's the only person on this earth I'll let talk to me that way."

"I know, Rube," she said, rolling her eyes at me.

"Jan's absolutely correct. I am an alcoholic."

I yelled, "That's good. At least you can admit it to yourself. You're a damn alcoholic. That's a good sign."

Elaine turned around to face him. "I know, Rube, she's lost her mind."

"I love Jan," he said. "She's my baby, Lannie."

I glanced at him through the rear-view mirror, still bewildered and hurt by what I'd seen. Our eyes periodically met when I glanced up in the mirror and I stared at him. "I don't particularly care about your love for me at the moment, Rube."

"You caught me, and I'm wrong."

"Yeah, I did. I watched you from the time you pulled the top off the garbage can. Rubin, only alcoholics drink first thing in the morning. That's the bottom line."

I had to focus back on the road, because I was approaching the entrance to the parkway. I looked in the mirror again at him as he bobbed his head up and down. He said, "You're right."

I thrashed out, shouting, "You *disgust* me. I know you don't think what you did is okay with me, because it's not. You of all people know how I feel about alcohol. Oh, hell, *no*, Rube! You know." I drove at moderate speed in the middle lane.

"I'm admitting it, Jan. What more do you want me to say?"

"You'd better admit it to yourself, not to me."

Elaine sat immobile in disbelief, looking at me. "Leave the man alone, Janet!"

We got off the parkway and I stopped at a red light, then turned in her direction and said, "What?"

"Don't be hollering at *me*," she replied. "I didn't do anything to you."

The light turned green. "Personally, Elaine, I don't give a shit how he feels right now."

Rubin leaned forward, placing his arm over the back of her chair. "That's right, Elaine. Tell her to leave me alone."

I turned towards him, and at the same time glanced at the road. "I'll leave you alone, alright. You fuckin' drunk. That's what you are. Uh-huh. Now, tell me to leave you alone again."

Rubin poked her on the shoulder, and then pointed at me. "I love that woman right there."

"You better worry about yourself," I said, trying to concentrate on the road, because I'd swerved near the other lane.

"Jan, that's not the first time I've drunk around you."

"No, it's not—but not at seven o'clock in the morning!"

"I've done it before. You hadn't seen me, that's all."

"Whatever. Are you bragging? You're an alcoholic, Rubin. I didn't know you were that far gone. You're worse than my grandmother was, and she only drank socially. I thought that was bad."

He sat back, rested his head against the seat, and turned toward the window.

Elaine shook her head at me. "Rube, don't listen to her." He sat silently. "She's just angry—she'll get over it."

I shouted, "That means you drink every day!"

"Yes," he said sadly.

Disgusted, I said, "Don't tell me any more."

What an eye-opener for me that day. I even noticed, for the first time, his face had the puffiness of an alcoholic's. Also, I recalled he never drank out of a glass—only the bottle—and didn't appear to be drunk or smell of alcohol. That's why he kept mints or Certs in his mouth at all times. Like an idiot, I'd thought he was keeping his breath fresh. Rubin Hurricane Carter was a functional alcoholic who had talked and walked around me for decades.

Now I understood those moments when he'd call me at any hour of the day or night. Once he'd cried on the phone because I hadn't waited for him at a turnpike exit. Another time could've been the night we talked about our spouses; that was a conversation I'd never had before in my life.

That day, the conversation was about his wedding band. I happened to look at it while we sat, watching a video when something drove me to say, "Rube, can I see your ring?"

"Sure," he said, pulled the thin band off his finger, and handed it to me. "You can wear it."

"Wear it?" I placed the ring on a finger. "Wow, I didn't realize your fingers were so big," I said, handing it back to him.

"Wear it," he said with his legs crossed as a bottle of vodka stood on the side of the couch near him.

"For real?" I asked and placed it on another finger.

He said, without batting an eye, "Keep the ring if you want to."

I was startled. "What? I can keep it?"

"Yep, you sure can."

I'd never expected him to say that. What man does? "You mean it? I can wear this?"

He smiled. "Yep. Wear it for the rest of your life."

I moved it over to my middle finger on my right hand so it wouldn't fall off. "Really?" I stretched out my hand and looked him in his face.

"Uh-huh, I don't want it. All the sentimental value got taken away a long time ago."

"How come, Rube? It's your wedding ring."

"That ring was one of my favorite pieces of jewelry. They even allowed me to wear it in prison."

"Oh. They did?"

"Yep." I turned slightly. He grabbed the bottle and quickly swallowed some down.

"Lisa took advantage of me at that time."

"How'd she do that?"

Candles flickered throughout the room. "Put on some music." I jumped up, scurried over to the entertainment center, and pushed the button on the stereo remote. A song by Roberta Flack echoed in the room. Rubin pulled me up to dance, which wasn't unusual for us; we always danced when we were together. We enjoyed it.

He whispered in my ear while we spun, "That ring is white gold."

". . .Oh, it is? I thought it was sterling silver."

"No, baby. There were twenty-four diamonds on it, too." We wobbled from side to side, and our shadows were plastered against the walls.

I held up my hand and looked at the ring. "Twenty-four? Where are they?"

"Lisa took them. She asked me if she could make our wedding rings out of it. I told her yes, not thinking she was going to take all the diamonds. She left me with that thin piece of shit. Besides, I felt obligated for everything she'd done for me. That's why I married her."

"You weren't in love with her?" I asked.

"No. I never loved her."

"I see. You think you were ripped off for the diamonds."

"Yep, Lisa has nineteen diamonds on her ring and I'm stuck with five diamond studs on a thin band."

"That was sneaky of her."

"It goes with her personality," he said, with his cheek pressed against mine, as we moved barefoot on the plush mauve rug. "But it doesn't matter now, because all I want to do is get as far away from her and those people as I can."

THESE YEARS HAD ZOOMED BY US. We had constant uncontrollable events and situations engulf us. I sat watching television on an eight-foot-long lime-green silk couch, with vertical white lines jetting across it, when my mind wandered, and focused intently on Rubin; soon his presence had taken over the room. I envisioned the two of us standing in a hotel room near a window with his arms around me. Rubin had been on a fishing trip in Alaska with some friends that cold rainy weekend. Shortly thereafter, he called. I answered; his deep voice captured my attention, sending butterflies through my stomach; I propped up straight, as I felt his joy when he said, "Hey, there, baby. What are you doing?"

I aimed the remote at the stereo to turn the sound down. "Lying on the couch, thinking about you,"

"Oh. I see you're working that stuff on me again, huh. I miss you, Jan."

I snickered. "I miss you, too. Where are you right now?"

"I'm still on the boat, fishing. It's cold as hell out here. I'm freezing my ass off, but we're catching some nice-sized ones. Girl, you sure know how to conjure me up, don't you?"

I stood up and headed for the bathroom. "You think? Not only that, I had a vision of us standing in a room in front of a window, and you kissed me as your arms were around me."

"I must have felt you, because I called." His voice echoed in the background. "We must have some type of mental telepathy, my love."

"Yes, I believe we do, Rube. That happens to us all the time, huh."

"Yes. Well, Jan, I called to say hello and let you know that I'm okay."

I returned to the living room, grabbed the TV remote, and surfed through the channels. "That's nice," I said as I picked the stereo remote up from the couch and turned it off. "We can literally think about the other, and then one of us calls."

"Yeah, we do, do that often. Isn't that beautiful?" he said with a giggle.

IT WAS FALL. I packed an overnight bag, that fall, to stay overnight, dropped my daughter off, and left for South Jersey. At dusk, I had maybe thirty minutes to enjoy the fall colors while driving down the turnpike in the Renault, listening to the radio, counting exit signs. I reached Exit 2, paid the toll, and took the winding roads into Monroeville.

My first visit to Monroeville was when I pulled into the horseshoe-shaped driveway and peeked to see if there were lights on in the house. I jumped out, opened the back door, grabbed my overnight bag and a brown paper bag, and scurried to the porch. The light came on, and the door flung open before I knocked. "Hey, Baby," Rubin said, and hugged me tightly. "You smell good, and you look beautiful in that skirt. Come inside."

I handed him the bag that had a bottle of vodka in it. "Thank you," he said as he tossed my garment bag on the couch. Rubin went over to the dining table and draped the bag on it.

I stood in the center of the room; he turned and smiled. "I stopped at a liquor store in Newark before I headed out."

He grabbed my hand and pulled me to him. Memories flooded back of how I used to come to the house, and the couch sat right where it had been, up against the wall. I'm sure the place did the same to him when he first got back.

"I'm glad you made it safely." We stood in the archway beside the dining room, where a white lace tablecloth hung from the table. The man was a passionate and romantic one. "Hi, baby," he said with his lips pressed up against mine. He squeezed me. "I've missed you."

I gave into the passion, melting in the heat that consumed and weakened me. "I've missed you, too, Rube."

He leaned over to the table, grabbed the brown bag, and pulled out the bottle of vodka. "Thanks for this, Jan."

"No problem." I said and turned towards the couch and took a seat.

He went to the kitchen, quickly returned, and took a seat in the chair next to the front window. "It's good seeing you, Jan. I love you."

"How was it in Canada?"

"It was productive. Matter a fact, it was great, because I wasn't around the Canadians the entire time." He reached for his pack of cigarettes, which lay on the round end table next to him, and lit one up. We sat in silence until he finished smoking and smashed the butt against the crystal ashtray. Then he got up, grabbed my hand, pulled me up, and led me down the long, narrow hallway to a bedroom.

From a distance I could see lights flickering. When we entered, there were two candles on a walnut dresser, casting shadows. A queen-size bed sat up against a wall near a window that faced the front of the house and the driveway. He had R&B playing in the background, from a station out of Philly, that elevated the mood.

I slid past him, and he rubbed his hand across my arm. "You always smell so fresh and clean, and your skin's as soft as a baby's behind, as they say." He laughed.

"You think so?"

"I know it, Jan. I like that fragrance. What's the name of the perfume you're wearing?"

"Its Opium oil. I don't wear perfumes." I sat down on the edge of the bed.

"It's a very clean smell."

I placed my purse alongside me. "You know, Rube, you're wild."

He smiled devilishly. "You think I'm wild, girl?" he said, hopping onto the bed, pushed me down, and slid his tongue over my lips. "This is what you call wild?"

"Yep, you know why my skin's soft, Rube? I've been putting lotion on my body every day, since I was little."

"It worked." He jumped up, walked over to the window, and turned back toward me. "Jan, get up and walk for me."

I frowned. "*Walk* for you?"

"Yes. Walk. I want to watch the curves of your body." I stood up. Rubin returned to the bed and sat. "Go ahead, baby," he said, motioning his hand.

I felt uncomfortable but glided back and forth because he'd asked me to. He watched intently. "Okay, is that enough walking, Rube?"

He laughed. "You're very tantalizing to my eyes." I blushed. "Sure, baby. Come sit down here next to me." I plopped down quickly, and he ran his hand across my thigh then slipped over towards the dresser and picked up the paper bag. "You're put together well, with those natural curves. Your ex-husband is a fool for letting you go!" he said, placing the bottle back on top of the dresser. I swung my legs off the edge of the bed, looked at my watch, and saw it was ten o'clock. "Jan, the bathroom's down the hall, first door on your right if you need to use it, or there's one directly across, in the master bed room."

"Okay." I went over to the doorway and looked at the empty master bedroom.

Rubin came up behind me and whispered in my ear, "I told you I was coming back to you, didn't I? Here I am, girl. I love you, Jan," and brushed his quivering tongue across my ear.

"My divorce papers finally arrived this week," I replied. "It's official now. Thanks for recommending Perkins, Rube."

We remained in the doorway. "Oh, baby, I was glad to help. Now you're free."

"I'm free from him, but we still have a daughter together. He still tries to control things and strip me of my self-esteem, by manipulating my character with assaults. I felt this feeling of emotional, spiritual, and physical incarceration—it totally depleted me when I was with him."

"Don't let him get to you, baby. You're a strong woman. I must say I have to commend you, too on going to college, getting the master's, and raising your son, on your own. You've done an excellent job with him. Fuck your husband."

"Now my ex-husband." We laughed. Rubin reached over, picked up his cigarettes off the dresser, lit one, took several puffs, and laid it in the ashtray.

ONE THURSDAY EVENING I SAT BY toll booths near the row of telephones at the Secaucus and East Rutherford exit, waiting for Rubin. He was driving back from Canada. I'd picked up my son from practice, who sat in the backseat, eating supper from Burger King. Eight o'clock came, but there was no Rubin, and I sat for another thirty minutes before I decided to go home. The reality hit me hard at that moment; I couldn't go to my aunt's place any more to pass the time away. The only people I had left in town were my sister and mother, who all lived together. Besides, I needed to go home, let my son shower, and get ready for bed. Rubin was late, and I never thought maybe he'd got stuck in traffic; I left.

The following day, he called. "Why didn't you wait for me, Jan?"

"I did. I waited until eight-thirty, with my son in the car. London was watching my daughter. I had to get back."

"You should have waited."

"I had my *son*, Rubin, and had to get home. My ex was watching our daughter. I didn't want to get into an argument over being late." I sat straight up in the bed.

"You still should've waited. That hurt me." All of a sudden I heard wracking noises and thought I wasn't hearing correctly.

"Are you crying, Rube?"

"Yes."

"Why?" I curled up.

"Why? I can't trust you." He began to gasp. "I thought you'd wait."

What the hell is this weird shit, I thought. "I don't know what any of this has to do with trust. I miss you too, Rubin. I had to go, can't you understand that? I would've loved to have seen you. I need to. You know how London is."

"You have to promise something, then."

I shook my leg. "What's that?"

"Whenever we wait for each other, we have to wait at least two hours."

"Two hours! I'll wait an hour an a half, but not two, Rube."

"Alright, an hour and a half, but I'll wait two for you or as long as it takes."

I thought about what he had said about trust and became agitated. "You said you can't trust me?" I got out of bed, went to the living room, lay stretched across the couch, and listened to him feel as if it were my fault. "I'm sorry for whatever it was you think I did, Rube."

He sternly said, "The next time, you wait for me. Do you hear me, baby, and promise?"

"Okay, I promise. I'll wait the next time."

"You don't even know what happened."

"Tell me, and stop saying you can't trust me. What's that about?"

"I was stuck in traffic coming out of Canada. That's what slowed me down."

"I'm sorry I didn't know that or think that could've of caused you to be late."

"Two hours. Hear me. That's in case something goes wrong."

"Two hours? That's a long time, Rube, but alright."

"An hour and a half. I'll compromise for you, baby, but I'm waiting for you."

"Now, Rube, when can I see you?"

"I'll come up on Friday."

"This weekend will be fine. London has DJ. I have to drop her off around seven."

Emotionlessly, he said, "That'll be great. I'll see you around six."

I began to realize how many memories I had of him involved with alcohol.

FIVE YEARS HAD SOARED BY since our reunion; before moving to Plainfield. Another winter arrived; Rubin began to look worn down from the road. He'd gotten thinner and complained of tiredness, felt cold constantly, had severe headaches, and later developed a terrible cough. I thought his thinness was from not eating properly, and he was a skinny man to begin with. He wore undershirts beneath a sweatshirt in eighty-degree weather, with thermal bottoms under his pants, and complained of being cold all the time.

His health worsened; it became evident after a weekend trip to Virginia, when he slept the entire time. When we returned to Jersey, he had to stay with me because of chills, coughing, and massively severe headaches.

He lay in bed, in a pair of red-and-white-striped pajamas, a thermal top and bottom underneath, looking close to death, as beads of sweat covered his forehead, with three blankets wrapped around him. It was evident how much weight he'd lost; he'd dwindled to a skeletal frame with a layer of skin. I sat on the edge of the bed, wiping sweat off his forehead. "Rube," I said as I bent over and kissed him.

He looked up at me with sick, glassy eyes and a stubbly gray beard. "Yes, my love?" he said, in a raspy voice.

"You have to see a doctor. I can call mine. Do you want me to?"

He turned on his left side, facing the wall, and mumbled, "I can't see a doctor here."

"Why not?" He was so sick I was afraid he was going to die on me at any minute.

His back touched mine. He said, muffled and horse, "All my medical benefits are for Canada."

"Can't you use your insurance here?"

"No, it doesn't work that way."

I rested my elbows on my knees and held my face in my hands. "You have to see a doctor, Rube."

"All my doctors are in Canada. Besides I don't trust the ones here. They have better ones there."

I jumped up and stood over him. "You look bad." I rubbed his face with the towel again. "Please let me call a doctor."

He twisted around. "I know I should, baby, but how am I supposed to get back to Canada? I don't have the strength to drive myself." I was afraid for him. He looked like he was going to die.

"I'll drive you. I'll take a few vacation days."

He pulled the blankets close to his neck. "Thanks, but you—know you can't do that."

I said frowning at him. "Why not? You're sick. You need to see a doctor."

Hurricane shivered. "The Canadians."

"How would they know? We can get a room, and they can pick you up there."

He peeked out from underneath the gold-trimmed silk blanket. "How do I explain how I got there? They can't see you."

"Why can't they? You're separated from that woman legally, aren't you, Rubin?"

"Yes, I am, but I have to be careful because of my business ties with them. This isn't the time, and the two informants would tell her."

Puzzled, I asked, "Who are 'the informants?"

"Sam and Terry," he said emotionlessly.

I became frustrated. ". . .Do you want me to put the television on?"

"No, it'll hurt my head. I have a splitting headache," he added, scooting up.

"Then let me take you directly to the hospital or to your doctor's office."

"I can't do that either, because the doctor knows them."

"I see." I walked to the window pulled back the curtain; shadows of branches flickered on the walls. The sun waxed the freshly grown burgundy and pink flowers, mixed with green leaves, as the wind made them move gracefully about in the neighbor's yard.

"They introduced me to him. They're friends, and he'd asked questions. They'd want to know where my truck was. I don't feel like going through that shit with them. You know what I mean, baby."

I turned back to him. "What are you going to do then, Rube? You need to get to a doctor."

He stared at the ceiling. "I don't know. I can't think right now."

"Personally, Rube, I don't understand any of this. It seems to me you're still under her control."

"If they see you, it'll make matters worse for me. That woman is upset with me because I left. She still hasn't completed my paperwork for citizenship. God only knows what else she'd do if she heard you were there."

I paused near the dresser. "I don't care what she thinks, and I'm sure she already knows about me. I've been there many times before. You've called her house from here." I lay beside him. "I know what I'll do."

He scratched his eyebrow and opened his eyes wide. "What?"

"I'll call Ken and Jean. I'll ask them to take you."

"Don't call them, Jan," he replied, but it wasn't convincing enough for me not to call.

I looked around the room for the portable. It was lying on the floor at the foot of the bed. I scooped it up. "What are you going to do, stop me?" I smiled at him. Rubin was weak. It took energy just for him to talk.

He placed his arm across his forehead. "You don't have to do that," he said, sliding down on the bed.

"I know I don't, but what else can we do? You're very sick—I can see it in your eyes." I dialed. Jean picked up. "Hey, Jean."

"Hey! What's up?"

I paced the room, watching Rubin's eyes follow me. "Are you busy?"

"Nah, I'm washing clothes, my usual daily chores." I could hear her turning the control knob on one of the machines.

"I called to see if you and Ken can do me a big favor."

"What's that?"

"Remember when we were down and how sick Rubin was?"

"Yeah, he laid around all weekend. He looked horrible."

I walked out to the dining area. "Well, he's been here ever since we left."

"What? That's been almost two weeks," she said as the water ran in the washer.

"He needs to see a doctor but needs to get to Canada. I can't drive him back because of the Canadians. I was wondering if you and Ken could drive him." I looked down at my toes, noticing that my toe nails needed to be polished.

"I can't go, but hold on, let me ask Ken. He may be able to do it."

"Okay." I heard a door close and waited several minutes. In the meantime, I walked back to the bedroom and stood at the doorway, looking at Rubin.

"Jan?" He seemed to have a little more energy.

"Yeah." I leaned against the door frame. "Hold on, Rube." Jean had returned.

She called out into the phone. "Jan?"

"Yeah, I'm here."

"Ken said he can take him, but it'll have to be in a couple of days because he has some work to finish up. Can he wait that long?"

"He has no other choice. He's waited this long. Thanks so much. Tell Ken thanks."

"I will. I'm glad we can help."

"Thanks, Jean, I'll talk to you soon." I hung up and and sat alongside of Rubin.

Hurricane stared at me in anticipation. "What did they say?"

"Jean can't go, but Ken said he can take you. But it won't be until the end of the week. He has some work to finish up."

He gathered the biggest smile he could and in a weak voice said, "That's fine. Thank you, Jan."

"I'm worried, Rube. You don't look well at all. You have to get checked. I don't want you checking out of here any time soon. If something were to happen to you, what would I do without you, huh?"

I gazed into his eyes, lifting my feet onto the bed, and lay next to him. "I really love you. I do," he said.

EARLY THURSDAY MORNING, KEN SHOWED up around one in the morning because they wanted to get to the doctor's office by the time he opened. I didn't hear from them for hours, until that evening. In a raspy voice he said, "Hi, my love," and coughed.

I was standing in the kitchen—large yellow square stone tile, surrounded by lime-green oval stone trim, circled the kitchen walls—cooking dinner. "Hey, Rube! Where are you? I've been worried to death about you. Is everything alright?"

"Yes and no, my love. I'm sicker than I thought. The doctor put me in the hospital."

"What? You're in a hospital? What's wrong with you?" I became nervous.

"You got me here just in time."

I sank onto a seat at the table in the corner near the refrigerator, kicking off my shoes. "Where's Ken?

"He went back to his hotel room to get some sleep before he leaves."

"Oh." I held my forehead.

"He met Sam and Terry today at the doctor's office."

"He did?" I said as nervous jitters attacked my nervous system. "They were there, too?"

He said softly, "I told you Lisa was going to send them."

"Why'd the doctor put you in the hospital?"

Rubin sighed, "I have tuberculosis."

My eyes grew wide. "*Tuberculosis?* How'd you get that?"

"I had to have gotten it while I was in prison, Jan. If it wasn't for you, Jeannie, and Ken, I wouldn't be here now."

My heart dropped into my stomach; I dragged myself over to the oven. "I knew there was something terribly wrong with you, but I'd never figured it was TB. Isn't that deadly, Rube?" I remembered the word from grammar school but had no idea what the symptoms were.

In a weak voice he said, "They're doing all types of tests right now, poking and stabbing at me. That's what's been causing the headaches, the tuberculosis."

"Is tuberculosis contagious?" I asked as I opened the oven door to pull out the roasted chicken.

"There are different strains. Some forms can be contagious, but I don't know if I have a strain that is. That's what they're doing all the testing for, to find out. The doctor did tell me, the stage I'm in right now, most people would've been dead. "He was surprised I'd made it this long. I'm in a bad way, Jan. You never get sick."

Wow, the doctor had admitted him immediately to the hospital. If he hadn't gone, he'd have been a dead man.

"I've never seen you sick, girl. You've been around people with colds and the flu, but it doesn't seem to affect you. Your immune system is strong." Rubin turned away from the phone and coughed.

I rested against the sink. "I do, but not often," I said as I walked over to the oven to baste the bird, then slid the pan back. "You looked like death, I must say."

"I was, literally near it, Jan. They're pumping a whole lot of fluids and antibiotics into me. I'll be alright, thanks to you, and I'll be back to you before you know it. Take down my room number, baby."

"Hold on, let me get a pen and a piece of paper. Are you sure you'll be alright, Rube?" I went into the dining room and found paper and a pen.

"Yes. I should get my test results in a few days, but in the meantime, you and DJ have to go get tested."

I went up to the living room and plopped on the couch, flabbergasted, with my mouth hanging open. "You said *what?* Give me your number. . . . What do you mean, we should go get tested?"

"The doctor suggested that anyone I had been in contact with should go get a tuberculosis shot right away." Suddenly now I had to worry about that. What if my daughter had it? How would I tell her father? I thought.

"You need to tell Jean and Ken the same thing."

"What the hell am I going to tell my ex?" I said.

"Don't tell him anything right now. Go to the doctor first. Most likely you won't have anything. . . .Oh Lord, I forgot you get bent out of shape over stuff like this. Don't stress over it. I'm sure both of you are fine."

"Okay, I'll call our doctors first thing tomorrow morning and make appointments. Get some rest, Rube. I'll call you tomorrow."

The next morning I called each doctor as soon as the clock struck nine and made the appointments. My daughter went first, then I, the following day. I called my cousins that evening to tell them about Rubin but they decided to wait for our test results to come back before they made any appointments. If we were negative, they felt they didn't need to go.

Each day we spoke while he waited for his results and ours. In the meantime I had broke out with tiny, circular red pimples and freaked out. I didn't call Rubin right away because I became angry. When I did, he said, "Jan! Where have you been?"

"Oh, going crazy."

"Over what? Worrying about the TB?" he asked in a clearer voice, and giggled.

"You sound much better. The hoarseness has almost disappeared."

"Yeah, I'm recovering each day. Tell your cousins I said hello. I truly would've left this place if it wasn't for you guys. You're beautiful, Jan. Hold on a minute—someone just walked in." I could hear them mumbling in the background. "Okay, my love, I'm back' and I have some news for you."

"What's that?" I said solemnly.

"I don't have a contagious strain of tuberculosis. You're not infected."

"That's great," I said with a sigh of relief. "But I know that already."

"I told you you weren't. You had nothing to worry about."

"Yeah, DJ's test came back negative. But guess what? Out of all the people in the world, I had an allergic reaction to the shot. I thought I had it and freaked. That's why I haven't called."

"Oh. . . . I'm sure you cursed me out, too."

"Yep, you know it. I called Lannie and had her take me to the municipal nurse at her office to check it out. I was afraid to go back to my doctor." Rubin cracked up laughing. "It's not funny, Rube. I had tiny red pimples that formed in a circular rash. It looked similar to what the doctor had described to me it would look like, if you had TB. I just knew I had it."

"Tell Lannie I said thanks for looking after you for me."

"She laughed, too. She told me it probably was an allergic reaction. Of course, I didn't believe her either. But I begged her to take me to the nurse."

"I can imagine how you were acting. You're a mess, girl. You know you turn red if someone touches you the wrong way, because you have sensitive skin."

"I know. What's important is we're okay and you're getting better."

"I'm still going to have to take antibiotics. Did Jean and Ken go get their tests?"

"No, they said they wanted to wait for our results."

"Okay, I guess that makes sense."

So, prayerfully, we had tested negative, and Hurricane had a treatable type of tuberculosis he'd contracted in prison from inadequate air circulation and, apparently, carried around for a long time.

A few days before Rubin was discharged from the hospital, I called his room. He sounded distracted and annoyed. "Jan, can you call me later on this evening?"

"Okay," I said but was puzzled.

I called back that night. "Hi, Rube. How come you couldn't talk earlier? Was the nurse or doctor there?"

He said unhappily. "No, it was Lisa."

"Oh. I thought only Sam and Terry came to see you."

"She came, too."

"You never said Lisa was there."

"She knew it was you I was talking to, and she made a smart remark about it today."

"What'd she say?"

"'Oh that's your girlfriend, Janet.' I was shocked she knew your name."

"Why? I told you she knows all about me. Why wouldn't she, Rube? That's who came into your room when you told me to hold on?"

"Yes. She stormed out and hasn't been back since. Now only Sam and Terry come. Would you do me a favor?"

". . . What's that?"

"Please hold off calling. I'm going to be leaving in a few days anyway. I'll call you."

"Why, because of Lisa?" I snapped. "Huh, Rube?"

"I'll call you, I promise. You know I will, as soon as I get an opportunity. Another thing, Jan—I have to go back to that house until I recover and get my strength back. As soon as I'm better, I'll be back in Jersey. Take care of yourself, my love."

Rubin was released into the care of the Canadians. Weeks went by before I heard from him again. He'd leave the house and make calls to me from pay phones or when he went to friends' houses. Lisa treated him—according to him—as if he was, a prisoner on the outside.

NOT LONG AFTER, WE SPENT a weekend at a hotel in Canada. Rubin threw his arms around me and kissed me on my cheek as we stood in front of a large bay window, gazing out at the Canadian skyline. I'd pictured this exact moment the day I lay thinking of him when he was in Alaska; the kiss brought everything to fruition. I said, "Rubin?"

"Yes, my love?" he replied, with his arms tightly around me.

I vibrated from the atmosphere of the evening. "This is the spot. It's the exact room I had envisioned. I told you about it when you were on the fishing trip in Alaska, remember? One of those awake visions."

"Yes, I remember you telling me that."

"It was here at this hotel." He said, shaking me from side to side.

"Hm," he said, and squeezed me tighter. "You're scary, girl, and something else."

Conflict had played a major part in our relationship since the beginning. The older generations had their backward way of thinking—for one, wanting to believe we were related, because my great-aunt Lil married into the Carter family. They wanted to believe we were all related because of their closeness as friends that built a union as a family would.

His mother, Bert Carter, and my great-aunt Lil were sisters-in-law and best friends. They developed a tight relationship, sharing the same religious backgrounds and beliefs, both married to Carters who were reverends. Through this united front my mother had become close, friends at one time with Rubin's first wife, Mae Thelma.

We are Jacksons and they are Carters. Great-Aunt Lillian Jackson— a Jackson White, who married Marshall Carter, who is Rubin's father's brother—his uncle—became Lillian Carter's husband. My aunt had five children from the marriage, Rubin's first cousins are my mother's first cousins, because Lil was a sister to my grandmother, Dolores Scudder, who was my mother's mother. Great Aunt Lil's children are my second cousins only through the marriage. I am a Jackson, and Rubin is a Carter. There is no bloodline to him that makes us related.

What a sense of thought, I felt the elders had, confusing the issue for years. Because of their distorted and warped sense of mind thought, Rubin and I chose to keep everything we did a secret. We knew we had no blood-line between us and we were not related. Nothing could be said to our families—and then there were the Canadians and the press. This made my underground, secretive, shadow life essential.

I'd attend events with him and wear wigs to disguise myself, not to have the Canadians recognize me. Once we were in Washington DC, at the Quality Hotel Capital Hill, at 415 New Jersey Ave NW, when Sam and Terry were around; I was right under their nose.

A SUMMER AFTERNOON IN '92 MONROEVILLE—I lay across his bed, arriving only moments before we heard a car pull into the driveway. The bedroom he occupied faced the front driveway, and he could see who pulled up and who got out. Rubin slid up to the window, peeked out, and turned towards me with a frown. "Who the hell is that? I don't recognize that car."

"Can you see who's in it?" I asked.

"No, I can't." He pulled the curtain back more. "I wonder who that is? Damn! It's my nieces. What the hell are they doing here?" The car doors slammed, and voices rang loudly as they approached the porch to ring the doorbell.

"Be quiet," he said. "Maybe they'll go away." I sat still.

They rang the bell then shouted, "Uncle Rubin, Uncle Rubin! We know you're in there! Open up. We're not going away until you do."

He arched his back and said to me, "Jan, go into the bathroom across the hall. I'm going to let them in and get rid of them quickly, okay, baby?"

"Yeah," I said, getting up quietly, sliding out and over to the master bedroom directly across the hall from his. I had almost closed the bathroom door when I realized I'd left my sweater lying on the bed. I ran out and caught Rubin before he walked down the hall.

The doorbell rang again. They yelled, "Uncle Rubin!"

"I'm coming! Hold on," he shouted.

I whispered. "Rubin, wait! I left my sweater on the bed."

He scurried back and snatched it up. "Here, my love." The bell squealed, and he yelled, "Wait a minute."

I hurried back to the bathroom, locked the door behind me, pulled down the toilet seat lid, and sat still as could be.

I heard him rush to the door. A voice shouted, "Hurry up, Uncle Rubin."

He opened it. "Hi," he said. "What the hell are you doing here, showing up with out calling?"

"We're on our way to Philly, and we had to use the bathroom, so we stopped here."

"Oh, you decided to come here and bother me."

One of them said, "We knew you were here, Uncle. We wanted to see you."

"It's nice to see you, too, but. . . . Get to the bathroom, and get out of here," he said as he closed the door with a chuckle. But we all knew he was serious about what he'd said.

I heard one of them come down the hall towards me. She shouted. "I'll use the other bathroom in the master bedroom, Uncle."

When she said that, I realized I'd left my purse on the bed, too.

She came closer.

Rubin yelled, "Come back her, girl." I heard his slippers scraping the floor as he rushed up behind her. They both stopped at the doorway to the bedroom. "Use the one your sister's in, wait for her to finish." I looked at the door, making sure it was locked.

She said in a sassy voice. "Who's here, Uncle, Rubin?"

"What? Go back up front." She laughed. "I'm not playing with you, either."

"Who's here? Tell me," she said. I heard her feet shuffling about.

"Why are you asking me that?"

I panicked. It seemed she had moved in the direction of the bathroom. Rubin said, "It's none of your business. Now, let's go. Your sister just came out." They went down the hallway, laughing.

"It must be someone I know," she said. "Whose pocketbook was that on the bed? And besides there's a car parked in the driveway."

"Next time, call before stopping. Hear me?" Rubin said. "Go to the bathroom and get the hell out of here." Rubin's voice got even deeper when he said, "I told you I'm not playing with you."

"Okay, Uncle Rubin." The door to the bathroom closed.

A few minutes later, one said, "Alright, Uncle Rubin, we're leaving." All the footsteps moved to the front of the house.

He laughed, but it wasn't one from the heart, I could tell. "Good, get the hell out of here."

"Bye. You're rushing us out, but it was nice seeing you anyway, Uncle."

He snorted loudly, opening the front door. They headed out the front door. He opened it. "It was good seeing you too, but as I said, next time, call. Take care of yourselves."

An unfamiliar voice said, "It was nice meeting you, Mr. Carter." That must have been one of their friends, I thought.

"You, too," Rubin replied. "Now, get out of here." I heard the door close and lock. Rubin stood at the door for a few seconds, watching them pull away. He yelled, "Jan, you can come out. They're gone."

I jumped up and scurried out, distraught from the shock of their arrival. "Oh, boy, Rube, I can't believe I left my purse on the bed. I wanted to drop dead when I heard your niece coming toward the bathroom."

"Yeah, me, too. That's why I hurried up to stop her." He grabbed me and held onto me tightly.

"Do you think they knew it was me?"

He laughed. "Nah, they probably thought it was one of our cousins, one of the Carters they want to believe I'm screwing."

"Why would your family think that about you? Are you messing with one of your relatives?"

He pulled himself away. "Get the hell out of here."

Hurricane chuckled, bent over, and kissed my forehead. "No, they don't know you were here." He grabbed my hand and led me to the kitchen. "Are you hungry?"

ANOTHER CLOSE ENCOUNTER CAME WHEN I'd gone down to spend the night. We'd settled in bed, candles lit the room, and music played softly in the background. Around nine thirty, a car pulled into the driveway. Thank God all the lights were out, which gave the impression no one was home. Rube jumped out the bed and quickly blew out the candles. "Good idea," I whispered.

He slid near the window and peeked out as the car parked. "That's Mickey."

I slid down next to him and looked. "Are you going to let her in?"

He looked again. "Your mother's with her."

"What? My *mother?*" I heard both car doors slam and their voices as they approached the porch. I jumped back near the headboard and pulled the blankets up over my shoulders.

Rubin pulled on the curtains slightly and looked over at me with a grin. "They're standing on the porch, but don't worry, I'm not answering that door. You can relax, baby. If Mickey was by herself, I would."

I heard my mother mumbling. "What's she saying?"

"Oh, lord. She's pointing to your car," he said.

"Oh, shit!" Petrified and shocked, I sat listening to the doorbell ring. Mickey said, "He's not here."

"Whose car is that parked over there?" my mother shouted.

"I don't know. Maybe Thelma's. That's whose it looks like. She's probably visiting, and they went out."

"Oh! It looks just like Jan's car."

Micky responded quickly and said, "Nah, Thelma has one like that, too."

Rubin said, "Mickey must have realized that's your car and covered it up."

"Good. I'm glad she caught on."

"Let's go," Mickey said. The screen door slammed, the car doors were next, and they drove off.

We both sighed, but I was flipping, though Rubin had been getting a kick out of the whole thing. He reached for my foot and pulled on it. "Of all nights they decide to stop by."

"And of all people, my mother. I know she knew that was my car but pretended she didn't."

He chuckled. "I don't think she did. Don't worry about it, I'll call Mickey in the morning and ask her what they were doing here."

"I bet my mother liked you, too, back in the day, didn't she, Rube?" I burst out laughing.

He looked at me solemnly. "I don't know."

"Oh, yes you do."

With a mischievous smile he said, "I don't."

"After seeing my car she probably wished she was in my position, huh?" We both laughed hysterically.

"You're crazy, girl."

I lay back on the bed, and Rubin ran his hand across my stomach.

HE AND I, IN A real sense, shared the same type of confinement when it came to our spouses. We were always in conflicting situations, even minding our own business. He'd been in prison and, since he married, had the same type of control in a marriage. I'd never been to prison, but lived with a control freak, a man, like his wife. Both with attitudes, that systematized and rearranged somebody else's life because they wanted to.

5

THE MIDDLE OF THE RING

I N 1993, A SUNNY SUMMER Friday afternoon in July, my daughter and I were heading down the turnpike to meet Rubin at Exit 7. We'd park around that exit, transfer over to his red Jeep Cherokee, and go to Virginia. This trip was going to be for a week.

DJ was strapped in the middle of the back seat as I drove in the middle lane. The brightness of the sun enveloped the powder blue sky with rolling, puffy clouds, but something terrible happened before we reached the hotel parking lot where he waited.

When we arrived, it was on a flatbed tow-truck that pulled up in front of him alongside the road. Rubin looked up in utter bewilderment, leaped out, leaving the door open, and ran up the incline to us. I opened the truck door, he helped us down, grabbing my daughter first, hugging her tightly, then me.

He kissed her forehead, laying her head on his shoulder. "What happened, baby?" he asked as she lay emotionless.

"A tractor trailer hit us," I said, shaking, and he took hold of my hand, pulling me close to him.

"What?" He leaned back, looked at the rear of the tow truck, and saw the totaled gray Renault strapped on it. "Are the two of you okay?"

He rubbed my daughter's back.

"I feel fine right now, but who knows? She's traumatized, I believe, because she hasn't said much, and she's holding her arm in a strange position."

"Jan, let's go get a hotel room. The two of you aren't getting back on the road today. If you feel okay in the morning, we'll go, or we can cancel the trip altogether."

"I'll see how we feel when we wake up. We need to see a doctor tomorrow, that's for sure, especially her."

He held us both close, as we went inside the hotel and got our room. All of us sat together quietly on the bed, myself between his legs—DJ on my lap; he held us tightly, one body on the queen-size bed, feeling safe and protected in Hurricane's arms.

Eventually, DJ fell asleep. Rubin whispered in my ear, "I love you, Jan."

I leaned back into his chest and whispered, "I love you, too. DJ's fallen asleep. I should lay her down."

"I'll slide out and put her on the other bed," he said.

"Okay." I sat up as he moved. He took her from my arms, laid her gently on the bed next to us, and covered her with the blankets.

He slid back behind me, rested on the pillows, and I lowered myself on his chest. "Now tell me what happened," he said, and reached for those damn cigarettes on the table.

"I have to call London, you know. I'm afraid to, because he's going to act like a maniac and blame me for the accident."

"Go ahead and call. Don't let him get to you, my love."

We sat for another fifteen minutes before I made the call. I told my ex-husband the story; he gave me attitude, yelling and threatening me. Rubin could hear him yelling at the top of his lungs like a maniac and motioned for me to hang up. I did. "What was he yelling at you like that for?"

"That's how he is. I told you. He was calling me an asshole and blamed me for the entire thing."

"He's the asshole. What's wrong with that man? You know, Jan, he did you a big favor by leaving you."

"I know," I said, almost in tears. He blew out smoke, and I swatted it away.

"Let me move, so the smoke doesn't bother you." He got up stood near the window, and air conditioner to continue smoking. "Don't let him get to you, baby."

"I won't. Rube, if DJ wakes up and feels okay, we're going to Virginia as we planned. I'll call Jean and ask her to call her doctor, and get her arm checked out."

He stood with the ashtray, flicking ashes in it. "Are you sure?"

"Yes."

"Her arm isn't broken, that's for sure, or she'd be yelling. She probably bruised it."

"That had to have happened when I fell on her. Let me tell you what happened." Rubin came back to the bed and sat beside me. "I was driving in the middle lane, saw three trucks ahead of me, and one started jumping around in and out of the lanes, from the slow lane, the middle, and into the fast lane—all over the place. I slowed down to fifty and pulled into the slow lane. All of a sudden, I looked over to my left and see the truck move straight across from the fast lane, to the middle, and headed directly over towards me."

"What?" Rubin said, smashing the cigarette butt, and sunlight suddenly poured in from the window.

"Before I knew it, he was on top of the car trapping us between the cab and the trailer."

"Lord!" he said, squeezing me tightly, shaking his head.

"The impact broke my chair, threw me to the back seat, landing me on top of her. Then we were dragged a hundred feet down the road, attached to the truck, wobbling. I thought we were going to be thrown into the ditch at first, or he was going to fall on top of us. Until he finally realized we were hooked on to the truck and stopped, but somehow we were released—loose from the truck."

He rubbed my shoulders and neck. "Oh, baby. I'm sure that was horrifying."

"Scary isn't the word for it. When we stopped, I panicked and frantically looked around for DJ, because I didn't see her. I happened to look down underneath me, and there she was, peeking up at me. I snatched her up so fast; to make sure she had no broken bones, and held her tightly, then looked for a way out. I noticed the right side of the car wasn't damaged, and quickly pushed the passenger's seat up, opened the door, and got the hell out of there."

"I'm so sorry that happened," he said, looking over at DJ.

"People slowed down but didn't stop. Only one man did. He came to us with a piece of gauze and wiped the broken glass from our faces, then helped me get the garment bag and her bike from the trunk. He walked us to the embankment, away from the car, in case there was a gas leak. Then he left."

"Only one person stopped to help you? No one else stayed around as a witness for the police report?"

"Nope. He left us with the gauze. Everything happened so fast, Rube. I can't even remember what he looked like. I held her tight, stayed calm, and tried not to act afraid or cry. We sat on the grass at the edge of the ditch, and I rocked her in my arms. Peripherally, I saw the truck driver walking towards us. I got up and moved farther down, but he kept coming. I stopped and sat; he stood alongside of us, apologizing in a Southern dialect. I was disgusted and didn't want to hear what he had to say."

"He was a Southerner? What part of the South?"

"Yep, I think the plates said South Carolina, or it could have been North Carolina. It was one of the two. He knew to get away from me and walked back down the road to the trailer. Finally a state trooper pulled up behind us, slid his window down, asked if we were alright, and told me another trooper was on the way."

Rubin's eyebrows rose. "He did what? He left the two of you by the side of the road and drove off?"

"Yep. It gets better. He was a White guy, and the next trooper was a Black one."

"It sounds like they were buddies. You were an attractive Black female who was stranded on the road. He was setting you up."

"Maybe. The other trooper didn't take long. He asked me to sit in the car, where it was cool, then grabbed his hat from the passenger's seat, and walked down toward the truck driver."

"Did he get his information?" Rubin said.

"Yeah, the trooper came back to the car and took down my information while that man looked in his cab for his insurance card. Then the truck driver walked back and climbed in the seat alongside us. He tried getting slick with the state trooper, too."

"Oh? What did he do?"

"He gave him one insurance card. It was the one from the trailer, and not the cab. The cop got mad and told him to get out and go get the other one."

"Good," Rubin said, glancing at DJ because she had moved.

"While he was doing that, the tow truck pulled up. We got out of the state trooper's car and walked down near the flatbed, carrying my daughter, hugging her tightly. The tow truck driver asked me to sit inside while he took down some information on the car. I found out from him he was taking the car to Exit 7. So, I asked if I could ride with him to the exit, but he told me I had to get permission from the trooper, that it was a state law.

"You had to get permission to ride with your car off the turnpike?" Rubin asked.

"Yep. While he pulled the car on the truck, I went back to the trooper and asked to ride with the tow-truck driver. He said it was fine, after I explained that someone was waiting for us at the exit."

Rubin said, "You know, that truck driver was trying not to get tracked down."

"How's that?" I glanced over at my daughter, feeling horrible about what she'd just gone through.

"That's why he gave him the one insurance card. . . . Are you okay, Jan?"

"I'm fine, Rube. I'm glad you were still waiting."

"I knew something was wrong because you were late. You're never late. I would've driven up the road first to look for you before I went home."

I slid my hand across his face. "You're so sweet, Rube."

"The insurance company should claim that Renault as totaled. When

I saw it sitting on the back of that tow truck, crushed and crumpled, my heart stopped. I was glad to see the two of you climbing out alive."

"I'm worried about DJ's arm."

"She's fine, believe me. You most likely bruised it when you landed on her. What you did actually was protect her from getting glass in her eyes."

"You're right. She would've had all that shattered glass in her face if I didn't go backward. My God, was I hoping we wouldn't slide off into the ditch and get seriously hurt!" I positioned myself on the edge of the bed and smiled. "My guardian angels were there protecting us."

"You're a strong woman. That's one of the reasons why I love you, Jan," he said, and bopped over to the entertainment center, grabbing the TV remote. We watched television the rest of the night, ordered something to eat, and DJ slept peacefully. Early the next morning, we left for Virginia to get my daughter checked out; she was moving her arm around.

When we returned to Jersey, Rubin stayed with us for another week. One day that week, he'd stepped out to the store and I received a phone call. He returned, "Guess what, Rube?"

"What, my love?"

"The state trooper called while you were out."

"He did? I wish I'd been here to answer the phone. What'd he want?"

"He claimed he'd missed a question on his report. I kept the conversation strictly on a business level."

"Good, baby. I told you he wanted to hit on you."

"I believe you now, Rube."

He snickered. "Yeah, he wants my woman. I knew it."

NEAR THE END OF 1993, Carter's mother's property was being sold; it was in the last phase of sale. I knew then that the time was drawing close for his departure to Canada. Besides, his personality had been changing; Rubin had a knack of crawling into his shell at will and wouldn't come out until he wanted to. He'd gone through so much and was nearing homelessness—nowhere to go but back to the Canadians or my house. He had my house keys and would come to stay for months at a time but he chose not to officially live with me.

Most people thought Rubin was extremely wealthy, living a fabulous life in Canada, but the environment he chose to live in, in South Jersey, wasn't anything near that, especially when he had moved in with Mr. Wilson.

I came to realize then that we didn't communicate as much as I thought. We discussed surface issues and talked about nothing important. Our conversations focused on him and his projects, even though our relationship had been solid for the those past consecutive years.

While he was going through another transition, he spent less time with me. Moreover, because of it, we got together and rode to the shore, my favorite place, Sandy Hook. It was a cloudy, warm day that looked as if it would rain at any moment. We spread a flower-colored sheet, sat, and watched the waves pound against the shore. He positioned me between his legs. "Please forgive me, my love," he said, laying his chin on my shoulder.

"Forgive you for what?" I asked, my head pressed against his chest.

"For not giving you the attention you've needed. I've been dealing with the sale of my mother's house. It's in lawyer review, and now I need to find a place to stay."

"You know, Rube you can always come stay with me."

"I know that. Thank you. But I can't." He began to draw circles in the sand with his finger.

When he made statements like that, pain always shot through me because I couldn't understand his rationale. He'd give logical explanations, too for his reasoning. I snuggled up close to him.

"Rubin, we practically live together, and you have keys."

He scooped up a handful of sand. "I can't." It trickled down through his fingertips. "I can't live with you, Jan."

I moved away from him and watched a wave roll up to shore with its white bubbled tip curling against the sand. "I really don't understand why not, Rubin."

"People who contact me can't call me in that area code."

"What? Oh. . .it's because of my area code. I still don't understand what you mean."

"All our business associates believe I'm still living in Canada."

"Yeah? So what does that have to do with the area code? Hm," I said, staring at the sea. What a crock of shit, I thought to myself. "That's why you always do those three-ways, to make them believe you're in Canada?"

"Yep, if you were in the 732 area code, it wouldn't be a problem."

"I'm 908."

"Yeah, they'll know right away it's a New Jersey number."

"I see," I said, saddened by him and focused on the lights from a ship out at sea, because I knew he could live wherever he chose to. That conversation made things even worse between us.

He moved towards me. "I'd love to live with you, baby. You and your daughter are my family. You're more my wife than my wife, whom I separated from physically, too. You have to know that. I've spent more time with you than any other woman on this Earth. There's no other woman on this planet who could say they've been with me as long as you have, Jan." A tear fell from my eye. I wasn't sure I believed what he had said. "I've spent more time with your children than my own. They're more mine than the two I have. I was deprived of them and the opportunity to be their father, and I unfortunately don't know them, because of being locked away in prison. The prison system is designed to separate Black men from their families. Besides that Jan, you're the only woman I'd live with."

"That's what you say—but you won't come live with me."

He kissed my forehead. "Understand my situation right now." Rubin choose to, and wanted to, stay underground while residing in New Jersey. "When things get better, I promise we'll be together, my love."

I didn't want to bring any more stress into his life, so I stopped talking about it, looked at him, and the years flashed before my eyes. Even with our constant conflicts, a deep spiritual energy bonded us. Each time we got together, it felt like our first; soul mates we were, with eighteen years between us.

"Rube, have you found a place to stay, or are you going back to Canada?"

"Hell, no! I'm not going back to that place now. Eventually, you know, I have to, but it won't be with the Canadians. I'm going to be staying at Mr. Wilson's place."

Each time he mentioned returning to Canada, I'd cringe, and my soul stopped dancing. He could see the sadness in my face. "Listen, my love—you know I'm going to have to return to Canada, because there's no way I'm living here in the United States of America."

"I know, Rube." I said and turned back toward the sea.

"But before I go back there, I have to figure out how to get away from those people and get hold of my own finances."

I quickly changed the subject. "Where does this Mr. Wilson live?"

"He lives around the corner from my mother's place, and down the street from Mickey."

Looking up at how gray the clouds had become, I said, "Oh. It looks like it's going to rain any minute."

"Wilson's a nice old man."

"How old is he?"

"He's in his seventies, has a farm, and raises pigs."

"Pigs?" I said with my nose in the air.

"He's a slob. The house is filthy, because he doesn't take off those muddy boots he wears outside and tracks mud all through the place. You know I can't stand filth. I'll have to clean that place up if I'm going to live there."

"Wow. It's that dirty?"

"But after living in a prison, I can live almost anywhere." He chuckled. "It's only temporary anyway."

I turned to him with my legs folded. ". . .By the way, how did you survive in prison all those years, Rube?

"I spent most of my time in solitary."

Surprised, I said, "Solitary confinement? Wow, Rube."

"Yeah. I refused to eat their food, wear that uniform, and conform to the rules of that prison. It's designed to dehumanize and degrade a human being, specifically one of color. Once, they slipped me a hallucinogen."

"What? How'd they do that?" It began to drizzle and we jumped up.

"Someone dropped it in my food or drink. It was such a bad experience, a friend from prison stood outside my cell all night, guarding me. He wouldn't let anyone come near me until I came down off that messed-up shit." Rubin snatched the sheet up and shook off the sand.

"Wow," I said, grabbing the corners of one side that had slipped because the wind blew it about like a flag.

"You know, they're always experimenting with inmates and drugs like that." We folded the sheet, and the rain became heavier.

"No, I didn't know that, Rube."

"When I clean up Wilson's place, I'll invite you down. His house is a pigsty. How'd you like that?" He tucked the sheet under his arm and we rushed toward the car.

"Okay. That would be nice."

"You can spend the night with me, my love."

BY 1993, HIS PROJECTS WERE MOVING along, and Hurricane was in and out of Canada on business. On one of his trips, I'd had a terrible loss in my family the day he left. Rubin called the next day to give me his flight information. I told him the news. "Hi, Rube."

"How are you? You don't sound too good. Is there something wrong?"

"Yeah, Aunt Judy died yesterday."

"What? Oh, baby, I'm so sorry to hear that."

"You know I go there everyday. Well, the night before, I waited there for my son, because he had basketball practice. She was getting ready for a dance the senior citizens were giving. As she shuffled around, we chatted about dancing and how much she loved it. I was tired from a hard day at work, and stretched out across her love seat. She stood near the walk-in closet, looking through clothes, and said, 'This morning, two sparrows landed outside my window sill. It was Harry and Dee Dee.'"

"What did she mean by that?"

"Well, it gets better. I said to her, in utter surprise, 'You saw two sparrows that were Uncle Harry and Nana?'"

"Umm," said Rubin.

"She says, 'Yes. I finally have come to grips with my brother's death. They sent me a message. In the old days, they'd say, when you saw birds, they were messengers from the spiritual world.'"

"That's an Indian custom," Rubin replied.

"I know. She'd always talk about birds. I'd never really listened until that point. I propped my head up with my hands, trying to understand where she was going with it. Those two siblings of hers passed on several years ago. I had no idea, Rubin; she'd never accepted Uncle Harry's death. That made me flash back to when I had to identify him, sitting in a chair, slumped over dead, in the same building in his apartment. That was my first experience with death of an immediate family member."

Rubin said, "Wow, that's creepy, girl. You've never seen a dead person before then?"

"Nope. I lay frozen, as an eerie feeling came across my chest because of the fact she hadn't moved on. At that very moment, a tear fell from my right eye. It had formed out of nowhere, because I wasn't crying or feeling sad. No other tear streamed down my face but that one. Aunt Judy didn't see it—her face was tucked in between the clothes. I wiped it away quickly."

"Oh, baby," he said sadly.

"The next morning I went for my morning cup of coffee and to see how the dance went. I stuck the key in the door, and a cold feeling enveloped me as I walked straight ahead towards the living room, and her shades were still drawn. Normally, they'd be up, and the sun would have been pouring in. I thought she was still sleeping."

"That's when you found her?"

"Yep. My pace slowed as I neared the sofa bed, gripping the plastic bag I held in my right hand, because the bed was still out. I saw her foot hanging over the edge and immediately knew something had to be wrong. Aunt Judy was lying there in her nightgown that had rolled up to her waist. That wasn't her. I reached over to touch her back. Her muscles had begun to harden, and her face faced the wall. One arm was stretched out like she had been trying to reach for the emergency cord. Clutching the bag tighter, I backed out the room, quickly turned the door knob, and ran to the elevator down to the nurse's office for help."

"Jan, I'm so sorry you had to find her that way."

"Me, too." I sat in silence for several seconds.

"I wish I could be there to comfort you. Ah, baby."

Tears came to my eyes, but none fell. "Thanks, Rube." I composed myself and said, "You've helped me more than you know already, by calling. That made me feel better."

"What did she die from?"

"They say a heart attack. She was reaching for the cord but couldn't get to it on time."

"I'll be back tomorrow. Do you want to meet me by the turnpike?"

"Where?"

"Over by the Giants Stadium, that pay-toll station."

"In East Rutherford near the boarder line of Secaucus?"

"Yeah, meet me there. I should get there around eight."

"That's tomorrow evening, Thursday?"

"Yes, my love."

"Okay."

I VISITED HIM THERE FROM TIME TO TIME at Mr. Wilson's, but not often because of the farm environment. Wilson had lived alone since his wife died, in a dreary-looking two-bedroom home that was still decorated as she'd left it. He grew his own vegetables. I'd pick Rubin up, mostly on our way out to Virginia, or on weekends and holidays.

Both men had invited me down for a dinner they'd prepared one weekend, my first visit to Wilson's. I approached the driveway on that hot summer day before the sun set, and the overwhelming odor of soured milk emerged swiftly, smacking me in the face. The smell devoured everything in sight; even if you only opened your mouth, the odor slipped in, causing you to taste that soured dairy smell. I gagged, as I parked, and watched the two of them lifting, tussling, and wrestling with a five-hundred-pound pig they were trying to get on to a truck. The pig somehow seemed to know where it was going. I got out and walked over to them. Rubin introduced me to a spry, tall, and medium-built seventy-something-year-old dressed in denim overalls, with a pair of green knee-high rubber boots encased in mud. "Mr. Wilson, this is Jan. Jan, Mr. Wilson."

I said shyly, "Hello. How are you?"

"Fine, and yourself? I'd shake your hand, but as you can see, mine are dirty. I have to take this hog down the road. I'll be back shortly for dinner." He hopped in the truck and drove off toward the slaughterhouse.

I waited for Rubin to finish what he was doing, and we went in the house. He directed me down the narrow hallway to a medium-sized bedroom he occupied. He stood there with his slim physique, in dirty jeans and tee-shirt, and said, "I need to take a shower, Jan," as he grabbed his robe from behind the door.

"Alright." I turned on the television and waited. Time passed; he was back, dressed, and we headed out to the kitchen. Rubin sat me at a small, square table; I looked around, noticing cluttered counter space and faint amounts of smudged mud on the floor—but the table had been set. Wilson appeared at the front door in his muddy boots and overalls, and moved toward the kitchen sink to wash his hands. Now I understood Rubin's feelings about the mud, after he'd mopped the floors.

"Do you eat pork, Janet?" Wilson shouted.

"Yes. Sometimes. Not very often, mostly holidays."

"Good. We made fresh pork chops."

"That sounds good." I replied, and made eye contact with Rubin, who stood near the stove. A pork chop's a pork chop, so I thought. What's he talking about fresh?

He came to the table and sat on my left near the black iron rails that ran across the raised floor that separated us from the living room. Rubin placed food in dishes, brought them over, and laid them down on the red-and-white checkered plastic tablecloth. Wilson got up again and went to the kitchen cabinets to grab a bottle of hot sauce.

Rubin sat with a weird smirk on his face. "What are you smiling at, Rubin?" I asked.

"Just smiling. That's all," he said and passed the dishes. I placed portions of food on my plate. "I hope you enjoy the chops," he said. I forked a large one off the platter.

Wilson said again, "They're fresh." He came back and said grace. We all dug in. I began to cut the chop in pieces, placing a piece in my mouth and chewing. "It's delicious," I said.

Rubin chuckled. "It's good, isn't it?"

"Um-hm. I'm not sure what fresh pork is, exactly."

With a mouth full of food Wilson said, "You're not?"

"That's one of Mr. Wilson's pigs," Rubin chimed in. "Remember I told you he sent one of them to the slaughterhouse last week?"

I swallowed and felt nauseous. "This is him?" I reached under the table to squeeze his leg tightly. ". . .Oh," I said, wanting to vomit.

Rubin grinned, rose from the table, and went to the refrigerator. He turned around, looked at me, and chuckled. "What do you want to drink, Jan? Juice? Kool-Aid? Water?"

Rolling my eyes at him, I said, "I'll take Kool-Aid, please." None of it was funny. I forced another piece of meat into my mouth, not to offend Mr. Wilson, and thought about the animal I was eating.

RUBIN STAYED WITH WILSON FOR about a year and a half. I'd roll down to south Jersey with a girlfriend to pick him up. Once, as we approached the house, we could see from a distance the tractor out in the field with two bodies on it. I pointed it out to Nadine, a preppie-looking, slim, dark-skinned Cuban woman in her middle thirties with shoulder-length black hair.

Mr. Wilson was driving dressed in his overalls and green boots, and wore a straw-hat. To my surprise, I recognized the other person, throwing seed, as we got closer. "Nadine, that's Rubin on the side of that thing. What the fuck!"

"That's him alright," she said, looking at me with a smirk, and laughed. We pulled in the long dirt driveway. "He looks funny—*ee-i-ee-i-o.*"

Laughing hysterically, I said, "Yeah, he looks like a professional."

"He's too much." Nadine said. We howled uncontrollably, until tears rolled from our eyes.

I parked. "Nadine, what's up with that? Mr. Wilson's tossing the soil, and Rubin's riding on the side of that damn thing throwing seed. What kind of shit is that? Now, that's the funniest thing I've seen yet," I said, laughing and gasping for air, while Nadine stomped her feet, rocking back and forth as tears rolled down her face from laughter. "We have to get our composure before they come over here," I said, turning the car off.

"You're so crazy," Nadine said.

"All Rubin needs is a straw hat. Can you imagine that?"

She opened the car door, got out, and stretched. I did the same and went over to her, as I listened to the pebbles crunch beneath my feet, both of us still laughing. "We have to get control of ourselves, *control*."

"Rubin grew up down here. That's why he has the farm thing in his blood."

"No wonder!" she shouted, wiping her teary eyes.

"Yep, he's a farm boy by heart."

Nadine peeked over at them and fell out laughing again. "Just call Rubin 'Jethro Bo Dean.'" She'd grown up in New York City.

"They look funny as hell out there." The tractor was headed toward the house, so we tried to compose ourselves before they reached us. Mr. Wilson parked the tractor behind the house, and Rubin hopped off then bopped our way, yelling, "Hey, you two."

We said in unison, with large grins on our faces. "Hi, Rube."

He hugged Nadine. "How have you been, girl? I haven't seen you in awhile."

"I'm fine, and yourself?"

He came over to me, and I began to tease him. "Come on," he said. "Let's go inside. I have to shower and change clothes, girl." Before we entered the house, Rubin snatched the mail, placing it on a small table that sat under the large window. Nadine sat in a high-backed, floral chair near him, and I stood at his side.

"I'm sorry for laughing at you, Rube, but I couldn't help it. You looked so funny out there. What the hell were you doing on that thing?"

"Yeah, you did," Nadine replied.

"That's okay, laugh," he said as he looked through the mail. "I was helping Wilson plant the seeds. Have a seat, Jan."

"I'm alright. I want to stand a few minutes, especially after that drive."

Nadine tugged on his pants and said, snickering, "You did look funny, Rube."

He smiled and turned toward the back. "I'll be ready to get out of here as soon as I take a shower."

"Okay, we'll be right here," I replied.

He whispered back, "I'm tired of this shit, baby, but I'll talk to you about it later." I took a seat across from Nadine. We looked at each other and laughed more.

AFTER FIVE YEARS OF SPENDING holidays together, including New Year's, things changed for us, because Hurricane was taking more trips to Canada. One of the longest was on the North American Indian reservation, with a chief and his tribe—friends of the Canadians, who traveled there during the week to provide their community with educational services, he told me. Rubin had business with Lisa and her crew but refused to stay with them.

He called me early one morning; the phone rattled me straight out of a deep sleep. I jumped and scrambled around in the dark for the cordless that was buried beneath one of the five pillows. I found it, quickly clicking the button, so I wouldn't have to hear it ring another time.

A voice said, "Hey, there, baby!"

"Hello?" I said, groggily as I tried adjusting my eyes to the darkness.

"I woke you, my love. I'm sorry."

"It's alright, Rube." I rolled over and glanced at the clock that read four in the morning. "What are you doing up at this hour?"

Vibrant and chipper, he said, "You know, I'm awake when most people are asleep. Go back to sleep, girl."

"It's okay," I said, trying hard to sound awake. "You know that's impossible for me once I'm up. I'll be up now for awhile."

"I wanted to tell you about the exciting experience I had."

I pulled myself up slowly, leaned against the headboard, and reached over to turn on the triangular lamp next to me. "It's that important to you, huh?"

"Yes. Besides, I haven't spoken to you in a few days, baby."

I squinted in the bright light. "No you haven't. Matter of fact, it's been more like a week, Rube."

"You know, I don't know one day from another. Days, weeks, and months don't matter to me."

I rubbed my eyes. "Yeah, I know," I said, fumbling with the pillows, searching for the television remote. "What do you want to tell me?"

"I went into the sweat lodge."

"What's a sweat lodge?" I knew I wasn't going back to sleep and had to get up for work in a few hours.

"It's an Indian custom and tradition where men gather."

I found the TV remote and pressed the red button. The television lit up the room with a soft background light that was better on my eyes. I turned off the lamp. "Oh," I said.

"Jan, it was a phenomenal experience, one I'd never had before in my life."

I stared stoned-faced at the television. ". . . Okay."

"It's extremely hot inside, so hot I sat naked. And you know it's cold outside, too."

Feeling the residue of sleep and drowsiness, I sat frozen in place. "Rube, you sat nude? It had to have been hot in there, as cold as it is."

He cracked up laughing. "I know."

"That sounds wild to me." I said, rubbing my eyes. I perked up somewhat.

"It felt as if I were sitting around in a sauna. They throw coals on the fire constantly to keep it burning."

"That must have been nice to witness, though."

"Jan, it was beautiful, absolutely beautiful!"

I tugged on a pillow, yanked it loose, and slipped it behind my head. "Go on. What else happened?"

"You heard me say only men."

I scooted back against the pillows. "What? No, I didn't pay attention to that, actually."

"They're the only ones allowed in," he said, chuckling. His cigarette lighter clicked in the background. "I didn't think you heard that."

I stretched and yawned. "No females are allowed?"

"Nope," he said, thinking it was funny; knowing it irritated me to death, he continued to laugh.

"Whatever, Rube," I surfed channels, finally finding a station to watch. "I don't think you're funny." He laughed even harder.

"That's their belief—one that's been around for centuries, Jan."

Feeling warm, I threw the blankets down towards my feet. "Yeah, yeah, yeah."

In deep thought, he said, "It's a spiritual experience."

"Spiritual? Meaning what? Was it like being in church?"

"Not quite."

"What is it then?" I said, tucking my neck into the soft down pillow.

"One time, I saw floating spirits circle the room."

". . .Flying around? You actually saw them?" I was skeptical.

"I did, Jan."

I shook my head. "You saw spirits. But with you anything is possible, Rube."

"Yep, they soared around. I'm not joking, I saw them with my own two eyes, but I guess if someone were to tell me a story like that, I'd have a hard time believing them, too."

My eyes opened wide, and my eyebrows rose. "Spirits! That would've unnerved me." Goosebumps spread quickly down my arms. ". . .Hm."

"Uh-huh, you had to have been there. It was beautiful. I've seen many things in my lifetime, but never have I seen anything quite like that, my love."

I rubbed my hands down each arm, trying to get rid of the goose bumps. "You sure you didn't pass out for a few minutes from the heat and imagine it all?"

"No, I didn't do that, nor did I imagine anything."

"Were you smoking the pipe?" I asked, laughing.

"Nope."

"That's deep. I would've loved to have seen that. That's a moment only God could've revealed, huh. And women aren't allowed. That's a shame."

While he was there with them, Hurricane had also traveled to the Arizona Mountains, a journey many North American Indians ventured upon in pursuit of their traditional beliefs, in prayer, and to collect crystals.

Before he returned to New Jersey, they had given him a warrior's name and a traditional, handmade dream feather that Rubin hung for his protection from the rear-view mirror of his red Cherokee pick-up with the removable blacktop. He drove that Jeep into the ground, traveling from Canada to Jersey and, at times, turned right back around once he arrived.

6

ANOTHER REUNION

I SAT STRETCHED ACROSS THE couch, glancing out the window at the half moon that shone brightly in the dark blue sky. Rubin and I were talking on the phone now because he'd been staying all over the place. We were catching up on what had been going on in our lives.

He said. "I'm going away to do a radio program in two weeks, my love."

"Where are you going now?" I replied, pulling my legs close to me, and leaned back against the pillows. "You're traveling a lot more these days." I knew it was a matter of time before I'd hear, *I'm moving back to Canada.*

"Back to Canada. I won't be staying with the Canadians, though. I'm so used to hearing from you, I had to find somewhere else to stay." He moved the phone away from his mouth and coughed. "Oh, my mother's property has been sold."

"It has?" A big lump developed in my throat making me sit straight up.

"You'll be the first person I see when I get back."

Prickly needles ran up my spine. "I miss you already."

"You do? I can't believe you're interested in this ugly old man."

"You're not ugly, Rube. And I *am* in love with you, old man."

"I'll be right back to you right after the show. I can't stay up there. Besides, I have to go back to South Jersey, to that house."

Hurricane returned to South Jersey within the week and called right away. "Hey, baby, I'm home."

"When did you get in?"

"A few hours ago. I missed you, Jan."

"Ditto."

"Are you coming to see me this weekend?"

"Yep."

I sat up to listen for my daughter, who was fast asleep. "Would you hold on a minute, Rube?"

". . .Yes." I heard agitation in his voice.

I walked to the room where the boys were playing. "Hey, you two." They looked at me like, What? "Be quieter. You're going to wake your sister up." I rushed back to the phone. "Sorry, Rube, I had to quiet the boys down."

"Boys?"

"Yeah, my ex asked me if I could watch his son today."

"Oh. . . . That's fine, baby."

"Rube, you know I had thought about how you're the only man who's grown up with me."

"What do you mean?"

"You've known me as a small child, a young adult in college, and now as a woman."

"Your right, Jan. I most certainly have."

"Its funny how fate works isn't it, Rube? How many times can one person run into another in a lifetime?"

"That's beautiful, isn't it—and we've fallen in love with each other, too. Not many people can do what we've done. There's something special that we have, and I feel we should hold onto it and not let it go."

"Time feels like it's stood still for us. Our separation wasn't anything we chose, it was apart from us—uncontrollable obstacles."

"It happened naturally with us." His voice was hypnotizing. "I feel complete with you, Jan. You have this calmness about you that I love.

There are many women—people in general—who wish they can get as close to me as you are."

Many people would've indeed wished they felt what we had deep down that made us soul mates, entwined on a plane or dimension that was very close to God, our souls connected. Fate had brought us together for the second time, and many years passed in which we had now the chance to get to truly know each other.

WE SPOKE EVERY DAY, MAKING trips back and forth from north and south Jersey. Rubin helped me spiritually get back to myself; the spark that had nearly gone out flickered still within me. One benefit from those telephone exchanges was the motivation and inspiration he freely invested in me. He must have realized the man I'd lived with had robbed me of much of my creativity. With him I was able to rebuild it.

Rubin and I never experienced hostility in our relationship, because of our special gift, true love, something most people look for and fail to find all their lives.

I wasn't blind either to the fact Rubin lacked some major skills when it came to a relationship, or he pretended he did. He had a habit of shutting down and retreating into his shell, so as not to show emotion or feel any, turning himself off from the world. I assumed that was a legacy of his incarceration. I loved him anyway.

I felt I had the best relationship I could choose with a man I admired, a Black hero, and most of all my soul mate. To me he ranked with Elijah Muhammad, Jesse Jackson, and Martin Luther King. Yet only when we were in public and someone pointed him out, recognizing him, did I realize who I was with.

Hurricane helped me capture what is meant by loving life and experiencing true happiness. I felt the purity of life with him, which is the closeness we have to God.

DURING THE SUMMER MONTHS WE'D sit around a barbecue and stroll through the woods; several years went by like that from '90 to '96. He enjoyed being with me as I did him, because of the peace and quiet that surrounded me; I don't like drawing attention to myself. We'd stop at our favorite stumps in the woods, among the colorful trees, and converse in south Jersey.

"Rube, you seem preoccupied today," I said, inspecting the stump before sitting.

Wrinkles formed across his forehead. "I'm tired of not having money," he said, reached in his shirt pocket, and pulled out his a pack of cigarettes.

I watched a cardinal fly past and land in a tree in the distance. "I thought you had money coming in each month."

"I do, but it's not enough for me to survive on." He yanked his gold lighter from his pants pocket and lit the cigarette.

"Can't your wife send you more then she does?"

"Ha-ha! She's not my wife. I'm divorcing her."

"What the hell!

"Yes, each month, she sends me five hundred dollars."

"That's all?"

He blew smoke in the air away from me. "That's why I had to get away from her. She expects me to live off that every month. I bring in thousands of dollars, and that's all I get allocated. Fuck that."

I squinted at him. "You bring in thousands, and she gives you five hundred?"

"Yep, I told you she's a control freak," Rubin said, blowing smoke, and flicked the ashes off the butt.

I swatted a bug away from my face. "I don't know how you deal with it."

"Lisa divides everyone's income up. She controls everything."

I looked up at him as I hung over my knees, pulling on the grass. "It sounds like she's ripping you off, Rube."

"Yeah, I feel obligated to them because they helped me with my case."

"I'm sure you do, but they're taking your money. When are you divorcing her?"

"I can't do that until after the movie. What I have to do is find a way to get control of my own finances."

I sat up. "What type of work does Lisa do?

"They're all professionals—environmentalists, educators, a whole bunch of different backgrounds with strong political connections."

I felt a stab of insecurity. ". . .Oh. She sounds like a pimp who pimped, everybody, even you Rube," I laughed.

He smiled. "That's a damn shame, isn't it?" he said and put out the cigarette butt.

"You're her prostitute," I said, cracking up. She's your madam."

He ran his fingertips across my hand. "Get the hell out of here." I pulled it away, and he quickly reached for it again.

"Think about it, Rube. That's what's going on. She's been doing it for a long time. All those people that were living there, and now there's only a few left. You're the one bringing in the money. Sounds like you're the goose who lays the golden eggs for them."

". . .You're right—she's had a relationship with just about every man that's came through that house, too. Then she had them get vasectomies."

"Oh, yeah," I exclaimed and stood up. "What the hell?"

"She tried to get me to do that, but I told her to go fuck herself." He laughed loudly, and his voice echoed through the woods. "Jan, when I think about that, it really pisses me off." Rubin grabbed my hand. "Hey, baby."

I looked down at him. "What?"

He looked straight ahead. "You know, in my life, you're the only woman I've ever spent such a long period of time with? I haven't spent this much time with my two wives. Not even with Mae Thelma." He stood up, smiled, and pulled me close. "Yeah, you've told me *that* before."

"You know, you are my wife."

I looked up at him and shook my head. "Get the hell out of here, Rube."

"Honestly, baby. You're the only woman I've shared that much time with. There's no one on this continent or planet I've been with like I've been with you, my love. No woman could come to you and say that she has, either."

I placed my arms around his bony frame and hugged him tightly. "That's nice you consider me to be your wife. I just wish it were true."

"I'm going to marry you, Jan, as soon as the time is right."

"When will that be, Rube?"

"I'm not sure. I can't do anything until the movie project is completed. We've been working on that for eight years. I can't divorce her until then, because they have business ties to the book and movie."

". . .Oh." I was in a sort of shock, feeling doubtful, and stared into space, because he'd never told me that before. How upset that made me.

"Sit back down, come on." We sat, but I felt like crying while glancing up at the powder blue sky that had clouds perched around looking like cotton. "I don't know, my love," he said in a melancholy voice.

I pulled on the grass below me and tossed it in the wind. Rubin laid his hand on my knee. "I'm still waiting for that woman to sign my papers for citizenship."

"You're not a Canadian citizen yet?" I replied, and pushed my sunglasses up on my head. The sun had a blinging effect on some of the treetops on the hill.

"Nope. I'm applying for dual citizenship, too."

"What does she have to with your citizenship, anyway?"

"She's my sponsor, and she has to apply for me as her husband, in order for me to get Canadian citizenship. It was supposed to have been done a year ago, but since our separation she's been holding it over my head. But I'm going to get it with or without her!" I watched a flock of geese soar by in the distance as chills ran up and down my spine, hearing Rubin refer to that woman as his wife. "She's being a bitch about it," he shouted cantankerously.

I said, "It's her way of still having some type of control over you."

"I hope she's not thinking that shit." He turned to me. "Jan, you do know, eventually I'm going to have to move back to Canada."

He'd added more salt to the wound. "I knew you were going to tell me that. I'd have to live in Canada?

"You sure would, because no way can I stay here. I'll send for you when it's time." I retreated into myself and sat silently for countless minutes. Rubin grabbed my face, turned it towards him, and said, "I love you, Jan. You have to know that."

"Yes, I know." I grinned, as I thought about my great-aunt Judy, and how she'd linked me back to him before her death. I wondered if that was a sign. Would I ever become Hurricane Carter's wife? Our silent years had strengthened our reunion, and we could now move on through life as a couple.

7

REVELATIONS IN SIGNS

CARTER'S FOCUS WAS ON HIS projects, the movie and book deals—his dreams were finally coming to fruition. He'd begun taking trips back and forth from Jersey to Canada for the final outcome, *The Hurricane*, until he left for Canada for good. There was no way in hell he would live in the States ever again, and nothing on this earth could have convinced him to do so.

When he left for Canada, I'd noticed for the first time the distance that lay between us again, and our relationship grew strained. It was harder for me this time, almost devastating, because it took him away just as our friendship was blossoming. Distance always crept up on us, sweeping us in opposite directions. We weren't strangers to it, but it hit me hard, and I adjusted, as I always had when distance had snatched him since 1976, sending him back to prison again for triple murder.

In our life, this was the third time we'd met after years had passed. It was a plan more powerful than the two of us. When we first met in '76, during Rubin's second trial, he'd made a promise to me he'd return, and he had. I found that in itself eerie when we met up again in 1990. How could it have happened? We'd landed in each other's lives for a second, third, and fourth time, though neither of us had gone looking for

SHADOW OF THE STORM

the other. Now was a time I'd begun to flash back on the events and sit-uations we had gone through, and put them all in perspective.

Now we were free, wanting to move further and develop the rela-tionship into something more serious. I had been mesmerized by the vibrant energy he possessed, especially for a man his age, eighteen years my senior, and I'd always believed that, in some odd way prison had pre-served him.

IN '97 RUBIN RETURNED TO CANADA for good—he and Lazarus had bro-ken away from the Canadians. They both searched for living quarters together—Carter's first time out on his own since he was thirty-two and his release from prison.

I hadn't gotten over the initial shock of him leaving New Jersey for good but knew it was inevitable. That summer the two of them stayed at a friend's beach home.

We communicated each day, but it was difficult not being able to physically touch or feel his passion any more. A month went by; each time I called Rubin, I'd began to notice, Lez would tell me he wasn't in. He'd return my call hours later or the next day, claiming he had been working or taken a walk on the beach. I wondered when he made time for fun—no one worked all the time, as he wanted me to believe, and I never questioned him because it all could have been quite possible.

In the middle of August, Rubin told me he and Lez were leaving the beach house because his friend was closing it down for the winter. This meant we'd have no contact again. He moved around like a gypsy.

Our relationship had changed in an instant, right before my eyes, and our talks turned into bi-weekly chats because he had to rely on other people's phones. Fall arrived before I heard from Rubin Carter again.

He called as I'd been lounging around, watching a movie after laying my daughter down for a nap. "Hi, there, Jan."

"Rube! Where are you? Found a place to stay yet?"

"I'm fine, baby. Yes, we found a house."

I lay stretched out, rose and said excitedly, "A house?"

"Uh-huh, in Toronto!"

"That's great. I'm happy for you."

"A friend of mine was renting it with an option to buy. He brought another home."

"You're going to buy it, aren't you, Rube?"

He said, "Yes."

"You sound good, Rube. How's your health? Is everything okay? I can come see you now."

He said giggling. "Yes, you can soon."

"Soon? What does that mean? How soon?"

"I'm not sure when, because my friend is still living here. When he moves, you can come. But in the meantime, I'll see what we can do to see each other, okay?"

"Alright." As usual, there was some kind of twist to our getting together.

"Let me give you my phone number, baby."

When I called Rubin at his new place, Lazarus would always answer, which allowed us to get to know the other. He'd began to feel like family; besides, Rube considered him a son. I meet him when I made the first visit to Canada the summer of '98.

Hurricane and I stayed at an efficiency hotel in downtown Toronto because of his living situation. Reality had sunk in for me; I knew we had a long-distance relationship that both of us were trying to cling to. I started to wonder if we were ever going to marry, as he had promised. He constantly called, keeping me abreast of his itinerary for months to come: book signings, television talk shows, radio interviews; he even sent me magazine or newspaper articles he'd appear in. Rubin had come full circle with the organization and his projects.

FROM 1998 THROUGH 2000, I visited Rubin's house twice. In the winter of 1998, my first visit to his home, Rubin picked me up from the airport in an old silver Mercedes that he and Lazarus had somehow kept from the Canadians. I walked through the corridor of the airport, crowds of people surrounding me. Suddenly, I saw him standing near an exit sign, wearing a black Sherlock Holmes-style trench coat and a black suede cowboy hat trimmed with a tan band.

When I reached him, we greeted each other, went to the car, and drove off towards downtown Toronto. Before I knew it, we were pulling onto his block; I noticed all the closely aligned houses, similar to homes in New Jersey. He pulled in the driveway at 155 Delaware Avenue, parked, then grabbed my rolling duffel bag from the back seat. We marched up to the porch. I stood there shivering, because of the freezing temperature, and I slid the bag from his hand into mine as he fumbled with his keys.

"You're cold, huh?" he asked, turning the key.

"Yep, hurry up. Get that door opened, Rube!" I said, shaking.

He finally let me through, and when I entered the house my mouth dropped. It was breathtaking. A mahogany staircase wound upward for three floors. I dropped my bag and pulled off my coat. Rubin snatched it from my hands and hung in the nearby closet along with his.

"I'll show you around the place."

"Okay. It's beautiful, Rube," I said gazing at the detail on the wood.

"Thanks," he said as he closed the door, and motioned for my hand, leading me into the living room, then through an archway toward a white-lace tablecloth draped over the dining room table, past another doorway to a black-and-white kitchen with a counter-top table and four high-back black leather bar stools lined up underneath.

I said, shaking my head, "This is nice."

"You like it? I'm not too keen about this kitchen."

"It's different."

"Huh. It reminds me of the Fifties."

"Oh."

"I don't have fond memories of that era. The basement's fully furnished with a bar, bedroom, and full bathroom," he said, standing near the basement door.

I leaned over and took a glance from the top of the stairs. "It's a little apartment," I said.

"Yep. Come on, let me take you upstairs."

We walked up that gorgeous staircase to the second floor and paused in front of an oriental bamboo door that stretched across a section of the wall. Rubin slid it open to a dark room; I saw a queen-size bed and, at the other end, a small end table with a lamp on top of it. We backed out and he pointed straight ahead of us. "Over there's the sitting area."

"This is a unique floor. I like it."

He took my pinky and led me to the other side, near the bathroom; a large and unusually shaped red tub sat in the middle. His office was to our left.

"What have you been up to, Rube?" I said, grabbing his arm.

"Working hard, that's all. I'm a workaholic, as you say." I smiled. He pulled on my arm.

"Come." I'll take you to the last floor."

"Okay." In the back of my mind I'd been thinking of what he'd said. No one works all the time with no play.

He said proudly as we marched up, "This is my floor."

". . .Oh," I said, walking behind him. "You have three separate furnished floors?"

"Yes." We reached the banister railing. I peeked through the bars at the master bedroom; a platform bed lay in the middle of the floor with a string of colored lights wrapped around the frame, a long window stretched behind it, and a black telephone and lamp on an end table next to the bed. Rubin walked over to the side of the bed. "I want to show you something," he said, bending over to turn on the switch for the lights. "Do you like that?"

Christmas lights shone underneath his bed. "Yeah, I'm sure they look even nicer at night." I thought how nice they'd be for a romantic evening and wondered who he'd been entertaining.

"You'll get a chance to see tonight." I scurried over and plopped on the bed. He snatched a sweater that lay on it and walked it to the heavy-duty sliding glass-mirrored closet on the other side that stretched across the entire wall of the room, slid it open, and hung his sweater on a hanger. I jumped up, wondering what his bathroom looked like, peeked in at the high ceilings and the large jacuzzi that was surrounded by plants and, across from it, a glass-enclosed shower.

I turned towards Rubin. "How's the movie going?"

"Fine, baby. We're changing directors right now."

"Really." I went back towards the bed and sat on the lounge chair tucked in a corner, looked across the room, and saw another sitting room with sliding doors that led to a small balcony.

The following day, after breakfast, Rubin took me to the kitchen door and pointed to his garden. It was freezing outside—so we peeked through the curtains. There was a replica of an oriental garden design; even in the dead of winter, it was a beautiful sight.

"That's my garden, baby. That's where you'll find me working in the summer, planting flowers. I just love that."

"Yes, you've called me at times from here." Rubin smiled.

I CONTINUED WITH OUR LONG-distance relationship based on his promise that, one day, I'd move up and spend my life with him. I wondered how that would be possible when, every time I turned around, he had someone living there or someone visiting for short periods of time. My life was centered on him and the "Hurricane" Carter story.

After that trip one evening in '98, around midnight I'd called Hurricane because we'd spoken earlier in the day, and he'd told me he was going out to a dinner party and would be in late. When he picked up, it sounded as if he'd been laughing or talking to someone.

"Hey, Rube," I said.

"Hey, there. Hold on a minute. Let me grab the phone upstairs."

"Okay." I was puzzled because I found it odd he had to go upstairs to get the phone.

"Here I am," he said.

"How was the dinner?" I sat in silence.

"Great."

I suddenly heard coughing in the background, but I didn't say anything to him about it. I listened intently for more background sounds with my legs crossed. "Was it a big affair?"

"Nah. Small sit-down dinner."

"Oh." High heels clicked across the floor. Apparently, it was a woman who wanted me to know she was there.

In a strange voice he said, ". . .It was nice."

I leaned on the table. "Who's that, Rube?"

"What?" he snapped.

"Who's the person coughing and walking around in the background?"

"A friend of mine," he said uncomfortably.

"A woman, from the sound of those heels," I said angrily.

"Yes. She gave me a ride home."

My pressure rose, even though I don't suffer from high blood pressure. "A ride home?"

He sighed. "You know I can't drive at night." Night driving became difficult for Rubin, because his vision had deteriorated, and from the tuberculosis he had been left with one eye.

"What? She was the only one that could drive you home?"

"Yes, she lived the closest to me."

"Well, how come she didn't drop you off and *leave?*" I shouted. "Why's she at your house at this time of the morning, Rubin?"

"Don't you ask me why someone's in my house!"

I banged on the table. "Why can't I? I'm supposed to be your woman, aren't I? That gives me the right to ask."

"I have to go. I'm not listening to this shit."

"Why, because you're guilty?"

"Get the hell out of here, guilty! Of what? I'm hanging up."

I stood up. "You're being mighty defensive. There's more to this story than you're saying, isn't there?"

"Stop this shit, Jan."

I screamed into the phone, "Can't you talk? Talk to me."

"I'll talk to you later, not right now. Good night."

I shouted. "No! Talk to me now."

The phone went dead. He'd had the nerve to hang up in my ear, which made me absolutely furious, and I immediately hit the redial button. The phone rang, but he didn't pick up. The answering machine came on.

Two days later, Rubin called, thinking I'd calmed down, and spoke to me as if nothing had happened. "Hi, my love. What's going on?"

I was surprised it was him. "How am I? I'm fine."

"I wanted to let you know what time I'm leaving Friday morning."

". . . You're still coming?"

"Of course I am—unless you don't want me to," he said, soft-spoken.

"Yes, I want you to." I was assuming he'd called to apologize but he hadn't. I tried hard not to explode. I wanted to confront him face to face; no way was I going to give him an excuse not to come.

"Will you be working Friday?"

"Yes. I have a meeting."

"That's alright. I'll be there when you get home. I have keys," he chuckled.

"It'll be nice to come home and see you there when I get in." He had no idea how furious I was: How dare he pretend everything was okay?

He left early Friday morning, reached Plainfield around eleven that morning, and called me at work after he settled in.

"Jan, I'm here."

"Already?" I said as I twirled a pen through my fingers.

"Traffic was light coming out of Canada this morning."

Wrinkles formed on my forehead. "There's food in the refrigerator if you're hungry."

"Okay, I'll fix myself something after I take a shower. It'll sure be nice to see you, girl. It's been a long time."

"Yeah. It sure has," I said, drawing stick figures on a piece of paper, and then looked up to see a student standing at my office door. I motioned for her to wait a minute.

"I can't wait," Rubin said.

"Listen, I have a student here. I'm leaving around one o'clock. See you later."

"Good. See you then."

Excited but furious, I watched the hours creep by, going over and over in my head how I should approach him. No matter how I did it, he was going to get defensive, but I didn't care.

That evening after I got home and changed into comfortable clothes, then sat in the living room with him. We talked with dimmed floodlights, and I sipped on a kiwi-berry wine cooler, while we both pretended nothing had happened, but I couldn't hold it in any longer.

I scooted closer to him. "Rube."

"Yes?" he said, placing his arm around my shoulders.

"Will you talk to me now?"

His shoulders stiffened. "Talk to you about what?"

"What was that woman really doing at your house at midnight?"

He pulled his arm from around me. "I don't have anything else to say about it."

I gave him a look. "I think you do."

He looked at me, wide-eyed. "I told you, we were both invited to the dinner and she drove me home."

I folded one leg underneath me. "Yeah, but you haven't told me the whole story yet."

There was a sharp edge to his voice when he asked, "What else do you want to hear?"

". . .Rube, do you think my head screws off?"

"She drove me home!" he shouted.

"I want the truth. There's more to this story than you're saying. I know there is."

"You're hearing the truth, Jan."

"Yeah, right. No. I'm not. Give me a break. I'm sure there were plenty of people who could've driven you home that night."

"As I said, she lived the closest," he barked, jumping up from the couch.

"That's the reason why you invited her in at that hour of the morning?"

He glanced down at me before he moved toward the other room. "Cut this shit out, Jan."

"Cut what out? I'm simply trying to get answers." I slid to the edge of the seat.

"This is bullshit." He turned towards the kitchen.

"Bullshit! That's what you want to call it, so you don't have to explain yourself."

"Stop this," he said when he reached the kitchen table.

"No. I'm asking you a question. Why'd you invite her in?"

"I'm not talking about this any more with you." He snatched his jacket off the chair.

"Are you having a relationship with her? Answer me, Rubin."

He said nothing. ". . .Nope, I'm not," he mumbled, putting his coat on.

"Why would a woman be at a man's house at that hour? She probably spent the night with you!" I screamed. "You're sleeping with her, aren't you?"

He stopped in the middle of the floor, his shoulders twitching. "You better leave me alone, Jan."

"I want to know. What's your relationship with her? Huh?"

He said nothing, only huffed angrily, than stomped toward the front door. "I've explained it to you."

"Why are you doing this to us?"

"I invited her in because it was the polite thing to do."

I snapped back at him. "Polite. . . . Please."

"Yes, it was polite," he said, reaching for the doorknob, but realized his keys were sitting on top of the table and rushed over to pick them up. I watched in shock as tears streamed down my face.

"Where are you going, Rube?"

He refused to answer, turned to the door, and walked out.

I cried hysterically, unable to accept any of it. Why was he hiding that relationship from me? He'd told me over and over I was the only woman for him, and I'd believed it. My life had always been centered around him, my soul mate. Rubin was the only man I'd let get close; he was my best friend.

I'd put him on a pedestal, apart from any other man. In my eyes he was flawless, because I loved him and considered him the most affectionate guy I'd known. What a perfect relationship I thought we had—for decades, blessed with true love; no one had been able to penetrate. But Rubin was turning out to be a man I didn't know.

A gigantic shadow of disappointment crept into the room, engulfing me; I'd never felt anything quite like it before. My heart had been ripped straight out of my chest. I realized I couldn't trust him.

He didn't come back to the house that night, nor did he call. I lay in bed with the lights out, looking at the ceiling, tossing and turning. I cried mostly, wiping away the tears that streamed down my face. I couldn't help but wonder where he could've gone. Before I knew it, the sun had begun to pour through the vertical mauve venetian blinds, another day had come, and I lay there with puffy, bloodshot eyes. I hadn't gotten a drop of sleep.

The two decades I'd known Hurricane, he'd never seen me cry. My mind wandered off in all directions. I thought he might have driven back home, or maybe called Lazarus. Rubin had recently given me Lazarus's phone number, so I looked around the room for my phone book and spotted it on top of the dresser. I leaped from the bed, grabbed it, seized the portable phone from its base, and stomped into the living room. I lumbered to the couch, anticipating the call, but decided not to make it until noon. I picked up the remote to the TV that lay next to me, clicked it on, and surfed from channel to channel.

The hours passed slowly; finally, noon came, and I dialed Lez's number. The phone rang several times. I listened closely, making sure it was his voice I heard, because I wasn't sure about what type of living situation he was in and didn't want to cause any problems. A voice answered. "Hello?" Again he said, "Hello?"

". . .Lazarus?" I said, as tears gushed down my checks.

Cautiously he said, "Yes. Who's this?"

I spoke up louder. "Hi. This is Jan."

"Jan? Hey, how are you doing? I haven't spoken with you in awhile."

"I know. I heard you moved out. How are you?"

"I'm fine and happy," he said. "How are you doing, Jan?"

Holding back my tears, I said, "I'm good."

"I'm in law school now."

I slid my bare feet across the cushion. "Rubin told me. Congratulations. I'm happy for you, Lez. When opportunity knocks, you have to go for it. You know what I'm saying?"

"Yeah, I've always wanted to go to law school, and here I am."

My voice quavered from time to time, and I sniffled from all the crying. "I'm very happy for you."

"You don't sound good. What's wrong?"

I said in a choking voice. "I'm a little upset."

"What's the matter?"

"Rubin and I had our first disagreement. He left my house yesterday, and I haven't heard from him since. I thought maybe you have."

"No. Last time we spoke was last week. He told me he was going down to see you. What'd he do?"

"How'd you know it was him and not me, huh?"

He chuckled, "Lucky guess."

"Well, last week I called him, and he had this woman at the house who made sure I knew she was there by coughing and pranced around in her heels."

". . .Oh," he said, unsurprised.

"You have any idea who she is?" I said.

"I believe I know exactly who that was." He said it as if he was smiling.

I sat up straight. "You think Rubin went home?"

"You know how stubborn he is. Who knows? I'm sure he's okay wherever he is. He'll be back, or he'll call you."

"Lez, you know her?"

"Yes."

". . .Oh, you do? How long has this been going on?"

"For awhile," he said.

"She's been there before?" I asked, rolling onto the rug as the sunlight beamed on my face.

"Yep, she's always there—and, personally, I don't like the woman."

"She's always there? . . .Why don't you like her? Does she live with Rubin, Lez?"

"No, but she might as well be. It'll just be a matter of time before that happens, because she leaves her belongings behind each time she comes."

"Huh. Rube's been seeing her that long?" I said as I hopped back on the couch.

"He's blinded by her right now."

My leg shook furiously. "Hm. How's that?"

"She knows I know that, too. Whenever she comes over, she's decorating the place with dried flowers."

"Dried flowers." I flashed back on my visit when Rubin told me how to dry them. They were all over the place; matter of fact, some had been hanging to dry. He had acted as if he knew how to do it on his own. I had been right. That's why he'd gotten so angry with me: I'd touched a nerve. My heart dropped.

"I can't believe Rube doesn't see her for what she is. She's just using him for his money. I'm glad I moved out when I did."

"Hopefully, he'll catch on, Lez," I said, slumped over, wiping my nose.

"I see right through that phony woman."

"Have you told him how you felt?"

"I tried, but he won't listen to me."

"I guess he has to learn the hard way. Lez, I'm not going to keep you. Thanks for listening. I honestly thought Rubin might have contacted you."

"Nope, but if he does, I'll make sure he calls you."

"Thanks."

"Take it easy, Jan. Rubin loves you, I know he does, and he'll call. What he should do is bring you to Canada with him, because he can afford to do that."

"Oh, really? He can?" I said, surprised, because he'd told me something else.

"Yeah, he has the money. Take care."

"Good luck in school."

"Thanks. Bye."

I hung up and began crying uncontrollably, replaying the conversation in my head, especially Lez's comment about her moving in; that disturbed me the most. I knew Rubin was lying, and there was more to his story; what a liar. He'd had the nerve to look me in my face and say it was the polite thing to do, to invite her in. Did he think I was stupid? What a lying ass. It would serve him right if that woman *was* a gold-digger and took him for everything he had. Hopefully, he'd see her for what she was before it was too late. The disappointment was killing my soul, and all I did was cry.

Another evening came, and no word from Rubin. I thought he'd gone home for sure; I was shaking nervously, staring out the window at the large oak tree that sat in the center of the courtyard. I picked up the phone, dialed Rubin's number; it rang several times before the answering machine picked up. I said, "Hey, Rube. Are you there? Pick up if you are. . . . Okay, give me a call when you get in."

I'd hung up and walked to the kitchen to find something to eat when, seconds later the phone rang. Leaping to the living room, I picked up the cordless from the sofa.

"Hello?" I said, but no one answered—I heard only silence. "Hello?"

Just as I was getting ready to hang up, a woman's voice I didn't recognize, said, "Hello."

I said, frowning, "Who's this?"

In an Island accent, she said, "Why don't you leave Rubin alone? He's with me now."

"What? Who is this?" I wondered how she'd gotten my number in the first place. How could she have called back so quickly? "Well," I snapped, "let me tell you something—whoever you are—for your information, Rubin happens to be here with me." There was silence once more. "A matter of fact, you can expect to see Rubin on Monday afternoon, when gets home. I guess he didn't tell you where he was really going. And another thing: Don't call my house again." I hung up.

She's at his house, I figured, and must have found his phone book, or maybe Canada had a new phone feature we didn't have here in the States. That took a lot of nerve, to call me back. She had to have listened to the answering machine when I left the message for him. Her insecurities and vulnerability had been exposed to me, too—that's why I'd heard her coughing, and clicking her heels around, that night.

That bitch is crazy, I thought. Lez is right. Rube better be careful with that. I'd never call another woman over some man. He must have talked about me to her before for her to react that way. I looked out the window with tears in my eyes at a sunset sky full of pinkish purple.

The conversation Rubin and I had had ran rapidly through my head, compounded into disappointment; everything was beginning to add up. It was a shame I could no longer trust or believe him as I'd done in the past; it ripped my heart out, damaging my soul. I'd always told him everything I'd done; look what I'd received in return.

Darkness rolled in; around eight o'clock, the phone rang, but I'd given up on hearing from Rubin. "Hello," I said sadly.

"Hi, Jan."

A sigh of relief ran through my body. "Hey, where are you?" I asked, rubbing my hand across the cushion.

"In South Jersey."

"I've been worried sick about you. I thought you drove back home."

"No! I'm still here."

I clenched a tissue in my left hand. "I see."

"Is it alright if I come back there? Is it okay?"

"Of course you can, Rube." I wiped tears away. "Come on. How far away are you?"

"About two hours, but the people I'm with have invited me to stay for dinner. I'll leave after that."

"Okay. That's fine."

"I'll be there as soon as I can."

I'd been up for twenty-four hours, and my entire body had gone through a physical transformation, as if it had been infected and consumed by the virus of disappointment.

More than two hours passed; I began getting anxious and paced the floor. I walked to the kitchen and washed a few dirty dishes that lay in the sink. I forced myself to watch a movie that didn't calm me down. Nothing helped me relax, so I lay jittery on the bed and waited.

Twenty minutes later, I heard keys in the door. It opened and closed, and I heard the lock click shut. My heart began to beat quickly as his footsteps came toward the dining room, then stopped. Nervous shocks scrambled through my body. All the lights were out in the house, and Rubin must have noticed I wasn't in any of the rooms out there. "Jan?"

"Yeah! I'm back here in the bedroom."

He appeared at the doorway. "Hi," he said, and approached me slowly.

"Hi." He came closer and dropped down beside me to kiss me on the cheek.

I was lying on my stomach in a pair of jeans and a tee shirt, bursting inside, wanting to get everything off my chest, but I knew I couldn't say anything or I might chase him away again. "It took you awhile," I said.

"They asked me to stay for dessert. That led to more conversation. What have you been doing, girl?" He rubbed my face with his finger.

He could tell I'd been crying, because my eyes were puffy and red.

". . .Oh, nothing," I said, propping my chin on my arm.

He rubbed his hand across my back but wasn't sure I wanted him to touch me. "I can tell you've been crying. I'm sorry, baby."

"You're sorry? You are?" I asked, looking up at him.

"Yes, I am. I never meant to hurt you on purpose."

I thought to myself, I know you're sorry. "Will you tell me the truth now? Who's that woman?"

"Yes, I'll do that. I love you, Jan. You have to know that."

"Uh-huh. What's her name, Rubin?"

"Velise."

"Where did you meet her?"

With his head hung he said, "At—at the beach house last summer."

I felt frozen. "Last summer? That's almost a year ago, Rubin!" I rolled over to the wall.

"Yes, I know. . ..Can you forgive me, my love?"

"Forgive you? . . . That's why she was at your house answering the phone?"

He leaned over me. "Why do you say that?" he asked, and pulled me around to face him.

"I called your house because I thought you went home, and left a message on the answering machine."

He held my hand tightly. "You did?"

I rolled onto my back. "Yep, that woman called me back." My eyes swelled up with tears. I quickly wiped them away.

"She did what?" he said, surprised.

"She called back after I left you the message."

He shook his head. "Called you here?"

"Yes, here. Did I stutter? . . . Is she living with you, Rubin?"

"Hell, no. She's not living with me."

He lay next to me, pulling me close to him until we were face to face, looking each other in the eye. "Why is she there?" I asked. "And why is she allowed to answer your phone? You never let *me* pick it up."

He threw his arm over his forehead. "She's not supposed to be answering my phone for any reason."

"Well, she did, and she's definitely listening to your messages."

"I asked her to stop by and feed the cat."

"Feed the cat?"

"Yes," he said, staring at the ceiling. "The cat has to eat, Jan, when I'm away."

"Buy a cat feeder, Rube. Then no one has to be in your house."

He frowned. "A cat feeder? What's that?"

"It'll be like the one I have for the bird, Frisky, but larger."

"Oh. . . I didn't even know they sold those for cats."

"It holds food and water for a week."

"I'll definitely pick one up when I get back."

"You need to," I said, sliding up against the wall.

"I'll do that. I'll go to the pet store."

"Yep. I'll remind you of that, too."

"I know you will."

He slid closer. "Jan, that woman means absolutely nothing to me."

"Evidently she does—she has keys to your place."

"Absolutely not! She has the spare set."

". . .Hm. She's probably made a copy by now."

He leaned near and pecked on my lips. "I doubt that. Besides, I'll change the locks."

"Rube, you don't know what that woman's capable of. If she had the nerve to call me back, she's capable of anything. What's her name again?"

"Velise?" He placed his arm around me tenderly.

"You told me your neighbor looked after the house when you're away."

"He usually does, but he's out of town. I had to ask her."

"Uh-huh. I called Lazarus, too, because I thought you might have called him."

"Nah. I wouldn't have called him."

". . .How could you have done this, Rube? You've been seeing her since the summer and never mentioned it to me?"

"Baby, I'm sorry. I'm sorry. Honestly, she's there only to feed the cat."

"Then why haven't you told me about her, huh? You were hiding it. Face it, Rube. I can deal with honesty easier than lies. Velise means more than you're saying."

"My friend from the beach house introduced us."

"Oh? That justifies your actions? It explains why you weren't around when I called and you claimed you were working or taking walks on the beach, when actually you were with her. Why didn't you say something? Stop lying! She means something, or you wouldn't have spent the time with her, Rube."

He held onto me tightly. "No, she doesn't. I'll prove that to you. When I get home, that woman's out of my house for good. I'm not going to let her or anyone else come between us, not like this. We've been together too long to allow that to happen."

"That took a lot of nerve, doing what she did. She told me I should leave you alone. That pissed me off."

Rubin wrapped his leg around mine. "She said all that?"

My eyes swelled, and tears ran down my face. I turned to the side and wiped them away, because I didn't want him to see. "Yep. She let me know you have been with her."

He tugged on my shoulder, pulling me around to him. "Baby, I don't want that woman."

"Well, Rube, somehow she believes you do," I said, staring in space.

"What makes her think that?"

"She didn't get that idea on her own. You must have made her feel that the two of you are a couple."

He was looking at me as if he was going to cry himself.

"We're not! I swear to you, Velise is out of my life. She stepped over the line. I promise you that, she's gone. I love you, I do, Jan. You have to believe that."

"You *love* me? If she hadn't called me back, I would've never *known!*"

"I would've said something to you eventually. I didn't want to hurt you."

"Yeah, right. But you did. The lie would've kept going."

"I don't want to lose you. Will you forgive me? Let's put this behind us, Jan."

"Then why did you do it, Rubin?"

". . .She reminded me of you, in one sense."

"What? How's that?"

"She's a single parent, like you, raising a child on her own."

"Oh, that reminds you of me? Get the hell out of here with that, Rubin." He squeezed my leg with his hand. "That sounds pretty lame."

"It's the truth. She does."

". . .I still believe she means more than you're saying."

"No, not like you want to believe, and it's nothing I'm willing to ruin our relationship over."

"Uh-huh."

"I promise you, she's gone."

"You're not going to do that. You're just saying that because you think it's what I want to hear."

"Honestly. I mean every word of it. I don't like that shit she did."

"Rube, think about it. If she had the nerve to call me, she'll call any-body."

"She's out of there! Really, Jan! Do you hear what I'm saying to you?"

"I hear you, Rube," I said, feeling totally destroyed. "She's probably using you anyway."

He stroked my arm. "You're probably right about that, too."

"Honestly, Rube? You're going to stop seeing her?"

"Yes. I apologize for what's happened." He pressed his lips to my forehead, slid me back onto the bed, and rubbed his body against mine, "She's gone," he said, kissing my neck, making me melt into his arms.

AT 2:00, MONDAY AFTERNOON, CARTER made it back to Canada. He called me late that evening, speaking in a soft voice, as if he was lying in bed. "Hey, Jan what are you doing?"

"I've been in the house for about fifteen minutes. How was the ride?"

"Great. I hardly had any traffic. I made good time."

"Nice," I said, looking over pieces of mail.

"When I got home and opened the door, Velise was standing at the top of the stairs, wearing a nightgown, smiling down at me. I stood there, looking up at her, stone-faced, and I said, 'Get your things and get the hell out.' She gawked at me in shock."

"You said it like that, Rube?"

"Yes. She was shocked, dressed in that gown, trying to entice me as if I'd be glad to see her after what she did. I was glad to see her, alright. Hell, no! I wasn't, to her surprise." He laughed

"You really meant it."

"I did. I told you, I love you, girl. That woman's out of her mind and absolutely stepped over the line. Now she's out of my life for good."

"Thank you for doing that for me, Rube," I said with a smile plastered across my face.

"It was for us. You're more than welcome, my love. I don't have time for that kind of bullshit. I love you."

"I love you too, Rube."

"Jan, no woman's going to come in between us like that and disrespect you. Besides, I like you."

"I like you, too."

"I do like you. That's nice, isn't it?"

I'd lost track of the conversation because I began to watch the television. "What's nice?"

"Being in like. . . . What are you doing? Are you listening to me?"

"Yes."

"It's good to like the person you love. That's how it's supposed to be, baby. You should like first before you fall in love."

I smiled. "Yeah. That does feels more natural."

Shortly after, we began encountering problems we hadn't had before in all the years of knowing each other. Months turned into years before I'd get the chance to see him; our relationship existed by phone, and long distance had taken its toll on us, too.

8

POTENTIAL FOR NEW LIFE

URRICANE HAD SUFFERED FROM ONE medical catastrophe after another, starting with the tuberculosis that later resurfaced and spread to the nerves in his right eye. Because of that, he'd had to get an operation to remove it, and replaced it with a glass eye.

The period from 1997 to 1998 was an emotionally trying one for Rubin and me; distance separated us, leaving him to retreat into himself. Usually when he did do that, it lasted a week or so, but this time, I didn't hear from him for almost a month. I called his house and left message after message, but he didn't return my calls. I decided to make one last attempt; out of clear blue sky, he picked up.

I couldn't believe it was him. "Oh, my, it's you, Rube. It's about time. Where have you been? Were you away?"

He said cheerfully. "Hey, baby."

"I've been worried out of my mind about you. You just vanished on me."

"Nah, I didn't do that. I'm still alive. I told you—if anything were to happened to me, it would be all over the news."

"I don't want to hear about you that way. You should let me know something yourself or get a message to me, Rubin."

He chuckled. "I've been away, sort of."

"What do you mean, 'sort of'? I've called for days, and I left messages. . . ."

"I wasn't here, Jan. I had to put myself in a rehab program."

"A rehab program? For what?"

". . .My drinking problem."

"You're *drinking* again? . . .You got that out of control, huh?"

"Yes, unfortunately. I've been hiding it from you, along with everybody else. I was doing it every day and spending about six hundred dollars a month buying liquor."

"What? *Six hundred dollars*? That's ridiculous."

"I drank every chance I could, Jan."

". . .So that morning, when you were at the side of the house drinking at seven o'clock in the morning, I was right about you. Huh, Rube."

"Uh-huh. I needed help badly, girl."

"You needed help then."

"Yeah, but I wasn't ready to do it then. I had to wait until I was ready. Nobody could've made me stop but me."

"I, uh, thought it was occasional drinking."

"Occasional my ass. I drank early in the morning, Jan, remember."

"I didn't realize you drank that much, Rubin."

"You didn't know? How could you not have known?"

"I didn't. If I had, I would've said something about it to you."

"You sure would've done that, girl."

"You hid it well."

"I know, but it'd begun to get obvious."

"That's why you were always popping mints and Certs in your mouth, hiding the smell."

"Yep, I was so far gone when I admitted myself into the center; they had to transfer me to a hospital."

"How come?"

"They didn't have the resources to help me. The hospital was the only place I could fully recover."

"Damn, Rube. I've never actually seen you drunk."

"I've been drunk, but you haven't noticed. And you've been the closet person to me, too. Well, Mae Thelma didn't know for a long time, either."

"You were a professional drinker. I guess, I can say that."

"If that's what you want to call it. Jan, you know nothing comes easy for people like you and me."

"Yeah, how well do I know that?" I said.

"My body's strong and fights off so much, that's how I've been able to control it for years. I use to make it in prison. That's where I got started."

"You made it in *prison?*

"Yep."

". . .Are you going to counseling?"

"I don't need that shit. When I put my mind to something, I do it on my own. Counseling can't do anything for me. It's no more drinking for *me*, baby. I mean that. You're the same way I am."

"What do you mean?"

"Once we put our minds to something, we do it."

"That's true."

"One of the attorneys I work with brought it to my attention. He told me it was becoming noticeable, especially when I spoke over the telephone."

"He was right about that. I've heard you slurring your speech plenty of times."

"I'm surprised you didn't say something to me."

"Nah, I wasn't going to."

"He suggested I clean up my act because my professional career and image were in jeopardy."

"Good. He was right."

"You know, I'm more a danger to myself than anybody else."

"I'm the same way. You think it's because we're Tauruses?"

"Maybe." We laughed.

So Hurricane came to grips with his alcohol addiction, and I continued clinging to him, hoping for the future promises he'd made to me.

His projects—*Lazarus* and *The Hurricane* and the reprint of *The Sixteenth Round*, were coming to fruition. The trips and telephone calls grew shorter because of his schedule, and his commitment to his organization, the Association in Defense of the Wrongly Convicted (ADWIC).

The distance got to me, making me go as far as wondering if I truly wanted to be with Rubin Carter for the rest of my life. Our age difference became a concern for me, too—one I'd never given much thought to before. I thought about how I could become unfaithful to him because my trust had been destroyed. Then there were those moments when he'd put me down, making me feel as if I wasn't good enough for him, as if I didn't have a sufficient amount of intelligence in my head. In his eyes I was still a twenty-two-year-old, maybe because I look ten years younger than I actually am. Marrying him, in any event, was becoming more of a dream then a reality. I faced the reality and realized I would be Rubin's third wife, as I'd been to my ex-husband, which left me with a nasty taste in my mouth. What a lot I'd begun to wonder about.

I met other men, but it was always Rubin for me. My entire life had been dedicated to him, including the past nine years we had just spent together. I wanted to meet someone else after all I was going through with him, even feeling strongly, knowing he was still seeing other women, even though he said he wasn't. I wasn't as simple-minded as he wanted to portray me to be in his mind—though he'd never admit it. There was no way he could make me believe all he did was work, as he once had before.

In mid-winter 1998, my prayers were answered. God threw a man in my path—interesting and attractive—who turned my attention away from Rubin. But as they say, 'Be careful for what you pray for': Free will changed my destiny.

Lee was his name, and I grew close to him after a year. He treated me with more respect than Hurricane—a golden-complexioned black man with hazel eyes, medium built, around five-eight, with wavy black hair, and a stylish dresser, Lee was. I wanted to tell Rubin about him because I felt we were best friends who talked about everything; besides, what was he going to say after all I'd gone through with him, especially after he'd ripped my heart out? Carter had his own philosophy about our relationship, though. He felt, no matter whom I came across, he didn't care, because he knew my heart and soul belonged to him. He was correct to a degree, my life centered around him, trying to be the woman he wanted me to be, not the one I needed to be for myself.

I made the call to tell him; Rubin answered in high spirits. "Hey, girl, where have you been? I've missed you, and I haven't heard from you in awhile."

"Rube, come on. If you missed me so much, why haven't you called or flown me up to see you?"

He laughed mischievously. "We'll get together as soon as things slow down. He repeated. "I asked you, where have you been, girl?"

"I've been okay." I said, even though I knew that wasn't what he'd asked me. I knew it wasn't going to happen—seeing him—because he'd been promising me for months. "I've been here, at home. Where else would I be, Rube?"

"No, you haven't, because I've called you a couple of times and you didn't answer."

"Did you leave me a message?"

"No. No, I didn't."

"Then how would I have known you called? I don't always come in and look at the caller ID, you know. What have you been doing, Rube? That's the question."

"I've been working. I love it! Just love it!"

"You're a workaholic anyway," I said, though I didn't trust his word.

"I know." He giggled. "I've been away for the past week and got in late last night."

"Oh. That's why I haven't been able to reach you."

"It was one of those emergency trips for the organization."

Not convinced, I murmured, "I see."

"I haven't listened to any of those messages on my machine, and there's plenty on that thing."

"Yeah, yeah, yeah. Why didn't you wake me up like you usually do when you got in last night?"

"I didn't want to wake you up."

"Why not? You've done it before."

He didn't comment. ". . .What's going on with you, Jan?"

I suddenly got very nervous but said, "I met someone last week,

Rube."

". . .You *met* somebody? Is that what you said?"

"Yeah, I went out on a date with him, for coffee."

He sounded a little disturbed. "Oh."

"He appears to be a nice person."

I could hear him pulling on a cigarette. "What does he do?" he said, with choppy breath because he was exhaling smoke.

"When I tell you, you're going to laugh."

"What profession is he in? You better be careful, Jan." He chuckled.

"What are you laughing at? Are you jealous?"

Rubin laughed. "No. I'm not worried about him or any other man, Jan. You're mine. Be careful, that's all I'm saying."

"You're going to crack the hell up when I tell you what his occupation is."

"What is it?"

"He's a reverend."

Rubin hollered. "Oh, Lord! *Reverend?* Get the hell of out of here. That's funny, you with a reverend."

I burst out laughing, myself. "Yep, I always run into them for some reason. It must be my spirituality, huh."

"Hm!" We both laughed until tears ran down my face.

"You didn't give my stuff away, did you?"

"*Your* stuff? I thought it was *mine*. It belongs to me."

"You heard what I said, Jan."

"Yeah, I hear you." What nerve he has, I thought.

". . .Jan, I want to see you."

What a change all of a sudden. "Oh?" I replied.

"Would you be able to come in a couple of weeks?"

"That's possible."

He said excitedly, "Hold on a minute, my love. Let me check my calendar. I believe two weeks from today will be fine for me."

I checked the calendar that hung on a wall near the kitchen. "That'll be good for me, Rube."

"Two weeks from today, plan on coming here to see me."

"I'll have to let London know I'll be away that weekend."

"I can Fed-Ex the ticket to you."

I moved back to the living room. "That's fine."

"I have to get back to work, my love. Don't forget what I said!"

"What's that?"

"Don't give my stuff away."

"Oh, sure," I laughed.

". . .Jan? I'm serious, you belong to me, and you better remember that."

"Okay," I said, not paying him any attention. It was part of the control thing he used on me.

"There's one thing, when you come."

"What's that?"

"We'll have to stay at a hotel. Remember, my secretary, her daughter, and the daughter's boyfriend are here."

"Oh, yeah, I forgot about that."

I was so tired of that situation. Since he'd been back in Canada, I'd been to his house twice. People were always there.

So in early December 1998, I went to Canada, somehow knowing it would be the last time there for me. We stayed in downtown Toronto, at the City Center Park Hyatt, at the corner of Bloor Street and Avenue Road.

Staying in a hotel in fact bothered me, but I had no other choice because of his house guest, and our relationship didn't seem to be working; the visit was going to make it or break us.

His secretary from the AIDWYC organization was living there because, Rubin told me, she had been going through a messy divorce and her husband had sold the house out from underneath her, leaving her basically with nowhere to go. Shortly after she moved in with him, her grown daughter, sick with AIDS, along with *her* boyfriend, had moved into his basement as well. Rubin had a house full of grown adults.

A part of me missed him, but another side wanted to get as far away from him as possible. The magic between us had gotten lost or misplaced somewhere.

As the Air Canada jet landed, I looked out the window at the snow-covered runway, early Friday morning. It was everywhere. I carried only an overnight bag, so I cleared customs quickly, entering the glassed-in passenger pick-up area, and saw Rubin standing near the front entrance.

At first, he failed to recognize me. Then he did a double-take and smiled, waving my way. He looked great with that big television smile. He gave me a peck on the lips and hugged me tightly. "We have to hurry, my love. I'm parked where I could get a ticket."

"Okay." He snatched my bag from my hand and led me quickly to a silver Mercedes sitting in the drop-off area.

As soon as we got in, we noticed a police car approaching. "You were right, Rube. Here comes a car," I said, looking through the back window.

"I didn't need to be ticketed or towed."

We drove to the Hyatt in downtown Toronto and parked in the underground garage, near an exit door. Rubin leaned over and kissed me. "It's good to see you, Jan. You look good," he added, popping open the trunk.

"So do you, Rube." I got out and met him at the rear of the car as he gathered our belongings. It was brisk and chilly, so we moved fast, almost running to the exit door and the nearby elevator to the lobby to check in.

We were standing at the front desk when a dark-haired, twenty-year-old clerk, conservatively dressed in a dark suit with an emblem blazer, appeared at the counter. "Hello, may I help you."

"Hello," we said in unison, pressing up against each other.

He looked at Rubin. "Do you have reservations, sir?"

"Yes, I do."

The young man asked with a pleasant smile as he clicked away on the computer, "May I have your name, please?"

"Rubin Carter." The clerk laid a registration card and pen on the counter for him to fill out. We let go of each other but stood close enough that, with each stroke of the pen, his arm brushed against my breast. He finished and slid back the card.

The young man looked it over. "Welcome, Mr. and Mrs. Carter."

Rube put his arm through mine. "Thank you."

"Do you need two keys?"

"Yes, please." Rubin replied as he replaced his Gold Master Card in his wallet.

He handed them to Rubin, who slipped one to me. "Here, baby." I put it away in the small zippered area of my purse

"Enjoy your stay," the clerk said.

"Thank you." Rubin reached for our bags. We crossed through the atrium to another set of elevators; as we approached them, the doors flew open. We stepped in, the doors closed, and he pulled me close into him with a fiery passion. "Here we are, Jan."

"Yep, here we are." By the time he tried to kiss me, the doors had opened to the fifth floor. We strolled down the long, dimly lit corridor, following the signs for our room number. We found it; Rubin inserted the card in the door slot, and a green light flashed, automatically unlocking it. We entered. He always had to inspect the suite before he settled in, because it had to meet his standards; standing in the center of the place, he looked around. "It's fine, my love," he said contentedly.

We stood in the sitting area with our coats and garment bags at our sides. "I'm glad."

Rubin picked up the bags and went to the bedroom; I slid up to the wide frost-spotted window near the brown leather couch. I was still able to look down onto Bloor Street and see people whose bodies seemed tiny as they marched up and down in the cold. After a few seconds of feeling the chill radiating off the window, I stepped back and sank onto the couch. Rubin came into view and sat alongside me.

"There's so much frost on that window, Rube." I was still thawing myself out and kept on my navy blue wool coat.

"Yeah. It's cold up here, girl."

"I know. It was freezing out there. We didn't have this much snow."

"It starts getting cold here near the end of August."

"What? That's early." I glanced around the suite, thinking of how I couldn't live there; it was too cold.

"I know you don't like the cold." He paced back and forth with a cigarette. ". . .This is a decent room, huh, my love?"

"Yeah, I like the view of the city." I wondered why he'd changed the topic.

He plopped on the couch. He grabbed the sleeve to my coat and pulled my arm out as I lifted my body off the couch so that he could pull the entire coat from underneath me. He rose and headed to the bedroom. I followed and jumped on one of the king-sized beds. As he moved around, I noticed a change in him from his body language. The spirituality between us still flickered and seemed to be intact, but something was different. Still, our sexual attraction remained strong, even if we'd changed. With that insight, I decided to make the best of a nice weekend because of our friendship and whatever love we had been hanging onto. I loved Rubin all the same, but he seemed to have changed towards me, pretending nevertheless that nothing had altered between us. Normally when we'd get together, even after years had passed, it would always feel like our first time, and we'd begin where we had left off—but not this time. I realized passion was the thing that was real to me. Few people in life genuinely had that—a gift of natural passion, and that's what Rubin and I had.

He reached across the bed, grabbed his duffel bag, moved it to the edge of the bed near me, and began unpacking it. He placed clothes in a dresser drawer and hung some in the closet, then took his black toiletries bag into the bathroom. I did the same, and put the music equipment I'd brought with me together. I muttered, shuffling around in my bag, "Oh, no."

Rubin turned toward me. "What's the matter?"

"I forgot the AC plug for the speakers." He was fumbling in the closet with hangers. "It won't play without it?"

"It'll play, but we won't be able to hear anything. There won't be any sound."

"Oh," he said, sitting across from me near the closets.

"I brought it so we could listen to music. I guess we just won't have any."

"We can go to a store and buy an adapter. There's an underground mall right here."

"Oh, yeah? Nearby here?" I asked, looking at him as if he was crazy because I didn't want to go back out in the cold.

"Yep. How much would one cost?"

"I think no more than ten dollars."

"We'll go get one then. Let's finish putting this stuff up first."

Unhappily, I said, "Okay, we'll have to go back into the cold."

"We'll only be in the cold for a minute, because it's directly across the street. We have to have music, Jan! I haven't heard Black music in so long, girl."

"There's an underground mall? That's pretty cool, Rube." I looked at him. ". . . You haven't heard any Black music? What do they listen to here?"

"Nope. They play mostly rock, pop, and reggae here."

"Oh. I don't know if I could handle listening to that all the time." He grinned, rubbing his hands together. "You're telling me it gets cold starting in August, and now you're telling me they don't play R&B music? I don't know if I could live in Canada."

He gave me a look, as if to say, *You weren't going to live here anyway.* He knew I'd caught his facial expression, though. "You'd get used to it like I did."

I said, shoving the extra cords back into the CD case, "I don't think so."

Rubin pulled our coats out of the closet and we walked to the front door, putting them on. We took the elevator down onto Bloor Street and crossed the street arm in arm, walking down into the mall. Right away we spotted a Radio Shack. He pointed and whispered softly, "Look, baby." I looked up. "I'm sure we can get one there."

"Yeah. This was easy."

"Excuse me," he asked a salesman, "where can I find an AC plug." The young man pointed to a wall down on our left side. Rubin glanced that way.

We went over, and Rubin pulled one from the shelf. He purchased it. As we walked back cross the street, I said, "You can bring the plug back once we're finished with it."

He frowned at me. "Why? What do I have to do that for?"

"You can get your money back, Rube."

He said flatly. "*I* don't need the money!"

I looked at him in amazement; not long before, he'd have done just that to have ten dollars back in his pocket.

"You can keep it," he said, pushing the revolving door into the hotel. We squeezed in together. You'll have another one in case you lose yours.

"Thanks," I said, and became silent. So much had changed between us. I was in love with a different man; the one who was down to earth, and saw life in its simplest forms, now had gone.

When Rubin was at the peak of his boxing career, I was young and had no idea how he was as a celebrity with money. The character he was showing must have been how he was then, I thought. I'd never seen him that way—only when strangers approached him, asking for his autograph or to discuss what he'd been through. I'd see a glimpse of his celebrity character then. I wondered if he'd behaved as cockily.

He's just Rube to me, I thought. That's what he respects me for, being myself, so I thought. But obviously money and stardom were changing him; it was all about his story. He knew I wasn't a materialistic person; that kind of stuff didn't interest me at all, nor was I going to start tripping on the "Hurricane" Carter title.

All those thoughts occupied my head as I stood in the elevator, pressed against the rear wall. When we reached the room, I went directly to the table, and threw my coat in the chair, to set up the CD player. I hooked everything together, and music poured out. Rubin sat on the side of the bed and pulled off his knee-high black leather riding boots, then slid out of his clothes.

I took off my turtle neck and kicked off my shoes. Rubin turned on the television and picked up his pack of cigarettes from the side table. "It's been a long time since we've been together, Jan."

"Yes, it has," I said, looking out at the skyline.

"Let's lay down for awhile and take a nap," he said, tapping on the bed.

"That sounds good. I feel a little sleepy. Something about that cold weather wipes me out," I said, sliding near him. We lay still, with me in his arms—watching the mute television, and listened to the R&B music play; not long after, we drifted asleep.

Our nap lasted for several hours. Music swirled through the air as we came out of our dreams to the darkness outside. I jumped up, sauntered in my bare feet over to the table, and turned off the CD as Rubin brought up the volume on the television. I shifted towards the bathroom as he sat up, fluffing the pillows behind him. "Jan, do you want something to eat?"

I stopped at the bathroom doorway. "Yeah, I could eat now. I haven't eaten a thing all day, when I think about it." I pushed the door back.

"Baby, one more thing." I opened the door once again. He said, as he smiled at me like a Siamese cat, "When you come out, would you hand me the menu over there on the table?"

"Uh-hmm." I closed the door and hurried out. "Here you go, Rube." After handing him the menu, I stretched over and turned on the lamp alongside of him.

He rubbed my shoulders. "Jan?"

"What now? There's something else you want, isn't there, Rube?"

"You sure do know me. . . . Would you go get my glasses out of my jacket pocket, *please*, baby?" I looked at him, shaking my head as I went to the closet to search through his pockets for them.

"You're something else," he said.

I shook my head and pulled out the glasses. "Something else, huh."

"Come sit right here," he said, patting the bed.

He put on the black-framed glasses close to his nose. I slid closer to look at the menu with him. He pointed to specials. "They all sound good—or maybe it's because I'm hungry?" He peered over the glasses and said, "I'm going to have a steak tonight, my love."

I held onto the edge to the menu. "I'm not *that* hungry."

He bent down kissed my forehead. "You don't eat much meat anyway."

I pointed to the chicken entrees and laughed because of the expression on his face. "I *love* chicken. I can't help it."

His eyes stretched up over his glasses. "You sure do. You're going to turn into a chicken one day." Rubin hated chicken.

I laughed. "I'll eat that before meat any day."

"I don't even know why I suggested anything else, when I *knew* you were going to eat chicken."

He reached for the phone. "You ready to order?" he asked, holding it in his hand. I nodded. "Hello?" he said. "I'd like to place an order for two? . . . Yes. The steak dinner with a baked potato, and the chicken in lemon sauce with mushrooms. Oh, and a pot of coffee. . . .Yes, salad for both."

I motioned for him to get me a soda. I whispered. "I want a soda, too. A Pepsi."

"Do you have Pepsi?" He looked at me and said, "They only have Coke."

"I'll take it," I said, getting off the bed.

"I'll take that. Thank you, sir." He hung up. "I forgot dessert. Do you want something, Jan?

"Yeah, a piece of cheese cake."

"I'll call back. . . . Hello, I just ordered for room 504? Can I add dessert to my order? Yes, a piece of cheese cake and a slice of chocolate cake. . . .Great! He called out. It's going to be about thirty minutes, Jan."

"That's not bad. I thought we'd have to wait at least an hour." I stood near the table, admiring the high rotating restaurant from the window.

Rubin leaped to the closet, reached in his jacket, and pulled out his wallet. I turned on the floor lamp in the corner near the table, flipping through the CD case. When I looked up, he was bent over the bed, scrambling around in his black leather bag.

"Oh, *damn!*" he screeched, picking it up, frantically hunting in the bag.

I stared at him. "What's wrong, Rube?" I asked as I read the list of songs off a CD case.

"I forgot my appointment book at home. I may have to go to the house to get it."

"Tonight?"

"I need it. I'll go after we eat."

I turned towards the television, twirling a CD on my finger. "By the time we finish eating, it'll be close to ten. I'll call Win." He strolled over to the phone, dialed, and stood there for several seconds before hanging up. With a puzzled look on his face, he said, "No one picked up. Where the hell is that woman?" I didn't say a word. "I'll call back in a few minutes. She never leaves the house."

"She doesn't?" I said, surprised. "You're telling me she's always in the house?"

"Yep. You know how you'll fly all over and go places by yourself? She won't do that," he said with a worried look.

"Maybe she's in the basement." I wondered why he was so concerned. "Hm," I said, softly to myself. "Maybe she's sleeping, Rube."

He replaced the bag on the closet floor and replied, "I doubt that."

"Why'd you say it like that?" I said.

"Because she's mad at me," he said.

". . .Oh. Mad about what?"

He reached for the phone again, dialed then hung up after several rings. "She's not going to pick up, damn her," he said. "It's going directly into voice mail. She cursed me out the other day."

I was getting annoyed. "Cursed you out for what?"

He sat across from me with a smirk on his face. "Well, I didn't know she felt like she did, until the time Curtis was visiting."

With a puckered brow, I said, *"What?"*

"When he was here, we were up late one night talking and laughing. I was telling him how much I love you."

"Oh? . . .You discussed *me* with *Curtis?*" Curtis is a cousin of mine because late great-aunt Lil's daughter Mickey is his mother. "He knows about us. I stayed at their *house,* remember? When I was in South Jersey, you came to visit that one time?"

"Oh, yeah, I forgot about that," I said, but still wondered why Rubin was discussing me with him for? They must have been drinking.

"We were on the second floor and didn't realize she'd been listening, from the other room, until, the next thing we knew, she came running out of nowhere, crying hysterically. She overheard us talking."

"Crying? Crying for what?"

With a straight face he looked at me. "I asked her the next day why she was crying. You know what she told me?"

"What's that?"

He fell back onto the bed, laughing. "She told me she was in love with me."

"What? In *love* with you? How'd that happen?"

"That's what I asked." I looked at him strangely. "I hadn't given her any reason to feel that way, Jan. I'm telling you the truth. I've never touched that woman. She's crazy."

"You had to have had sex with her. Come on, you must have at least *once. Didn't* you, Rube?"

"No, I haven't." He looked at me wide-eyed. "I *didn't!*"

Once again I repeated, "How'd that happen? People don't fall in love just like that. Where did her feelings all of a sudden come from?"

"I swear to you, Jan, I haven't touched that woman. I don't want her. Besides, she's a *White* woman."

"What does that mean? You're *married* to one."

He reached for his cigarettes; there must have been five in the ashtray already. It sounded like a crock of shit to me, but I went along with him. "She overheard us talking, I told you. I'm telling you the truth."

I laughed. "Well, *damn*, Rube. Are you *sure* you didn't do her?"

"Positively not," he said, placing the burning cigarette on the edge of the ashtray.

"Why don't you try calling one more time?" I said. Personally I was getting a kick out of all of it, even though my doubts remained.

"No. I'm not calling her again. I'll just go to the house." He was still standing when there was a knock at the door. "The food must be here."

I looked at my watch. "Yep, thirty minutes have gone by, Rube."

He snatched his wallet from the table and scurried over to the door. "I guess so." His words faded in and out as he stepped toward the door.

I heard the waiter say, "Thank you, Mr. Carter."

"You're welcome," Rubin said. I could hear the door close and the wheels rolling on the food cart into the room.

"Rube, does Win know you're here with me?"

He stopped at the table. "Yep," he said.

"You told her that knowing how she feels about you?"

"Yep." He laid the dishes on the table. "That's her problem. He lifted the lids off the entrees. "She's a nosy bitch, always in my business. I'll try one more time, being you said so." Rubin stepped over in between the beds and placed the call, but he had no luck.

"She's not picking up. She thinks she's funny."

I opened a napkin and placed it on my lap. "I guess you have to go home."

"Yes. Would you drive me over there, baby? You know I don't see well at night."

I reached for the salt. "In this weather? It's that important? It's cold out there, Rubin."

"I know it is, but we won't be out in the cold, and it won't take long." He pulled out his chair finally and sat down. "I'll drive myself," he said, pouring us both a cup of coffee.

"Rube, stop being silly. I'll take you to the house."

He chomped on a piece of steak. "Okay. Will you be okay to drive?"

"Yes, why wouldn't I be? I'm fine. It's just cold out there," I said, turning towards the window, and watched the lights of an airplane approaching the airport.

Patting his mouth with a napkin, he said, "Thank you, my love."

"It's Friday night anyway." I had just realized I hadn't said grace and took a moment to do so before I dug into any more food.

"That's right—if you were home, you'd probably be getting ready to go out around this time."

"Maybe. That would depend on how cold it was."

He'd cut another piece of his steak, then sliced the rest, and tossed his baked potato. "Alright!" he shouted.

I picked up the can of Coke, poured some into the glass of ice, and sipped on it as I peeked at Rubin, who was glancing at the television.

We finished eating. "We'll wait thirty minutes before we go." Rubin turned his chair sideways to watch a movie. Thirty minutes into the movie, he jumped up. "Okay, let's go, baby."

We put on our heavy clothing, layering up for the cold. Down to the garage we went, hopped into the Mercedes, and waited until it warmed up. I pulled onto Bloor Street. To my surprise, people were still roaming around.

Rubin said, "Turn here, Jan."

I said slightly agitated. "Turn where?"

He pointed. "Right there?

"Rube, *please* let me know where to turn before I get up on it the next time!"

"Okay, baby." He pulled his gloves off. "Make a right at the second corner."

I glanced at him. "That's better."

He smiled. "Then at the third light, turn left."

I pulled the hat off my head. "Do we have much farther to go, Rube?"

"No—the next block, make a right, then start slowing down so you can pull in the driveway. He pointed to a house on my left."

My eyes followed his finger. "Right over there?" I remembered the outside from the last time I was there.

"Yes. Pull in." I did, and he said, "Turn the lights off."

"What? I just pulled up. Give me a chance to put the car in park." What the heck is he *thinking*? I wondered.

The drive had taken fifteen minutes. His entire house was lit up, and I noticed Rubin looking upward. My eyes rose automatically with his, because I wondered what he was looking at; all the lights were on in his bedroom, too. Who could possibly have been up there? I wondered. Why would his secretary be upstairs in his bedroom?

Rubin appeared jittery but tried to cover it up and rushed out, quietly closing the car door, and slid into the house. Minutes passed. He appeared on the porch, locked the door, and scurried back towards the car. Sneaked a glance up again, but I saw that, too.

He said in a rushed manner. "Let's go."

"Okay. Don't *rush* me, Rube. You wanted the lights off right away when we pulled in, now you're rushing me out. Let me put the car in gear first. Thank you."

"You have to go to the left." He pulled off his scarf.

"I know I do, this is a one-way street." I backed out, noticed approaching car lights, and slowed to a stop.

He snapped, "Why are you stopping?"

"A *car's* coming, Rubin," I shouted as I watched him every so often glance up at his bedroom window.

"Hold it, baby!" he shouted.

"What do you *think* I'm doing? That's why I stopped. I told you a car was coming. You're getting on my nerves, Rube. I do know how to drive!" The vehicle passed, and I pulled out.

He smiled. "I know you do. I was trying to help out, that's all. Okay, let's go."

He thought I wasn't paying attention to him when his head tipped upward once again. My head was turned, so I glanced up without him noticing me because I thought someone was standing there looking out.

"I'm out of the driveway now. Do you feel better?" I asked.

He gave me a strange look. "Uh-huh. I know you're a excellent driver, Jan. I feel safe riding with you. You're one of the few woman I trust driving me around."

I laughed then, became silent, wondering who was in his bedroom. I knew that was why he'd kept looking at the window. I was about to ask him about it but changed my mind. Instead I drove back in complete silence.

When we reached the hotel, I didn't want him to touch me at all. I'd had enough of him, wanting to go directly to the airport. Spiritually, I was very much connected to him still, but I wanted to get away from Rubin Carter. I'd never felt that way before in all the years we'd been together.

I hung up my coat, marched over to the drawer, and grabbed pajamas. "I'm going to shower," I said as I closed the bathroom door.

"Okay." He sat on the edge of the bed, holding his coat. He had to know I was annoyed with him. I finished in the bathroom, climbed into bed, and fell asleep while he watched television.

The following day we didn't wake up until late afternoon. I'd turned over on my back when Rubin said, "Good morning."

"Good morning," I said, glancing at the clock.

"You feel asleep on me last night."

"Yeah, I was tired. How long did you stay up?" I asked.

"Late. You know I'm a night person. I watched you sleep and the television."

". . .Oh." I fluffed the pillows behind me and sat up. He reached for his morning cigarette. I hopped up and stepped over to the table, rumbled through the CDs, picked one to listen to, put it in the player, quickly got back in bed.

Rubin began rubbing his hand across mine. "Jan, do you want breakfast?"

"Are they still *serving* it? It's lunch time."

"I'm sure they are. You can order it anytime," he said, reaching for the menu as the music softly played in the background. "I'm getting the sampler and a larger orange juice."

"That sounds good. I'll have the same."

"Maybe we should get two pots of coffee, one for later on in the day. We can heat it up in the microwave."

Breakfast in bed was nice as the day slowly moved and we slumbered around. I couldn't keep still much longer. "Rube, I'm taking a shower. It's three o'clock in the afternoon."

"That sounds good. I'll join you, baby, if you don't mind. Do you?"

"No. Come on," I said, sliding into my powder-blue slippers, then grabbed a white bathrobe the hotel had provided off the door. I was standing near the side of the tub, adjusting the temperature of the water, when Rubin walked in. We stepped in, and hot water ran down our bodies. I picked up the soap and spread it over the washcloth; he pulled me close to him. "This feels good, doesn't it, Jan?" Water trickled between our bodies and down our sides.

"Yes, it does," I said, turned, and he washed my back off. We rinsed the soap from our bodies, got out, and dried off.

He turned his skinny frame to me. "Jan, could you dry my back for me, please?"

"Sure. Turn around," I said, wiping his shoulders first, then proceeded down to the back of his legs.

"That's good," he said.

I walked out. Rubin stayed behind in the bathroom, grooming his face, while I turned the music up, and fifteen minutes later, he emerged. "Are you watching those soap operas?"

"No, I haven't seen them in a while. Besides it's the weekend, Rube. They aren't on."

"Good." He walked out to the sitting area and shouted as he stood near the window, "You want to go for a walk?"

I lay stretched across the bed. "A walk? Are you out of your mind? Out there in the cold?"

The sun was shining brightly, but it was bitter cold; I got up and slid in front of him. He wrapped his arms around me, pressing his cheek up against mine. "The sun's bright."

"Yeah——but it's freezing out there, Rube."

He nibbled on my earlobe. "We'll dress warm, bundle up, baby. You'll be fine. Did you bring warm clothing?"

I snickered. "Of course I did. It was cold in the States, too, you know. I have turtlenecks and heavy sweaters. I can layer myself."

"Then let's go!" he said, pulling on my hand.

I stumbled behind. ". . .Okay."

It was four o'clock by the time we left, and the sun was sinking in downtown Toronto, which meant it would get colder. I gathered my clothes, sat on the edge of the bed, put on a pair of heavy black Danskin stockings and a pair of jeans. Rubin had his thermals on under his bathrobe and put his jeans over them, then slipped on a black turtleneck. He sank down next to me.

"I wish I had thermals, Rube."

"You'll be fine with the heavy stockings you put on," he said as he fixed the collar on his shirt.

"I hope so. It's brutal up here."

He went to the closet and pulled out his high riding boots. He loved those boots and always wore them. "We'll stay out for twenty minutes. How about that, baby?"

"Okay, I think I can handle that, Rube." When I finished dressing, I went to the closet and pulled out my brown boots. "Rube, are you ready? I need to get out of here soon because I'm getting hot with all these clothes on."

"I'm ready." He came over, reached in the closet, and set his black suede cowboy hat on his head. I pulled my long wool coat from a hanger. Rubin looked down at my feet. "Are those boots new?"

"Yes and no. I brought them last year on sale. I'm just getting around to wearing them."

"They're nice," he said, reaching for the red Roots jacket that hung next to my coat.

I grabbed my leopard hat with matching scarf from my bag. As we headed toward the door, I set the hat on my head. Rubin turned around and looked at me with a big smile.

I continued to button my coat. "What?"

"I *like* that hat, girl."

I smiled. "You do?" Wrapping the scarf around my neck, I knew that for some reason the leopard style gave me a classy but foreign appearance, one I knew he'd appreciate.

"It looks very good on you, my love."

"Thanks, Rube."

"Uuh-*hmm*." I slid my hand into his jacket pocket while he zipped it; then he bent over to kiss me. "Let's get out of here before I want to do something to you."

"That would be nice. Then we wouldn't have to go out in the cold."

"Come on." We entered the elevator and down through the lobby arm in arm, and through the revolving door. The wind smacked us in the face as soon as we hit the sidewalk

"Wow! Did you *feel* that?" I stammered, pulling my collar up higher.

"I sure did. Let's cross the street where the sun's shining. It'll be warmer over there."

I slid my hand into his pocket. "I'm feeling you, Rube."

We moved slowly up the street, as the wind whipped against our cheeks, looking in store windows, and stopped inside some to warm up. Rubin paused in front of one of the clothing stores, pointing to a display in the window. "Jan? See those clothes?"

"Yeah," I said as I shivered.

Steam was rising from his mouth. "That line of clothing is made by Roots."

I rubbed my hands together and moved from side to side. "Roots?"

"The jacket I'm wearing is made by that company."

"Oh, *that's* why those words are on it," I said, trying to stay warm as I watched the wind swirl snow around like a hurricane.

"Yeah, Roots clothing apparel."

"I see," I said, and tugged on his arm so that we could move ahead.

"The president of the company is a Canadian. He gave me this jacket."

"That's nice. It looks warm, but it's short."

Chuckling, he admitted, "It is," as he pulled a handkerchief out of his pocket and wiped his nose.

"They've sponsored the Olympics."

Rubin, in the past, had always displayed a generous quality that I reciprocated, but that trip was different. It revealed another side of him, one I hadn't seen before—the self-centered one. When we shopped, he usually asked me if I needed or wanted anything, but that trip it didn't happen. He'd seen a buckle he liked in one store that specialized in handmade leather belts and buckles; we stopped. I stood on the side, silently, and watched while he talked with the salesman. "I'm going to buy this," he said, turning back toward me.

"That's a nice one," I said. That was another eye opener for me, the first being the AC plug. He hadn't offered to buy me a thing; that wasn't like him, though it didn't matter to me because there was nothing I wanted. It had truly become Hurricane Carter's world.

After the purchase we went further up the block until we reached the top, where there were fewer stores. The sun had gone down, which made it chillier, and the wind had picked up; whirling, whipping snow around everywhere. It scratched my face, turning it a beet red. I'd begun to shiver.

"Jan, it's gotten colder. I think it's time for us to start heading back down."

"I'm glad you said, that, because I'm freezing."

"Your cheeks are red, baby. You should see them. I know what I'll do, haul down a cab. We won't have to walk back."

I clung to his arm and quivered. "Thanks, Rube. That sounds good."

"The heck with walking, we've done enough. There's nothing else to see anyway."

"Yes, we have. I mean enough walking."

"Let's cross while we have the chance. The hotel's on that side of the street. We'll walk until I see a cab." He grabbed my hand. I rose up on the balls of my feet and kissed him on his cold cheek before crossing.

"At least we're heading towards the hotel, in case we can't get a cab." I said.

"I'm sure we'll get one," he said, turning around to see if any cars were coming.

When we reached the other side and chucked down, Rubin glanced over his shoulder periodically. "I see one coming."

"You do?" I turned around quickly in his direction. "Where, Rube? I don't see anything."

He pointed. "See? Back there. Here it comes. Do you see it now?" My eyes followed his finger, but all I saw was a bunch of car lights up on the hill.

"Nope, I don't see anything. You have good vision. It's that extra sense you have in that one eye."

"Yeah, that's just what it is, baby."

Rubin stepped closer near the curb. I turned around slowly, frozen, feeling as if I had frostbite, and the next thing I knew he was waving his arm out. The taxi pulled over, Rube quickly opened the back door, and we hopped in the back seat. "Thank God," I said, because I had been shivering with each step we took.

The driver wore a cap and had an olive complexion, a pointed nose, and a thick black mustache. "Where to?" asked in a deep Canadian accent.

"The Hilton, please," said Rubin, pulling his hat off, and cuddled close to me. I sat rubbing my hands together, and he placed his hands on top of mine as we both tried to warm up. "You can stop trembling now, my love."

I looked at him, wide-eyed. "I hope so, its cold out there, Rube."

"I know, but you'll be warmed up soon." He pulled me closer and rubbed his hands up and down my arms.

OUR FUTURE AND THE PROMISES Hurricane had made were, meanwhile, being ignored. Our dreams seemed lost; everything was about him and his projects. I believed he'd been deliberately trying to push me away from him. He began twisting my words around, making it appear as if what he'd promised was all in my imagination. Our conversations contained no real substance, but I still believed he loved me, even after he'd cheated on me; what a unique and solid relationship we had without trust. The years apart had brought us to the point where we hardly saw each other. No longer was I included in his everyday activities, as before. The eighteen-year age difference between us began to bother me; I focused on it more than ever before.

WHEN I LEFT TORONTO I prayed, asking God to help me move on with my life, though I knew it would change our destiny as a couple forever.

A long time would elapse between us because of the busy schedule he claimed to have, not leaving him with much free time. Rubin's itinerary was planned yearly, beginning always with September speaking engagements, book tours, and the movie, combined with his work at the AIDWYC, of which he was the Executive Director. At this time he had also been associated with the Southern Center for Human Rights, in Atlanta, Georgia.

He no longer loved me as he once had, although he'd tell me he did, and flew frequently to the States but didn't call to let me know he was here. I'd kicked many men to the curb for him, then became more and more frustrated by the situation, wanting out—to walk away and never turn back—but part of me couldn't. Twenty-four years had gone by; how many more were we to go? My heart and soul couldn't take it any more.

IN THE SUMMER OF 1997, I lost my job at the university. I was laid off. My disorientation made me call Rubin and tell him the news.

He answered in a chipper voice, "What's going on, Jan?"

I sighed, "Quite a bit today." I knew I had to be sounding upset.

"What's wrong? You don't sound like yourself, baby."

I told him.

"*What?*" he shouted. "Get the fuck out of here!"

"Yeah, they claimed it was because of budget cuts, but I know it was that punk-ass bitch director. He's afraid of strong women."

"He sounds like a punk, from what you've told me about him, baby."

"He is," I said, scribbling on a pad that lay on the table.

"I'm sorry to hear that, but it'll be alright. You'll bounce back on your feet as you always do."

"Yeah, I'm sure I will, but right now I'm so pissed, I could beat his ass like a man."

Rubin laughed hysterically. "You probably could too, you're so mad. You're physically strong, too. But I'm sure it's a blessing in disguise."

"That's usually how it goes. Something better will come along. Besides, I haven't had a summer off in twelve years."

"Twelve *years*? Why is that, Jan?"

"Because every summer we've had to do a summer program for incoming freshman. It would start in July and go through August, so you'd only be allowed to take vacation before or after it."

"Oh, I see."

"Now I can spend the summer with my daughter. We never have before. She'll love that."

He said with real compassion in his voice, "It'll be alright, my love. I know it will."

"I know." It was a blessing in disguise in a sense, because that was the first time I had the chance to spend a summer with my daughter; but when September rolled around I couldn't sit much longer and had to find work. I began looking for full-time employment but couldn't find anything, so I did temporary work for several agencies. An agency called Accue Staff placed me on assignment at a company in Berkley Heights, New Jersey, called Oakite Products, for six months. I ended up there until the summer of 1999.

While working there that spring, I familiarized myself with the two women with whom I had to share a large open spaced office. Both had worked for that company for years. Jan, Irish and skinny, with dyed black stringy hair, in her late forties, had recently returned to the engineering department after being laid off. She was a nervous individual who was a compulsive cigarette smoker, married with a grown son. She sat directly in front of the office door. Then there was MaryAnn, plump, Italian, married with children, in her late forties too, with short brown hair—our supervisor—who watched us both like a hawk from her perch to Jan's left and directly behind me. Both of them lived in prestigious conservative communities.

My desk faced a wall. The two of them were near the large window that stretched across the back wall, giving them light and a scenic view of the Berkley Heights Mountains, the parking lot, and highway 78.

The main focus in that department was taking orders for large generator equipment the company built and sent all over the world. The disadvantage of us sitting close was that, whenever your phone rang, we could hear each other's conversations unless we zoned out. Rubin and I conversed while I was there many times. On a few of those conversations Jan had picked up, to ask who was calling. On one of those calls, she became really inquisitive.

I'd stepped out when he called. I came back and continued to go through my stack of papers. She said, "Janet, the man with the deep sexy voice called? Rubin Carter?"

I turned toward her. "Okay, thanks."

"I don't mean to be nosy, but would Rubin Carter happen to be the boxer by any chance?" she asked as she was typing up an order. I didn't say a word. "Is he?

I wasn't sure if I wanted to answer the question, but for some reason I said, "Yes."

"Really?"

I hesitated, then turned sideways. ". . .Yes, it's the boxer."

"Rubin Hurricane Carter? I remember him." She said it with a huge grin. "I'm sorry for asking, but I got curious."

I thought, Here we go with the questions. "Uh-huh. It's alright," I said, and continued to enter information into an Excel spreadsheet.

". . .How long have you been seeing him?"

"I met him while I was in college in 1976. I've known him now for twenty-three years and been with him for the past eight."

"Oh, my God! That's a *long time*." I could peripherally see her staring at me. "You're dating Hurricane Carter. I've seen him box on television several times. That was years ago, of course."

I stopped what I was doing, turned around. "You have?"

"Yeah. He was a good boxer. That was a shame what happened to him."

I had no response and turned back. I'd thought she was in her forties; had I been fooled. And I also knew the entire company was going to know about us now because she'd tell MaryAnn, who'd blab it to the bigmouth mail-room clerk, Cliff.

"Where's he living, in Jersey?"

"No. He lives in Canada."

"Oh. . . ."

At Oakite they'd always gossiped about someone or something that went on in the company, because it was a small one. The biggest gossiper, as I've said, was the mail-clerk Cliff, a short, chubby, golden-complexioned Black man in his late fifties who spoke at a fast pace. There were only two Black employees in that place besides me, and both were men who worked in the mail room. I was there as a temp.

Besides doing generator orders, I'd been nominated to go to the reception desk three times daily—for two breaks and a lunch hour—which was at the front of the building, where the customers entered. I had to relieve Joan, a sixty-five-year-old with short gray hair, who lived in Berkley Heights. She was friends with Jan and MaryAnn, and another gossiper in that inner circle, but she did it quietly.

Several days later, I was sitting at the receptionist's desk with the sun pouring through the tall glass windows that surrounded me that spring day. There would be days when that sun was so bright I'd have to pull the heavy faded velour curtains closed. I had glanced down the corridor because I heard voices approaching, leaned forward, and saw Cliff, along with the president of the company. They passed the huge oval desk, then stopped alongside me.

The president—tall, thin, a young man in his mid-thirties with dark black hair conservatively cut—who had never spoken to me, all of a sudden said, "Hello, Janet." I knew then he'd heard about Rubin and me.

Laughing to myself, I lifted my head and said with a straight face,"Hello."

"How are you doing today?" he asked. He was wearing a white shirt and colorful tie that hung perfectly center, and he had one hand stuck in the pocket of his black slacks.

I looked at him with a puzzled expression. "Fine, thank you."

Cliff was positioned at his side, smiling, wearing tan khakis and a blue shirt that was snug around his belly. He knew I wasn't very fond of him because he talked too much for me—as bad as a woman. "Janet?" he said.

I looked him in the eye, almost intimidating him with my stare. "Yes?"

He tilted his head slightly to one side. "We heard you know Hurricane Carter."

Emotionless, I looked on. "Yeah."

The president stood there, cocky, not saying anything. "How long have you known him?"

"At least twenty-four years."

He faced showed his surprise. "Wow, that's a long time. I thought you were going to say two or three. You really do know him," he exclaimed. "I've done a little boxing myself."

What'd I care? I thought, but smiled. "Really? I don't like boxing, actually," I said, picking up a pen, and doodled on a piece of paper in front of me.

Cliff moved in astonishment. "You don't?"

"Nah, I don't watch many sports. The only way I'd see them would be with other people who were watching."

Cliff said, "I train young boys as boxers."

"That's nice," I said with a grin, but it wasn't the one he thought it was. I couldn't believe those big-mouthed women I worked with had spread it that fast.

"You're not into boxing, but you're dating one," Cliff replied like the short jovial gofer that he was.

I looked at him as if he was a fool. "Nope, Rube doesn't watch much of it himself."

"Oh."

The president rested his foot on one of the stairs. "Do you know that, each year, our company sponsors the Golden Gloves? Have you heard about it?"

"No. Never have." I leaned back.

Cliff said, "It's held in Plainfield each year."

"I live in Plainfield."

"You do? I've never seen you around town."

"That's because I only live there. I usually go from my block to Route 78."

"That's it?"

"Yep."

"The young men we train as boxers make it to the Golden Gloves."

"Oh. . . ." My eyes went from one to the other.

"We were—uh, wondering if you could ask Rubin if he'd like to attend the ceremony this year."

I looked at them as if they were both crazy. The phone rang, and I had to answer it. "Good morning, Oakite Products. May I help you?" I asked, and then switched the call.

I replaced the receiver and looked up at them seriously. "I don't know if he'll do that."

Cliff said, "Will you ask him anyway?"

I tipped my head to the side. "I'll ask, but I'm not promising you anything. I'm sure he'll do it for me, though. Maybe I can ask him that way. He'll do it then."

"Whatever way it'll get him to come, I'd be so honored to have Hurricane there. I'd love to see Rubin," Cliff exclaimed.

I folded my arms. "I'll see. I'll call him later."

The president started up the stairs to his office, stopped, and looked back. "Thanks, Janet. When Hurricane comes to town, why don't you bring him to my office? I'd like to meet him." He turned back down the corridor to his office.

"Okay." I was thinking how he had nerve asking me, when he'd never spoken to me before. If he thought I'd bring Rubin in to introduce him to him, he was crazy.

"I turned back to Cliff. "You're going to have to give me more information about the tournament."

"I'll give you my number. He can call me."

"When is it?" I'd gotten much joy from them knowing, because they thought I was a quote-unquote "temp" who had no brains, but I had a graduate degree and dated a celebrity. Was I being looked at differently now.

"Each year it's held at the Black United Fund Building in April."

I had no clue where that was. "I'll ask him. That's all I can do for you, Cliff." I turned abruptly and began to flick through papers.

Cliff headed towards the staircase that led to the bottom floor. He shouted back, "I'd love to see Rubin."

"He'll do it for me, I'm sure," I shouted back as I watched him disappear down the stairwell.

"Thank you, Janet."

"You're welcome," I whispered, because I couldn't see him anyway.

Late that evening, I called Rubin. "Hi, Jan, How are you doing?"

I lay across the bed in a tee shirt. "I'm fine, Rube. How are you?"

"Things couldn't be better. What are you up to, girl?"

"Nothing much. I do want to ask you something, Rube."

Sounding suddenly preoccupied, he asked, "What's that?"

". . .You know I never ask for anything." I rolled onto my stomach.

"So this must be important. What is it?"

"You know that temp job I'm working at?"

"Uh-huh."

"I found out today they sponsor the Golden Gloves Tournament each year. It's held in Plainfield?"

He chuckled. "Oh?"

"Well, let me tell the story. It started with those two women I share the office with. You know the two who answer the phone?"

"Yep."

"Remember the one who answered a few days ago? Jan. She asked me if you were the boxer. At first I didn't answer her, but she became persistent, so I said yes. She told some people there, and it got back to the president of the company."

He laughed heartily. "She did?"

"You think it's funny. I don't. Cliff, who's one of the two only black men that worked in the mail room, runs his mouth like a bitch."

Rubin laughed hysterically. "Oh, he does. I know how you feel about that."

"Yep, it gets under my skin. Well, he and the president of the company approached me today."

"Oh, Lord. What did they say?"

"The president, for one, never speaks to me. They began with, Oh! You know Hurricane. Then the questions came—How long have you known him, etc. They were telling me how the company sponsors Golden Gloves. . .until they came to the part where they asked if I could ask you to attend."

"Oh, they did."

"I told them I'd ask you, but I'd ask you to do it for *me*. Before they found out about us, they paid me no attention, especially the president. He'd walk straight past me and not utter a single word. To top it off, he had the nerve to ask me if I'd bring you to his office so he could meet you, whenever you came in town. How about that shit, Rube?"

"You said that president has never spoken to you? I'm not going to go to his office."

"Good. I didn't think you would've done that anyway. I was hoping you'd say that.

"You know what, my love? I'll do it, but it's only for you. You let them know that, too, I'm only doing it for you. Make sure you emphasize that. When is it?"

"I believe he said the first week of April. Cliff gave me his telephone number to give to you."

"I'm not calling anybody. If they want me to come, tell him to call me. Give him my office number. I shouldn't do it at all, the way they're treating you."

"It's up to you, Rube. I don't care."

"No, I'm doing it."

"Thanks, Rube."

"I love you, Jan. Do you know that?"

"Yes, I love you, too."

"This will give me a chance to get to you again."

SO APRIL 2, 1999, HURRICANE, my daughter, and I attended the Golden Gloves Tournament at the Black United Fund Health and Human Services

Center in Plainfield. When we entered the room, all heads turned our way, and local newspaper reporters rushed up, approached us with flashes of blinding lights, snapping shots as we were escorted to a small table near a wall on the opposite side of the room. Each of us took a seat on one of the folding chairs and glanced around, feeling the atmosphere of the place. The night began in a dimly lit room with a buffet-style dinner and people of every nationality standing around or sitting at cloth-covered folding tables, conversing.

I wore an eggshell-and-tan pants suit; Rubin was in a black suit, and my daughter wore a long, black flowered spring dress.

People came over to talk with Rubin or get autographs. While he did that, my daughter and I went up to the buffet table and fixed our plates, including one for him. People stared, glanced, and peeked at us while we ate. Soon after, Rubin was pulled to the other side of the room by reporters to answer questions and take pictures.

We were told, after dinner, to go over to the Plainfield High School, where the tournaments were being held. Rubin had no idea he was going to be honored that evening; Cliff had told me weeks before. I hadn't told him.

I'd passed the high school several weeks before, for the first time, which was good, because otherwise I sure would have had no idea where to go.

When we pulled into the parking lot of the school, I was amazed at the number of cars and the crowd. People were everywhere. We entered the gym, walked to the front of the line, and we were escorted to our ringside seats, listening to the loud chatter. We walked in and ran into the president of Okaite and his son. I grabbed Rube. We stopped, and I explained who the person in front of us was. The two were introduced; the rest of us were, too—his son and my daughter. As soon as we sat down, once again people approached Rubin, asking for autographs. Many used the program books they'd received at the entrance. He ran into many of his old friends from the area, too. "I didn't know you knew so many people from this town," I whispered to him.

"Yes, this was one of my stomping grounds back in the day."

"Is that why you told me to be careful when I moved down here?" I asked, looking behind me to see if anyone had heard me.

"No, girl, I told you a lot of rapists in the prisons were from Plainfield, and to watch yourself."

"Oh, yeah. That's what you said. I remember those words."

The ring sat in the center of the gym. My daughter and I had never been to a boxing match before, and all we did was gaze around at the excitement, energy, and intensity. The children raced up and down the floors in the bleachers that were opened on both sides. Rubin sat quietly, then said, "Jan, I'm going to step over to the other side for a moment. I see some people I want to say hello to that I haven't seen in years."

"Okay." I looked across following his eyes. He got up, strolled to the back of the gym, passing crowds, and shook hands as he moved through. When he reached the other side, he sat next to three men at ringside directly across from me. They shook hands, embraced, and conversed for at least ten minutes. I'd turned away briefly because a very attractive man came and took the seat that Rubin had occupied next to me.

"Hello," he said, smiled, then looked around at the crowds.

"Hello." I turned quickly back to Rubin, looked through the ropes to see where he was, and noticed he was sitting by himself, staring at me in a strange manner, with his legs crossed. I looked at him, and he turned away. He sat several minutes longer before heading back our way. I thought what he had done was very bizarre. In the meantime, the man who'd sat next to me had gotten up and moved away before Rubin got back to his seat.

Rubin sat down pleasantly but quietly until a thin brown-skinned man, around 5'8", who looked like he had a hard life on the street, came down the isle. Rube recognized him and called out his name. The man stopped, shook his hand, and began conversing with Rubin about people they had known. My daughter, who sat intently swinging her legs, had been busy looking at the people roaming around. I hadn't been listening closely to what they were saying but turned Rubin's way and happened to hear him say, "Thanks, man. It was nice seeing you again. Take care of yourself."

Rubin looked at me and smiled. I didn't ask him who the man was because, suddenly, the crown roared, a woman stepped in the ring wearing hot pants and pranced around, holding a sign high in the air above her head. The ring announcer stood to the side of the ring with a mike in his hand and made announcements that grabbed the audience's attention. Then he strolled to the center of the ring and shouted, "I'd like to ask Middleweight Champion of the World Rubin Hurricane Carter to come up to the ring!"

The entire place went wild; people cheered, clapped, stomped, and banged everywhere. I saw a surprised expression pop out on Rubin face, who stood up slowly from the shock, straightened his suit jacket, and hurried over to the ring with that unique walk of his that made him look as though he bopped some. He lifted the ropes and entered the ring, then approached the announcer, who embraced him. Hurricane waved at the crowd as he walked around with that television smile and the people cheered him on.

BEFORE THAT SUMMER OF '99, days passed before I heard from Hurricane. I called him more than he'd called me, wanting to catch up on what he'd been doing. One conversation went like this: "Hey, there, baby! he exclaimed after he heard my voice. "Where have you been?"

"Where have I been? What about you?" I realized when I was annoyed or upset with him, I called him 'Rubin' instead of 'Rube.' "I'm surprised you're at home.

"I've been away, working, as usual."

Pushing my bangs from in front of my eyes I said, "I left you messages."

"I know, my love, but I haven't been able to get back to you. Several emergency situations came up with AIDWYC."

I said, annoyed, "Oh, it's like that?" I kicked a toy that my daughter had left in the middle of the floor to the side and out of my way.

"Baby, you know I would've called if I had the opportunity. What have you been doing, Jan?" It seemed as if he hadn't acknowledged a word I had said.

"Nothing much. The same stuff I normally do. Why?"

". . .I apologize. The organization has me running, girl. I'm in the office right now, as we speak.

I sat at the kitchen table, looking over at the parakeet that was bobbing her head to music. I shook my head because he didn't seem to get it. "In your office? Which one? At home or AIDWYC?"

"I'm home. . . . Hey, Jan? Do you remember me telling you I saw my angel?"

"No. Not really." I thought, Okay, here we go.

"I mentioned it to you once before."

"I don't remember you telling me anything about angels. You know I love angels."

". . .Well, I saw my angel again last night."

"You did?" What do he mean, *again?* I was surprised he even believed in angels.

"I've seen her before."

". . .Uh-hmm." I tried to figure out where he was going with it.

"It's a woman."

I leaned back in the chair. "You get that close to her, you can tell if it's male or female?

"Yep."

I grabbed the cup of tea off the table and walked to the living room to stretch across the couch. "A woman? You're sure it's a lady? What does she look like, your angel?"

"Yes, she's a dark-skinned black woman."

I took a sip of tea. "A black angel?" I gulped down the tea so fast, I almost choked on it because it was so hot.

He heard me. "Are you okay, my love?"

I cleared my throat. "Yes. I'm drinking tea, and it went down the wrong pipe."

"Oh. . . . Don't you remember me telling you the first time I saw her was at the sweat lodge."

"No, I thought you said you saw spirits." I coughed again.

"Nah. . . . Are you sure you're okay?"

"I'm fine, thanks. Somehow I thought it was spirits you saw, not an angel." I should've seen then he was setting me up for something right then and there, but it seemed to make sense at the time.

I could hear papers rustling in the background. "I believe she watches over me," he said.

"Really, you see her that clearly, Rube?" I jumped out of my seat, wanting to throw the phone at the wall. I didn't believe him.

"Yes. I see her that clearly. Then she quickly goes away."

"You're not afraid when she pops up out of nowhere?"

"Oh, no, she's a *guardian* angel. She stood right next to me at the dining room table."

Plopping down again, I picked up the cup and blew on the tea. "I see." I had a tear in my eye and no idea why I was feeling sad.

He said, "She comes and goes more often now."

"Alright, I guess that's good." I didn't know or understand all of what was being said.

LATE ONE CHILLY FEBRUARY AFTERNOON that year, he called. "What are you up to today, my love?"

"Hey. I just came in from work not long ago. I just started preparing dinner."

"I was thinking about you and wanted to give you a call."

"Thinking about me. That's nice," I said, washing off the pieces of chicken thighs.

"I thought about how we haven't seen each other in awhile. I miss you, girl."

I rested the phone on my left shoulder and held it with my ear as the water ran. "You've been busy and haven't had time for me, Rube."

"I always have time for you. That's not true, girl," he said with a giggle.

"Yeah, right. You don't anymore, Rube."

"Okay, you're saying that. Would you like to come see me?"

"See you when?" I said, turning off the faucet.

"How about next weekend? My schedule has slowed down, and I have some free time."

I laid the pieces of chicken in a Pyrex dish. "I guess I can do that."

He said in puzzlement, "You *guess?*" I could tell he couldn't believe I might possibly have been turning him down.

"Yeah, I guess, I do want to come." I reached in the cabinet for the seasonings.

"You said it as if you weren't sure."

"I'm sure," I said, but I knew that wasn't true. I dried my hands on a nearby hand towel and pulled out the spices.

"Are you?" he responded so strongly it felt as if it had plastered itself on my forehead.

I listened to him blowing smoke. "I want to come, Rube," I said, squeezing lime juice over the chicken, washing it again, then dashed each piece with Paprika, garlic powder, and *adobo*.

"Okay, I'll call my travel agent tomorrow to have her arrange your flight, and she'll Fed-Ex the ticket to you."

I couldn't help but feel all I was to him was a piece of meat, which was the only reason why he'd called me. I sprinkled freshly chopped garlic around the chicken and said, "Okay." What did I say that for, when I felt the opposite?

Two days later, I received an overnight package with the tickets but couldn't get past that fact I was nothing more than a sex object to Rubin, and that he made it so obvious. All the suspicions I'd had were being confirmed. That night Carter called to make sure I'd received the tickets. "Jan, it's Rubin."

I said to myself, Yeah, I know it's you. "Hey, Rube," I said as I deliberated about what I was getting ready to say to him.

"Did you get the tickets?"

I shook my right leg feverishly. "Yes, they came this afternoon."

"That's good. I booked the flight so close to the departure date, those tickets cost me a thousand dollars."

I walked over to the stereo in the bedroom and turned it on. "A thousand dollars," I said, feeling guilty, almost changing my mind about the decision I'd made. I'd finished with the food and went to the computer desk.

"Yep. It sure did."

"Wow." But it didn't take me long to come to my senses; especially when I began feeling like his prostitute, I didn't care what it cost him. He couldn't spend that on a *ring?*

"I can't wait to see you, baby. I've missed you."

"Really?" Feeling like a horrible individual—but I felt, who did he think he was? How dare he, I thought. Nor did I like what I was feeling towards him—"I've missed you too, Rubin." I slid the computer chair out from under the desk and looked at the faint light that shone in through the sides and the slits, of the vertical blinds from the light poles. "I have to call you back, okay? I'll call you right back, Rube." I hung up, gazed at the ceiling, tossing everything around in my head, but I wasn't *feeling* him and decided to send the tickets back. I returned the call but never revealed my thoughts.

The next day I called Air Canada. I tapped on the table as I waited for a voice to answer. An agent picked up. "Hello, this is Cindy speaking. May I help you?"

"Hi, Cindy—I'm calling to find out what type of refund I'd get back on a ticket I have?"

"Okay, where are leaving from? And I need the date of travel?"

"From Newark Airport to Toronto, Canada, on February 15. I have the flight number, if you need it."

"What you gave me is fine." The agent responded. Then she said, "You have a fully refundable ticket."

I stood up and stepped toward the window. "Good. Oh, Cindy, the ticket was purchased through an agent. Is that going to make a difference with the refund?"

"No, you'll just lose the agent's fee."

"Okay. Thanks, Cindy."

"Is there anything else I can help you with today?"

"No, that's it, thanks."

"Thank you for calling Air Canada."

I couldn't get myself to call Rubin at the time and decided to wait, because I knew he wasn't going to be happy about my decision. The next day, I did call. I pulled over in a park and called him from my cell. When he answered, I said with anticipation, "Hey, Rube, what are you up to?"

"Hey, baby!" he said with such excitement.

I glanced out the window to see bare branches of cherry and weeping willow surrounding me. "What are you doing?"

"Working. Are you packing?"

"No, I haven't started yet." I watched cars and several people come pass.

"What are you waiting for? You only have a few days."

"I know."

". . .What's wrong, Jan? I can hear it in your voice."

I said with a smirk, "Hear what?"

"There's something on your mind. You have that same feeling with me, Jan, when something is bothering me."

I rolled down the window and the chilly wind blew in. "Yeah, you're right. . . . I'm not coming, Rube."

"You're *what?* Jan, what did you just say?

"I'm not coming, I said."

"You're *not?* Has something *happened?* What's wrong?"

"No. Nothing happened. Nothing's wrong. I changed my mind. I'm not coming."

"You changed your *mind?* Just like that?" he said angrily.

I snapped back, "Rubin, you only invite me when it's convenient for you. I'm nothing more than a booty call for you."

"That's not true, Jan! You *know* that."

I became heated. "It's true. Maybe you don't want to *admit* it to me." I slid the window back up.

He became silent. "Come on, baby. Come see me. I miss you, Jan."

"Nah, you probably do miss me, but I'm not coming, Rube. Oh, I called the airline to make sure you get a full refund. The only thing you'll lose is the agent's fee."

"You're a trip," he replied.

"*I'm* a trip?"

"You are."

All of a sudden the phone went click.

That made me absolutely furious. I shouted, "Who the hell does he think he is? He's fuckin' crazy."

It was disheartening, but I had to come to grips with the reality; I knew that what I'd done had ruined our relationship for good. I'd changed our destiny.

THE IDEA OF MARRIAGE WASN'T a reality for me any more, nor was living in Canada. I had grown tired of Rubin Carter and his broken promises. I began to think how I'd be left alone, would get lonely, and wind up, most likely, having an affair. Especially, with the extensive traveling he did. I wasn't so sure I could trust him as I'd done before. Anyway, I was feeling he had been manipulating me all those years; horrible things passed through my head.

I felt like a fool, because I'd given up my entire life for Rubin. He'd only told me what he thought I wanted to hear, not actually sharing his true self with me, though he'd tell me I brought so much more to his life than any other woman in the world had and kept me hidden from the world, in his shadow.

As the years passed, swiftly leaving us with no physical contact, I'd become leery of him, didn't trust him, and the mutual respect we'd had for one another dwindled. I felt I'd become his private, personal concubine. There had been nothing but drama and conflict in the relationship since the beginning. We had baggage, our families: my great-aunt Lil, who married into his family and was his mother's best friend; my mother, who'd become friends with his ex-wife, Mae Thelma. He had his life to live in Canada, and I needed to go on with mine—somehow. I didn't stop seeing Rubin, but I was feeling the pressure and no longer wanted to continue being whirled around like an object in a hurricane.

9

OUR FINAL BOUT

THE FIRE, SENSUALITY, AND INTIMACY that made up our relationship remained intact, but the trust I had for Rubin Carter had evaporated. No man could compare to him, because of the spiritual connection we had together, and I couldn't imagine life with anyone else whose soul wouldn't dance with mine as his did. But I knew I had to make some kind of change.

I'd met a man named Lee, with a golden-brown complexion and hazel eyes, a very handsome man with style, and I continued to see him—the first man who ever captured my attention—but he too was no match for Rubin Carter. We had fine-art interests in common; he wrote songs—for himself—and played piano and harmonica, which revealed, to me, his kind heart. He had what I needed, though Rubin had been right when he said that no other man mattered, because he knew my heart and soul literally belonged to him.

SINCE 1998, AUDITIONS HAD TAKEN place for the movie *The Hurricane*. Rube's first choice had always been Denzel Washington. The first actor to be considered was Charles Dutton, who had starred in the sitcom *ROC*, followed by Wesley Snipes—but Rubin didn't want him, because he considered him to be an "All American-Black-White boy," as he put it.

August 1999 was fast-paced for both of us. Hurricane began to travel on planes the way people ride buses each day. We moved about quickly; he'd begun to bring me out more in public with him, making me feel as though I had finally emerged from underground.

He'd made a trip to the Boxing Hall of Fame in upstate New York, because he had been placed among the greatest boxers in the world. The Boxing Confederation had given him the middleweight belt—soft green leather with a flag of every country on it; I'd worn that belt around the house myself.

Mostly he'd end up in Manhattan, where we would meet at hotels all around that borough because that's where the publishers and lawyers were who spearheaded his projects. He'd been working out the rewrite for the second edition of *The Sixteenth Round* and *Lazarus,* and *The Hurricane* was being published in Canada.

Rubin had been getting back responses from the publishing companies they'd choose, and one American company's response stuck in my head. He showed me a letter that had upset him deeply, because it basically said Black people don't believe in Black heroes, and Black people don't read. That was disheartening to me, especially in this day and age.

RUBIN SURPRISED ME ONCE, ON one of his many visits to New York City. The week before we spoke, I'd just stepped into the shower and had grabbed the phone that sat on the cabinet. "Hey, baby. I'm coming into Manhattan next week."

I said excitedly, "You are?"

"Yes. Can you meet me there? I'll be in on Thursday, and I'll be staying until Sunday."

I stepped out not to get the phone wet. "I can do that. I miss you, Rube."

"I miss you, too, baby. I can't wait to see you to get my stuff." He giggled. "When I arrive, I'll call and leave the hotel information on your machine, because you'll be at work."

"Okay." I snatched a toweland threw it around me.

"I have a short meeting that evening, but I'll call as soon as I'm finished, alright?"

"That'll be fine. I'll need to go home to change and pack a small bag anyway."

Rubin said, "I love you, Jan." A wide grin shot across my face, as if he could see me.

THE FOLLOWING THURSDAY HE FLEW IN. I checked the answering machine while I was at work, and he left the hotel information on it, as he said he would. After listening to his voice, I grew anxious and couldn't wait until Friday, wanting to call him right back, but couldn't because I knew he wasn't in his room.

The time at work couldn't go by fast enough that day, but when 5:00 p.m. eventually rolled around, I gathered my things and hurried home. I had been in the house no longer than thirty minutes before the phone rang; to my astonishment, it was Rubin.

I paused near the oak wood bookshelf with a big grin. "I thought you had a meeting, Rube."

"It was pushed back, and we decided to hold it here in the room."

"Will it be over by seven?"

"Jan, even if it isn't, I want you to come. Do you hear me?"

"Are you sure?"

"Yes. Come. I want you here with me. You can sit in the bedroom while we wrap up. Watch television."

"I'll leave around seven, and then I should get over there by eight with the Friday night traffic."

"I miss you, girl, and can't wait to see you, so get ready."

"Alright, I hadn't long ago got in."

"Come when you're ready, okay, baby?"

"Okay. Let me go shower and pack a bag."

"Come *on*, baby. Come *on*! Come *see* me!" He laughed.

"I might make it by seven-thirty."

"Good. We should be finished at that time. Then I'll be able to give you all my attention. I love you. Oh, Jan—I forgot to tell you, we're going out for dinner tonight with a friend of mine."

"Dinner! Now I have to find something to *wear*."

"You have plenty of clothes in that closet. Pick out a nice dress."

"Let me get ready."

I hung up and rushed to the bedroom, pulled my black duffel from the shelf of my closet, and prepared a overnight bag; opening dresser drawers, I began throwing garments into it, then went back and posed in front of the closet, deciding what to wear for the evening. I thought about it until I spotted a short black spaghetti-strapped sequin number. I reached down among my shoes, pulled out a pair of black heels, rushed into the bathroom, and jumped in the shower.

It was the end of September 1999, still warm outside, and the humidity was high. I dressed swiftly, grabbed the overnight bag, and sauntered out to the car. Looking up at the sky, I noticed it was clear enough to see the Little Dipper.

I drove into midtown Manhattan in the middle of rush hour, feeling the electricity of the city even before I reached it, and unexpectedly made it inside in an hour because the traffic was light.

As I left the Lincoln Tunnel, and made a right onto Forty-second Street; smack into flickering and flashing lights all around Times Square. I made a left onto Sixth Avenue, taking it all the way up to Central Park and the corner of Fifth, to the Trump Plaza. I pulled in front of the tall black-glassed building with small white lights on all sides of it. A valet attendant in a black uniform trimmed in gold, with a matching hat, came over, opened the door, helped me out, grabbed the overnight bag, and handed it to me as I passed him my keys. As I climbed the flight of stairs a bellboy opened the door to the lobby for me. I made my way to the left, towards the black-and-gold elevators to the seventh floor. I strolled down the corridor, looking for Rubin's room number. When I found it, I stood there feeling jittery with excitement, and adjusted my dress before knocking on the door.

I knocked and heard his footsteps approaching the door; butterflies ran through my stomach. The door flew open. There he stood, smiling, wearing a long-sleeved beige shirt with slacks. I slid in alongside him, and he reached for my hand. "Girl, *look* at you!" he said as he hugged me tightly, gazing intently into my eyes. "How are you?"

"*Fine*. You look good yourself, Rube," I said, hugging him back.

He laughed and swatted me on the ass as I passed through. He said, "Nah, not this ugly guy."

I stood near, leaned up, and kissed him on his cheek. "You're not ugly, Rube. You look good to me, always have."

"Come in here, girl. Let's get out of this doorway." I slipped inside the suite, and he closed the door behind us. He guided me towards the bedroom. "You came right on time—the meeting ended fifteen minutes ago." Another pair of slacks, shirt, and a tie lay across the king-size floral bedspread.

I strutted over to the other side, laid my bag on a chair near the window, and sat on the edge of the bed, crossing my legs. Was I glad we were alone before we had to leave for dinner.

Rubin straddled me. "Bob's going to call before he comes to pick us up."

"Okay," I said with a devilish look.

He slid off and sat beside me. "You still working out?"

"Yep. You can tell?" I asked, smiling back.

"Yes," he replied, laying me back onto the bed, running his hands slowly down the sides of my body. "I was just checking to see for sure," he added, cupping my breasts with his hands.

The phone rang. "That figures, huh, baby?" He leaped up and scurried across the room.

"Hello? . . . *Hey*, man. How are you? . . . I'm doing great, and yourself? . . . What time? . . . It's fine. . . . Okay. We'll meet you out front. . . . Good. See you then." He hung up. "Jan, that was Bob. He said he'll pick us up in forty-five minutes." He smiled over at me with his pearly white teeth.

"That's good—it'll give us a little more time alone."

"Um-hmm." He pulled me up from the bed; engulfed in passion, we sank back onto it. "I'm going to mess you up. I need to get myself ready. If we keep this up, we'll never get out of this room."

I looked up at the ceiling. "I know, and he'll be here before we know it."

"It's so good to *see* you, Jan."

I stroked his arm. "Rube, we're seeing less and less of each other, you know."

"I know. I've been running up and down these roads, flying everywhere. You know I don't like those planes, especially the prop ones. But it'll all be over soon, baby. The movie will be out in January."

"I know, but. . .I miss you, Rube."

He pulled me close. "I miss you too, my love. You know I love you, don't you, Jan?"

"Yes." I said in a soft voice.

He circled my ear with his tongue and rose to gather his clothes. He walked to the bathroom, leaving the door open as he dressed. "How's my daughter?" he shouted.

"She's fine," I shouted back.

Chuckling he said, "That girl's a trip."

"I know. I didn't tell her I was coming to see you, because she would've wanted to come with me. She misses you, too," I said, peeking in at him putting his pants on.

"Tell her I said hello, and I miss her."

I stared hungrily at him. "Okay."

He came out, adjusting his tie. The phone rang again. He rushed near it and picked up. "Hello? . . . Okay. In twenty minutes. . . . Great. We'll meet you downstairs."

"Wow, the time went by fast." I strolled over to the mirror. Rubin stood posed in front of it, looking himself over; I came up alongside him, checking my lipstick, making sure I looked presentable.

"Let's head down, baby." He slid his wallet into the breast pocket of his jacket. "You look good the way you are. You don't need that stuff on your lips."

I laughed. "You rubbed most of it off." He snatched my hand, and we walked out, emerging outside holding hands as we walked down the stairs and hit the sidewalk. There stood a tall, slim, well-dressed White man smoking a cigarette, who took one last drag and flicked the butt in the curb. He looked up and saw us approaching. "Rubin!" he shouted.

"Yeah. It's me." Rubin smiled from ear to ear. "Bob? How are you doing, man?"

"I'm doing fine. It's good to see you, man."

They laughed and embraced. "I wasn't sure it was you, with hair on your head. How the hell are you, Rubin?"

"Perfect. Absolutely, perfect. How have you been?" Rubin asked as people around us hopped in and out of yellow cabs lined up in front of the Trump Towers.

"Good. You look great, Rubin," he said, looking at me.

"Bob, this is Jan."

"Hi, Jan," Bob said, reached for my hand, and shook it. "It's nice to meet you."

"Nice meeting you, too," I replied.

"Are you ready to grab a cab?" he asked, motioning to the bell boy. "We're going to a restaurant downtown, the Village."

"Let's go," Rubin said, straightening the sleeve of his jacket.

The bell boy signaled for one of the yellow cabs to pull up and opened the back door. Rubin slid in first, I climbed in next to him, and Bob slid in alongside me. We headed downtown as the two of them smiled from ear to ear and conversed.

THE FOLLOWING MORNING I LAY in bed, watching Rubin gather the items he needed for his grooming ritual. He had a meeting with the publishers. He made a pot of coffee, poured a cup, and took it to the bathroom with him. He prepared the magic shave potion, the one in the blue-and-silver can. He used that brand because it was the only one that didn't give him hair bumps. But it stank to high Heaven, and because of the stench he always closed the door in the hope that it wouldn't slip out to the other rooms.

He bopped out in his blue-hooded velour robe with a cigarette in one hand, laid it in an ashtray on the dresser, turned to the closet, pulled out a shirt, pants, and a tie, and hung them behind the bathroom door.

He shouted, "Baby, I don't know how long I'm going to be today. I may not be back until late this afternoon."

"What's late afternoon?" I said as I watched him prepping his self.

"Around four o'clock," he said buttoning his shirt, and turned my way.

"That's practically all *day*! What time are we going to have together?

You're leaving on Sunday." I felt as if I should've stayed home, especially knowing I couldn't stand the fact he was leaving me again. We hadn't seen each other for six months. I was tired of being separated from him, and I didn't want to go on like that any more.

He replied, "I know you can find something to do while I'm gone. You spend a lot of time in the city."

I tucked and fluffed pillows under my neck, and turned away from him, my back faced him, lying frozen and upset. I stared out the window. Startled, glancing up, I noticed he was bending over me to kiss me on the forehead.

What was I going to do all day? I thought. I sure wasn't expecting to spend the entire weekend alone; I'm nothing more than a piece for him, I told myself. I jumped up and scurried to the bathroom, hoping the smell of the shaving cream had disappeared, holding my breath I hurried in and out. Rubin was putting on his suit jacket when I returned and hopped back under the blankets, exhaling deeply.

He came close again, looking immaculate. "I'm going, Jan. I'll see you later, my love." I was lying with the covers pulled up to my chin. I sat up; he squeezed me, kissed me on the cheek, and left. I heard the door slam shut, scooted over to the window, grabbed hold of the plastic rod, and pulled the floral curtains apart that matched the bedspread. Looking down, I could see people across the street setting up booths for a sidewalk flea market. That's what I'll do, I thought, quickly moving back over to the bed because the air conditioner was on. I lay watching television, but shortly after getting into it, I fell back to sleep.

An hour and a half passed; when I woke, I got up, showered, dressed, and strolled across the street to Seventh Avenue to wander around, stopping at each booth on the block. People scrambled about everywhere; one booth in particular captured my attention, stopping me in my tracks, played sounds of American Indian music. The instruments were soothing to my soul, but I didn't know any of the artists. I stood there, though, and still tried to decide on what CD I should choose to buy.

BEING BY MYSELF WHILE HURRICANE took care of business matters wasn't unusual at all for me; I'd become accustomed to it, actually. By nature,

I'm a loner, and I function that way every day of my life—a characteristic Rubin seemed to be attracted to, because it apparently worked for him, and he could keep me out of the public eye that way, too.

I spent several hours out there with strangers who came across from Central Park and others who looked on at the shops. I bought this and that, and got exhausted from the heat of the sun, before retreating to the hotel. My feet were hurting because I'd taken a walk in the park. When I hit the room, I immediately removed my shoes and threw the bags on a chair near the table. I stripped out of my sweaty clothes and propped myself up against the headboard, wanting to watch television, but realized the remote was on the table. I lay there disgruntled in silence for several minutes before I dozed off again.

When I again awoke, I was cold, because I hadn't put a blanket on. I jumped up, reached into my bag, grabbed a tee shirt, snatched a pillow off the bed, and slid into the sitting area. Propped on the couch, I surfed the channels until I found an interesting movie. Twenty minutes into it, the phone rang; at first I wasn't going to pick it up, but I thought it might be Rubin. "Hello?" I said as I lay stretched across the couch.

A woman's voice answered, "Hello? May I speak with Rubin?" I recognized the voice right away; it was Win, his secretary. I felt a certain pleasure knowing it was her, because I knew how she felt about him, and I knew she knew who I was.

"He's not in," I said. "Can I take a message?"

"Yes. Would you tell him his secretary called."

"Yes, I will."

"Thank you," she said. I hung over the arm of the couch, placed the receiver back, and turned back to the movie.

Thirty minutes later, I heard keys in the door; Rubin was back. He sashayed in and sank into a recliner parked diagonally across from me. "Hey, Jan," he said, grinning.

I looked up at him. "Hi, Rube. How was your meeting?"

"It went great. What'd you do all day?"

I said, scratching my arm, "Went across the street to the flea market."

He tugged on his suit jacket, pulled it off, and folded it over his knee.

"I knew you'd find something to do."

"I brought you something from the market."

Elatedly he said, "You *did?*"

I glanced back in the direction of the television. "Your secretary called."

From the corner of my eye, I could see his body language change. He began to move around nervously in his seat. "What time?"

"About a half hour ago," I said, watching him fidget in the chair.

He kicked his shoes off one by one. "You answered the phone?" he asked, looking at me wide-eyed and strangely.

With spunk in my voice I said, "Of course I did. How else would I have known she called, Rube? I thought it was *you* calling."

He stood up over me. "Did she say what she wanted?" he asked, glancing out the window. He even appeared to have been annoyed about me picking up the phone all of a sudden.

I snapped, "She just told me to tell you she called."

He stood holding his jacket over his shoulder and turned in my direction. "Why did you answer the phone?"

"Because I thought it was *you,*" I said. "I've answered the phone many times before. What's the matter with that? It's nothing new. What's the problem?"

He said, "You shouldn't have done that," and stormed off to the bedroom.

I shook my head and shouted, "Why not?" I didn't understand why he was acting that way. "Why? Are the two of you having an affair?"

He peeked his head out of the bedroom, and I stretched back to look at him, following him as I spoke. "No, what I'm saying is, you shouldn't have picked the phone up, especially with her."

"Rube, *please?*" I said, turning around, and sat back on the coach to watch television.

"There's nothing going on between us, but you know how she feels about me, Jan."

"That's *her problem!* Isn't it, Rube?"

I heard him shuffling over to the closet. "I don't want her in my *business*, that's all!"

I frowned. "Rubin, I only answered the phone. What's the big deal? What are you making such a big deal out of it anyway for? I can't help it if she has feelings for you. It has nothing to do with me. . . . I'm not getting all of this. I apologize for answering the phone, but no, I'm not sorry." I slid into the couch and focused on the movie.

"Don't worry about it. It's my problem. I'll deal with it," he said, coming back in with only his slacks and a tee shirt on. "She's always in my personal business."

I asked in puzzlement, "Why do you say that?" I sat up.

"She's always answering the phone."

"Well, not for nothing, Rube—she's your 'secretary'. That's her *job*, isn't it? That's what you said her *title* was, right?"

He appeared frozen as he stared out in space. It looked as though he was looking at the television. Maybe, he wasn't. "What are you watching?"

"A movie that was already in progress. I don't know the name of it."

He asked me, but I knew he was trying to distract me, "Where's the remote?"

"Over here, by me." I handed it to him. He changed channels but stopped back at the movie. I became angry, knowing he had refused to answer my question. I moved into the bedroom and turned on the television there to watch the rest of the movie.

BEFORE I MADE THAT TRIP, in August 1999, I'd called Rubin. He had been having problems getting Win's grown daughter and boyfriend out of his house. "Hi. How are you doing, Rube?"

"I'm great, girl. I'm tired of these people being in my house, though. I've been trying so hard to get them out of here. They have no idea, but they're getting the hell out of here very soon."

"Who? *All* of them? Your secretary, or her daughter and boyfriend?"

"Not Win, but her damn daughter and boyfriend. They told me they were going to be here for a few months. It's been a year. They've taken over my house. I hate going home every night."

What he had said confirmed my suspicions. I knew I wasn't moving to Canada any time soon. Now was the perfect opportunity for me to move up there with him. Rubin had started with Lazarus, who had lived with him; then his son had stayed for a short time—they hadn't seen eye to eye, so he was sent back to his mom. Now it was his secretary and her family.

Rubin couldn't have intentions of me moving in with him at all, and he didn't appear overly concerned, either about me losing my job, or that it might be a good opportunity for me to move in with him. Though we'd spent decades together as combined souls, I knew in my bones we'd never marry.

"Rube, you know this is the right time for me to move up. I have no obligations here now."

"I've thought about bringing you here, but not until I get these people out, my love."

"I have no job. It's the perfect time."

"I've been tossing the thought around in my head, baby. Don't think I haven't."

"It's not going to be simple getting these people out."

"Win's not the problem. She takes care of my business for AIDWYC. But she needs to stay out of my personal life. I can't stand that she has to answer the phone all the time. I only have that one phone that I use for business and for my personal calls."

"Get another phone line, Rubin."

"Another line—that's a good idea, Jan!"

Tears swelled in my eyes as I said, "Let her keep that one for business." He was only interested in his cause. He wasn't concerned about me. "Use the new line for yourself. Rube, you had to have known that was going to happen—it comes with the territory."

". . . What do you mean?"

"She's your secretary."

"You're right, but I didn't think about her intercepting my personal calls at the time. I just never *thought* about that. You know how I am, Jan. . . . That's a good idea, to get my own personal line."

"Yeah, you should do that."

Hurricane didn't think about the little things because his mind was usually on deeper thoughts. "That'll put a stop to that shit. I'm going to call the phone company today. Thank you for that idea. You know that's why I love you." He chuckled.

"Then she won't know when I call, either. That'll keep her jealousy level down. Right, Rube?"

". . .It most certainly will."

AFTER NEW YORK, RUBIN DECIDED to make a trip down to Plainfield and see me, so I always thought.

We'd been dancing around in the living room at my place to a twelve-inch record produced by Quincy Jones, *The Secret Garden*, stopping in the center of the floor to candle lights that flickered throughout the room. He whispered in my ear, "Jan, I'm happy."

"You are? What's up?" I said with my cheek pressed so close against his I could feel his cheekbones moving when he spoke.

"Denzel's going to play my part."

"Really!" I said, pulling slightly away from him. "You found a good actor for it, Rube."

"I sure did, baby. I told you before, I *wished* he'd do it. I've dreamt of this day, having Denzel Washington portray me."

All I could see from the side were his pearly whites. "I know," I said as we spun around.

"He was in Canada. We went out for dinner in Toronto."

We paused. "Oh? When was this?"

He snatched my hand and pulled me down on the love seat. "Last month. When we were eating dinner, he began mimicking me."

"What exactly was he doing?"

"At first I *wondered* what the hell he was doing. He watched my body language in that short time and captured my every movement. He had it down to a science."

"He did?" The floodlights were dimmed, and soft music played in the background.

"He came out and asked me if he could play my part."

"I know you were surprised," I said as I slipped out of his arms and went over to turn off the floodlights.

"Where are you going?" he asked as I walked away. I told him. "Surprised? I was flabbergasted. I was so amazed at how well he'd captured me. I said, absolutely. Then he said he'd be *honored* to play my part."

"That's nice, Rube," I said, sliding back into his arms.

"He even imitated my speech pattern, the way I spoke. I'm ecstatic, baby."

"I'm happy for you, Rube. Where's the premiere going to be?"

"In California, in January," he said, turning toward the entertainment center.

"Can I, uh, go with you to the premiere, Rube?"

He turned around with a bizarre look on his face, looking me directly in the eye. "I'd love to take you, my love, but I promised my mother I'd take her."

"Oh, okay. I can understand that." I felt slighted and hurt, but what could I say to that? I grew quiet and thought how odd it was that he would take his mother—they didn't have a close relationship that I knew of, unless it had recently turned to the better. I moved to the couch and tumbled in the cushions.

I BEGAN TO THINK ABOUT how I was thankful for still being in the relationship with Lee because he lived in Jersey, only fifteen minutes away from me, and had provided me with the attention, romance, and creativity I'd stopped getting from Rubin. Lee and I had conflict in our relationship, too, because of his position as a reverend with the church. Lee didn't compare to what Rubin Carter had given me those twenty-something years, though. In reality, Rubin had been telling me what he wanted me to hear all that time, for years.

HURRICANE BEGAN FLYING FROM CANADA to California, New York, and internationally. The producers of the movie had changed, and the publishers were at the final stages. The world was approaching the millennium, and our rocky relationship lay in the middle of it all. Hurricane Carter now had his opportunity to show the world his story.

Every few months, he'd pop up. One of those times, he called to say, "I'm here in New York, baby."

I asked with enthusiasm, "Can I come see you?"

"I don't know if I'll have the chance to see you this trip."

Disenchanted, I muttered, "That's alright."

"I'm only going to be in the States until tomorrow."

"Tomorrow! . . . I haven't seen you in quite awhile, Rube."

He laughed. "I haven't seen much of myself, I've been so busy."

"Oh really," I said, throwing a pillow across the room because I didn't see any humor in that.

"This was a last-minute business trip. I have to meet up with Denzel tonight."

"You do? Wow, Rube. Can I meet him? Can I come over? Huh, Rube?"

". . .Yeah, I can arrange that for you, my love."

"Thanks. What time should I meet you?" I said excitedly, wondering what to wear.

"I'll call you later and let you know. I wanted to call and say hello to you, because I'm so close. I love you, Jan."

"Love you, too." I hung up and placed a call right away to my son.

HOURS PASSED; THERE WAS NO further word from Rubin Carter, so I called his hotel room but got no answer. That following morning, as soon as I woke up, I called him. "What happened to you last night, Rubin? You told me you were going to call when you got back, and I'd meet Denzel."

"I apologize for that, but we rode over to Paterson."

"To *Paterson?* I thought you said you'd never set foot in that place ever again."

"We were in Denzel's stretch."

I said with much disappointment, ". . .I see."

"We picked up Mae Thelma," he snickered.

"You picked Tee up? Why would you do that?"

"Denzel wanted to meet her."

". . .Oh." Once again Rubin had lied to me, and to top it off he'd come over to Jersey. I was sure he'd known all of that beforehand; he'd bullshitted me once more. I was absolutely furious, and tired to death of the way he was treating me.

NEAR THE END OF THE summer of '99, Rubin was back at my place in New Jersey. We were dancing around, as we usually did, to music. Rubin placed his soft, flat lips on my ear and whispered. "Jan, I want you to do something for me."

"What's that?"

"Remember when we attended the Golden Glove tournament?"

"Yeah," I said, hypnotized by his deep voice.

"I found out an old prison friend lives in Linden, and I want you to take me there on my next trip back."

"Linden?" I said as we wobbled from side to side. "Yes, I'll take you."

"I'd love to see him. I had no idea he'd been released from prison. He doesn't have a phone, so we have to drive over and take the chance and hope he'll be home."

"That's no problem."

We stopped dancing; I stepped back to watch Rubin break out in the Running Man dance. "He looked after me while I was there," he said, bouncing up and down.

I cracked up laughing as I watched his moves. "What street does this guy live on?"

"St. George Avenue—what's so funny?" he asked, legs moving, arms flying all over.

"I have an idea where that is."

"Good." He stopped and sat down.

I stood in front of him in my cut-off jeans and a white tee shirt. "You looked funny doing that dance."

He pulled me to him and ran his tongue back and forth across my ear lobe, leaped up, and dragged me with him to the bedroom. I took a seat on the edge of the bed near the computer table. He picked his black leather duffel bag off the floor and dropped it on the bed beside me, reached in the large zipper area, and pulled out a pair of pajamas, toiletries, a set of keys from a side pocket, and dangled them in front of me. "Remember these."

"Of course I do. They're my house keys," I said, looking at him strangely.

"I keep them right here in this bag all the time," he said, pointing to the side of the bag. "Do you want them back?"

I looked at him crazily. "*What? Have I asked* you for them? Do you *want* to give them back, Rubin?"

"No, I was just checking," he said, throwing them back in the compartment.

I went over to the bathroom that was adjacent to the bedroom, and stopped at the mirror to look at a pimple that had popped up on my face. The bathroom and bedroom were close enough; I could see Rubin from there. I shouted across to him as he fumbled around with his garments, "Nope, I *don't* want the keys back!"

He was acting evasive with me, though, and I couldn't understand why. Ever since he moved back to Canada, our destiny had changed. He wasn't the same man; his personality switched so quickly, I thought the tuberculosis had spread to his brain. He'd also stopped wearing jeans and sneakers and gone back to tailor-made suits, ties, and polished shoes because he had to be groomed at all times for the public.

By then we'd been together for ten years, and it still didn't feel complete. While in New Jersey, he kept a low profile, and my laid-back personality helped; he knew I'd never draw attention to the media, and we could hang underground. When he was here and did interviews for radio, magazines, newspapers, or television talk shows, they were done on the phone usually, using the three-way system with the Canadians. That way, people always assumed Hurricane was in Canada with them.

A MONTH LATER HURRICANE CALLED, but I'd become uncertain about our relationship and wasn't sure I wanted to see him anymore. I was just not strong enough yet to resist him, though I knew he had a hidden agenda. "Jan, I'm going to be in the States this month."

"Where, New York?"

"No, Philadelphia. That's not far from you."

"Philly. No, it's not. It's only a two-hour drive."

"I'm not going to be in Philly, but on the outskirts near the airport."

"Oh, I can drive down."

"I was hoping you'd say that. You can pick me up. I can stay a week with you afterward. How'd you like that?"

"That'll be great, Rube." He seemed sincere about wanting to make up time that had been lost. "That sounds good."

"I need to relax, and you're the one person I can always do that with. "Don't forget, baby, I want you to take me to Linden."

"Oh, okay. We can do that."

In his sexy and masculine voice. he said, "I miss you, my love. I do."

Melting as I'd always done when I heard his voice, I said, "I miss you too, Rube. We haven't seen each other in a while. Is this a business trip?"

"Yes, for the organization. We're trying to keep an inmate in the Pennsylvania Penal system from getting executed."

"When are you coming?"

"In about two weeks."

I walked over to the calendar that hung on the side of the kitchen cabinet. "I'll have DJ that weekend."

"That'll be fine. You know I don't mind her being with us."

"I know. But I'm just saying, especially since we haven't seen one another in awhile."

"She's my daughter, too. Don't forget that. I've been around that child since she was two years old. I'd love to see that girl because we haven't seen each other in a long time. Besides, I'm going to be with you for a week, maybe longer."

"She'll be glad to see you, too, Rube. And she'll be happy to hear she's taking a trip with us."

IT WAS JULY, AND IT HAD BEEN extremely hot out, in the hundreds. The week before Hurricane came down, he called to give me the name of the hotel in Philly, the Hilton at the airport.

I'd reserved a rental car from Enterprise because my car wasn't reliable enough to make a two-hour trip, and besides, the air conditioner wasn't working.

The day we were leaving, Enterprise picked us up from home and took us to their office in Scotch Plains, off Route 22. I lucked out, because they had run out of cars and only had a Honda CRV left, which was fine with me because my daughter could ride more comfortably, stretch out on a seat, and take a nap as she always did with the motion of a car. The temperature, at ten o'clock that morning, had already reached the high nineties.

After they placed us in the small-size Jeep, I drove over to McDonald's in Berkley Heights and got her breakfast, then headed towards the Turnpike south. She ate, and within the hour, I looked up into the rear view mirror—black shades up on my face—and saw she had fallen asleep. The sun shone brightly, the radio played in the background, and I bopped to the beats while looking around at the greenery and cars speeding past.

DEFENDING THE WRONGLY CONVICTED WAS SOMETHING close to Rubin's heart. It turned out that day that it hadn't been quite a productive one for him. When we got to the room, I could see something was wrong as soon as he opened the door and embraced me.

My daughter hugged him, then ran ahead and jumped on one of the king-size beds. Rubin closed the door behind us and approached at a snail's pace in silence. I stood there, purse dangling from my shoulder, as he kissed me on the cheek. I placed my hand on the bag to stop it from swinging. "Is something wrong, Rube?"

He sat on the bed, and DJ jumped behind him. "Jan, I apologize for not being very talkative right now. I'm just trying to sort out the day in my head."

I went over to the round wooden table and sat in one of the chairs. "That's fine."

He said with a serious expression, "Today wasn't a good one."

"Oh. What happened?" I said and hung my purse on the back of the chair.

"I couldn't get inside the prison to see the inmate."

"Why not?" Now I understood his mood. Rubin took his work seriously and personally, feeling responsible for each one of his cases.

He said, with a pissed-off inflection in his voice, "The warden wouldn't allow me to enter the prison."

"What?" It was the first time something like that had happened to him that I knew of.

With his head hung, he said, "I couldn't help the brother."

"I'm sorry, Rube." I wanted to jump up and go over to comfort him.

Sadness spread across his face, and he sighed, "Ah, baby." My daughter jumped on his back. "Hey, there!" he said, turning around, and put his arm around her; she quickly rolled back onto the bed.

She stood up behind him and hung over his shoulder, throwing her arms around his neck. "Hi, Rube." He turned toward the side and kissed her on her forehead.

I sat ,winding down after the two-hour drive, and motioned to my daughter to get off Rubin, making sure she wasn't being a nuisance to him. "She's fine," he said.

"Well, we're here." I smiled.

It was apparent he wasn't himself. "Yep," he said. I sat alongside him.

DJ stood behind us in her powdered blue short set and ribbed white socks. "Ma, I have to go to the bathroom."

"Go ahead. Why are you telling me? You know where it's at."

"Okay," she said, jumping off the bed, and skipped off.

Rubin sat emotionless.

She came running back and jumped straight up on the bed behind him. He reached around, pulling her over to him, and put her on his lap. She placed her thumb in her mouth, held onto his ear lobe, and gazed at the television.

Suddenly, the phone rang. Before Rubin slid over to pick it up, he let it ring several times. "Hello?" he said. ". . .Hey, baby."

I looked at him strangely, wondering who the hell he could have been possibly calling "baby" besides me. Then I figured he must call everyone special to him "baby". I wasn't as special as I'd thought at all after hearing that.

I moved back to the chair at the table while he talked and grabbed the television remote. My daughter slid from behind him and dashed toward the bathroom.

"I'll be back next week," he said as he smiled.

All of a sudden I heard water running in the bathroom. I moved swiftly toward it, pushing back the door, and saw her playing in the water with soap all over her arms and hands. I snatched a towel from the rack, dried her off, and slid her out. We stood in front of the mirrored closet, and I watched Rubin talking—his back was towards us.

"That's great," he replied.

Whom was he talking to? I wondered. I left DJ in front of the mirrors amd took a seat; sun poured through the window, hitting me on the back. She came over and positioned herself on my lap while I surfed for cartoons so she could settle down.

A commercial came on. She pointed to it. "Mommy, why'd they do that?"

"I don't know," I said in a whisper.

Out of the corner of my eye, I thought I saw Rubin motion to us with his hand, gesturing us to be quiet.

"Mommy," she said again.

He waved his hand again—I wasn't imagining it. I frowned as he put his finger up to his lips. I bent down to whisper in DJ's ear, "Please be quiet, because Rube's on an important phone call, okay?"

She held onto my head and whispered, "Okay, Mommy," then turned back to the cartoons.

I looked over at him wide-eyed, as if he was crazy, but he pretended he didn't see that. Children being children, she forgot and spoke again, and I placed my finger gently over her lips. "Remember, you have to be quiet, Rube's on the phone." I didn't pay close attention to his conversation but would hear bits and pieces of it at moments.

"Okay. Take care of yourself," he said finally. "I'll see you when I get back next week." He hung up with a big smile on his face. "Come here," he said. I thought he was talking to me but noticed he was looking at my daughter. "Come give me a hug." DJ's eyes were glued to the television, and she didn't hear him or budge.

I gently tapped her on the shoulder. "Hey, little girl, did you hear Rube calling you?"

She glanced at him quickly. "Come over here," he said again. She turned back toward the television with a smirk on her face and shook her head back and forth, grinning.

"Yes," he said.

She turned again, stared at him and a gigantic smile came across her face. "No," she said.

"Please?" he said, smiling back as he nodded his head up and down.

She jumped off my lap, leaped onto his, and sat sucking her thumb.

"Take that thumb out of your mouth," he said, pulling on it until she slid it out of her mouth.

She said, "Rube, can we go to the pool?" DJ hugged him.

"To the pool? Sure we can." He began to kiss her all around her cheeks. She laughed and did the same to him. He looked over at me. "Okay, but we have to give your mother more time to relax. Give her time to rest after driving, okay? Will you do that?"

"Okay," she said, sliding from his lap back onto the bed.

While tumbling behind him, she said, "Mommy's resting."

"Yes," Rube replied and reached back for her legs. "Come here, Jan," he said.

"What?" I hesitated but moved near him anyway.

"What? I said come here." He stretched out his arm.

I sat next to him, and he wrapped his arm around me. "How are you doing, my love?"

My mind was still on the phone call. "I'm fine. Why are you asking?" Perhaps he had felt guilty.

"I love you," he said, rubbing my shoulders.

My eyebrows rose as I moved his hand away. "You do?"

"Yes, I do," he said, reaching across me to grab his pack of cigarettes from the end table. DJ rolled back and forth across the bed behind us like a disturbed person, excited because she was going to the pool. She rolled towards Hurricane after he lit his cigarette, stopped, and laid her head in his lap. "Are you ready yet?" she said, looking up at him. He held his arm out and the cigarette in his other hand.

He turned to blow the smoke out. "No, you have to wait until I finish this cigarette. Is that okay with you?"

"Alright," she said as she curled herself into a ball.

"I have to get your bathing suit out of the bag. Be patient."

With her thumb still stuck in her mouth, she said, "Are you going swimming with me, Mommy?"

"Nah, I don't want to get my hair wet, but I'll put on my bathing suit. I'll get in with you for a little while, okay?"

"Yeah. Thanks, Mom. . . . Goodie!" she screeched, looking at Rubin as she lay behind him on the pillows.

He smiled back at her. "You know *I'm* not getting in the water," he said.

"Yep, I know that, Rube."

"You're a little smart aleck, you know." They both burst out laughing.

We sat in silence for several minutes; then DJ jumped from bed to bed, once in a while stopping to hug Rubin. He finished his smoke. "Jan, are you ready?" he asked, and placed the butt in the ash tray.

"Yeah," I said, getting up to get my overnight bag off the floor near the dresser, pulled out our bathing suits, and a pair of shorts and a tank top for DJ. "Come on; let's go put our bathing suits on." She hopped down from the bed. I took her hand and escorted her to the bathroom.

"Remember, I'm only getting in the pool with you for a little while. Then you'll have to play by yourself, okay? We'll sit on at the side of the pool and watch you while you do that."

Taking off her clothes and dropping each piece on the floor, she said, "Okay, Mommy."

WHEN WE REACHED POOLSIDE, RUBIN WALKED ahead, gathered three long adjustable beach chairs, and set them down side by side; there were plenty to choose from, because it was a weekday. My daughter immediately took off her shorts, draped them on a chair, and pulled on my hand. "Come on, Mom."

"Alright, hold on. Let me take my things off first."

"You have to take that tank top off."

Both of us strolled to the lower end of the pool. I pointed to the water level marks. "Do *not* go any further than number *two*. Do you hear me?"

"Yes, Mommy," she said as we stepped in the water.

The sun shone brightly all around through the glass roof and walls. Rube sat and watched us play for about twenty minutes, smiling the entire time. I got out, came back, and laid the towel over my chair. He said, "Have you heard from Jean and Ken?"

"No," I said, pushing the shades up on my head.

"What about Micky? Have you heard from her?"

"Nope, I haven't heard from her either. You know how I am, Rube. I don't actually keep in touch with anyone, remember?"

"The only time I hear from any one in my family, the Carters, is when there's a death in the family."

I glanced in the direction of my daughter splashing around in the water and turned back to him. "Get out of here.!" I said in surprise. "That's the only time they call you?"

"Yep, or if they want something. They don't call me to see how I'm doing."

DJ shouted, "Look at this, Mom and Rube!" We turned towards her and watched her disappear underwater.

"That's great!" Rubin yelled. "Jan. . .are you going to take me to Linden next weekend?"

"Yes. That weekend she'll be with her dad."

"Great. You do realize we're heading out tomorrow afternoon, baby?"

I rested my head against the chair. "Yes, I know," I said, pulling the shades back down over my eyes.

Even though Hurricane was there with me, he seemed preoccupied with something else. "I'm getting ready to go on a lot more trips to California within the next several months, my love."

"Oh?" I said, turning in DJ's direction.

"It's for the movie. It'll be out in January."

"Really, that's great, Rube. It's finally come!"

"After ten years in the making," he said proudly.

"You deserve it, Rube." He watched a family pass by and set up down from us.

THE NEXT DAY WE DROVE BACK to Jersey, arriving early Friday afternoon. That week moved swiftly, and before we knew it, another weekend had come upon us. Friday evening, we dropped my daughter off at her father's house, turned around, and hung around at home, in the living room as the television remained on mute, music played in the background, and candles sparkled throughout the living room. Rubin said, "Tomorrow afternoon we can go to Linden, hear, Jan?"

I stretched out on the wall-to-wall carpet in the condo and said, "Uh-hmm."

He sat with his legs crossed on the coach and asked, "Do you know exactly where we're going?"

"Yep. I asked my son where St. George was."

"Good. How's he doing?"

"Your son's a good young brother."

"Thanks. He's fine. They're on their way to Portugal."

"Oh! He and his wife. One thing I can say, your son sure takes after his mom."

"What makes you say that?"

Unfolding his legs, and leaned back. "He knows how to travel around like his mother."

"Ha, ha! You said your friend doesn't have a phone, right?"

He pulled a piece of paper from his pants pocket. "Nope."

"What if we go and he's not home?"

"I was told he should be there because he cuts hair on Saturdays."

"Oh, okay." Rubin seemed to be acting strangely towards me. I wondered why and was getting fed up with what I was feeling, got up and headed to the bathroom, and yelled, "Rube?"

"Yeah, baby?"

"Remember the last time you were here?"

He said with caution, "Uh-hm."

"You asked me if I wanted my house keys back?" I heard his voice getting closer. I looked out, and his skinny body appeared in the hallway, and he stopped in front of me at the door.

"Yeah," he said.

I'd been patting my face dry with a yellow hand towel. "You can give them back to me," I said with a straight face.

He looked at me coldly, walked into the bedroom, snatched his bag from the floor, searched in it wildly, and emptied all its contents onto the bed. "I don't seem to have them with me," he said as he continued to rummage around.

"I thought you told me you kept them in that bag all the time."

"I do, but I must've accidentally taken them out."

"Ah," I said, replacing the towel on the rack. Everything Rubin had been telling me lately had been contradictory or a bold-faced lie. The tension was getting high between us.

BEFORE RUBIN LEFT CANADA TO COME to Philadelphia and Jersey, I'd asked him if he'd buy me a ring which he'd agreed to, and told him, I had a friend who was a jeweler, in business for twenty-five years in New York; she'd give him a good price.

The Saturday afternoon before we left for Linden, I said, "Rube, I'm going to call Pat now and get a price on a ring, okay?"

"Go ahead, baby," he shouted from the bathroom.

I grabbed the portable phone to place the call. "Are you sure you want to buy it?" I shouted.

"Yes, I *said* I would—but I'm not spending a lot of money for it, though." I strolled into the bedroom to talk, and he went into the living room.

"Okay," I replied, grabbed my torn burgundy phone book from the computer table to look up her number. I dialed. She answered. "Hi, Pat. This is Janet."

"Hi. How've you *been*? I haven't heard from you in awhile."

"Yeah, I know. I've been busy. Oh, I'm also not at the university any more."

"Oh, that's why. So how *have* you been?"

"I'm good—and yourself?"

"I've been busy, too, working long hours."

"I see. You know, I'm calling for a reason. I want to know what type of price you could give me on an engagement ring."

"Engagement ring? You're getting engaged?"

"Yeah," I replied.

"To whom? Not that I'd know him," she chuckled.

"Rubin Carter." I paced the room. "Have you heard of him?"

"Who's that?" she replied. "I never have."

I leaned against the wall. "A middle weight boxer? He's a black celebrity."

"I don't watch sports. See, I don't know him."

"He has a movie coming out in January with Denzel Washington playing his part," I said, walking in the bedroom.

"Oh! Haven't heard of him, but that's nice. Congratulations."

"Thank you." I plopped on the edge of the bed.

"What style are you thinking of?"

"It has to be 18-carat, because I'm allergic to 14-carat."

She laughed. "You are? You sure are an expensive, woman."

"Yeah, the set of rings my ex-husband gave me—I developed a rash on my fingers. It was so bad I had to go to a dermatologist."

"Oh, my. No problem. I'll give you a good price on it."

"I'd like an emerald stone with a sapphire cut to it, and a set of small diamonds around it."

"How many carats would you like it to be?" Pat asked.

"One to two," I said excitedly.

"Okay. I can give that to you for about a thousand."

"Really, Pat?"

"Yes. I'll give it to you at that price because you've been a good customer."

"Thanks. I'm going to get Rubin and give him the phone, so you can talk to him about it, okay?"

"Sure. I can do that. Good."

"Hold on." I yelled out for him in the living room.

"Yes, my love."

I walked out to where he was sitting on the couch. "Talk to Pat, please." I handed him the phone. "She has a price." I felt a thousand wasn't a bad price for what I was asking.

He took the phone, began talking, and walked to the bedroom. I could hear him say, "Fine, and yourself? Um-hm. Yes. . . . How much?"

I turned toward the room but didn't go in right away because of the sound of his voice. "What?" he said. "A *thousand*? I'll give you seven hundred. . . . Hell no, I'm not paying that." I slid in and sat down on the bed behind him. All of a sudden, he threw down the phone and stormed out, waving his hands as if to say *forget it*. I looked up at him strangely, because I knew he could afford that, but where was his anger coming from? I felt awkward as I picked up the phone. ". . .Hi, Pat. I'm sorry for his behavior. I don't even under stand what just happened."

"Wow!" she replied. "He doesn't want to pay a thousand.".

"What? He *doesn't*? Did he say why?" I asked in disbelief.

"I'm giving you a good price. Honestly I am. He can check out other prices," she said.

"I know you're giving us a good price, especially for what I'm asking for, Pat."

"He's just being cheap right now, I guess."

"I'll find out what his problem is." I was totally embarrassed. "I don't know what's wrong with him. I apologize for his rudeness."

"It's okay. I'm sure he makes good money—a thousand dollars is nothing for him."

"You're right. Let me talk to him, and I'll get back to you."

"Okay. Thanks, anyway."

In shock, I stared out the window into the bright sun, fighting back my tears. I couldn't help but wonder why he felt I wasn't worth a thousand dollars. I'd spent more than that the entire week. I walked out to him. "Rube, what's wrong?"

"I'm not paying a thousand dollars. I told you, I don't have that kind of money right now."

"A thousand dollars? That's not a lot of money. It would cost you a heck of a lot more if you were buying it from somewhere else."

"I'm not spending a thousand on a ring, so forget about it."

"Fine," I said, stormed off to the bedroom, and stayed there until it was time to drive to Linden.

We got off highway 78, entered Elizabeth, and passed Warinanco Park. About a mile down the road, we went over railroad tracks and crossed into a ghetto-looking area. The buildings were decrepit; people walked the streets wearing shabby clothing, showing signs of drug or alcohol abuse.

Rubin sat in the passenger seat, casually dressed, scouting for house numbers. He pointed to an abandoned-looking building. "There it is."

"Where?" I said, glancing quickly to my right.

"Over there, that brown one."

I'd passed it by then and had to make a U-turn. I couldn't believe anyone was living there; the place was boarded up. "Are you sure this is the right place?" I said as I stared at it.

"Yes, this is the address. Pull over there."

It was a broken-down, dilapidated store front. "That one there, Rube?" I said as I pointed to it.

"Yes. Pull over, my love."

He had no idea how wide-eyed I was, because I had on a pair of dark brown shades. I parked, we got out, and cautiously approached the door, which was cracked open slightly in the ninety-degree weather.

He knocked on it. A man shouted, "Come in." We entered a large, dark open-spaced room, Rubin first and me behind him. My eyes adjusted to the dark. I'd been busy thinking of how hot it was outside, and there wasn't a window open in that place, no air circulation anyplace. I noticed a golden brown-skinned man in his early sixties with a muscular body, wearing a muscle shirt, standing in front of a barber's chair, holding a pair of clippers in one hand, cutting the hair of another man who was wearing a tee shirt with a white towel draped around his neck. The barber looked up, stared, and said, "Rubin? Rubin Carter? Is that you?"

Rubin's face beamed. "Yes, it's me, my brother."

"Rubin Carter. Man, how did you find me?" In the blink of an eye, he'd laid the clippers on a table, dashed over, and embraced him.

I stood worrying about the nasty condition of the place, because I was skived out by it and absolutely didn't want to sit anywhere. The floors were so dirty they had outside dirt on them, the kind that gets caught between blades of grass.

They both had grins plastered on their faces. "Oh, man. It's good to see you," Rubin said, embracing him.

The barber stepped away from him and asked, "Man, where are you living?"

"I'm in Canada now," Rubin replied. He didn't seem concerned at all about the way the place looked.

"Oh, yeah," the barber said, stepping over near his customer. "Canada?"

Rubin said, "How long have you been out of prison, Charlie?"

I stood praying no one would ask me to take a seat.

"I've been out about five years now," he said, shaping the back of the thin dark-skinned man's hair; the customer didn't appear to be hot either. Sweat was building up all over my body. I felt as if I wanted to faint. There was no air circulation whatsoever.

Charles turned the chair forward, and the man asked, "That's Rubin Carter, the boxer?"

Charles said, "Yes."

"Oh, man. It's a pleasure to meet you, Mr. Carter."

Rubin shook his hand. "It's my pleasure, my brother."

"We looked out for each other in prison," Charles said.

Rubin said, "I'm so sorry, Charles—this is Jan. Jan, Charles."

"Hello, Jan," he said.

"Hi. How are you?" I said, still standing close to the door, wanting to make up an excuse to step outdoors.

It's good to *see* you," Rubin said, turning towards a stool that sat near a wall. I was surprised he was so comfortable there, because he couldn't stand to live in filth.

"It's been such a long time," Charles replied, bouncing from side to side, clipping the man's hair.

"Have you heard from any of the other people we knew?"

I continued standing until Rubin looked over at me. "Why don't you have a seat over there, Jan?" He pointed to a grimy chair that had turned gray with dirt. Charles motioned with the clippers in his hand to have a seat, too. I cringed but moved slowly towards it and sat down on the edge of the thing.

They reminisced about their prison episodes, catching up on where people were. The man in the chair rose and got ready to leave. "Well, it was nice meeting you, Mr. Carter," he said to Rubin.

Rubin rushed up to him and shook his hand. "My pleasure, brother." The man opened the door; sunlight flooded the room, and hot air rushed in. I sat, wishing a breeze would follow.

Rubin sat with one leg perched on the rim of the stool. "Jan, that guy there saved my ass in prison many times."

"Really?" I said, faking a smile as beads of sweat rolled off my forehead.

"Jan, once they'd put a hallucinogen in my drink. I freaked out, and

Charles stood outside my cell all night, making sure nobody would come near me."

"Yeah, I remember that night, Rube," Charles said as he put his clippers away.

Before I knew it, thirty-five minutes had passed in that sauna room. Rubin looked at me. I assumed he saw the moisture on my forehead and the uneasiness my body language gave off. "Hey, man, we're going to have to get out of here," he said, rising from the stool. As soon as he did, I jumped up off that soiled chair. "I want you to come visit me in Canada, soon, this summer, matter of fact."

Charles said, "I'm not flying on any airplane."

Rubin laughed. "What?" he said, standing in the center of the room.

"I'm afraid of flying. You won't get me on one of those things."

I sauntered closer to Rubin and near the front door.

"Even if I fly with you, you won't do it? I'm sending you a ticket."

"Nah, Don't do that. I'm not flying."

"Don't tell me you're *afraid*, man," Rubin said as he moved towards me.

Charles chuckled. "Yep. I don't care who knows, either."

"Think about it. What if I fly with you, man?"

"I don't know, but I'll think about that, Rubin."

I slid closer to the front door, sweating, in desperate need of air.

Rubin said. "Man, I'm coming back next month for you, and we'll fly back together. How would you like that?"

"Okay. We can do that," Charles replied.

"I'll contact you in a couple of weeks. I'll have Jan come back and let you know."

"Alright, Rube, I'll wait to hear from you."

What a quick change, I thought. It hadn't taken much to convince him. Rubin turn towards the door. Was I happy? Before we exited, Rubin said, "I'm going to do that, so get ready, my brother."

I held onto the door knob and pulled it open. He came closer and I scurried out, trying not to rub up against anything on the way. Rubin and Charles walked to the door. "I'm serious, man," Rubin said. "You'll be hearing from me."

"Okay." They hugged, slapping each other so hard, you could hear the echo.

"Bye. It was nice meeting you," I said as I inhaled and exhaled the warm air.

OUR FINAL VISIT WAS ON A SUMMER EVENING when Rubin sat parked on the love seat with a smug grin plastered on his face, in a pair of black slacks, dress socks, and a custom-made dress shirt. The sun had recently gone down, leaving a faint hint of daylight in Plainfield, New Jersey. We sat on opposite sides of the living room, listening to music, with the television on mute in the background, as usual. Normally, we would've been cuddled up together.

Stretched cross the couch, I asked, "What are you grinning about, Rube?"

He chuckled. "Oh. Me."

"You?"

"That's what I'm smiling about."

"*You're* making you smile like that?"

"Me being just enough? Yep. I'm just enough."

I tapped on the cushion to the music. "What do you mean by that, you're just enough?

"I'm enough for whatever it takes." He burst out laughing and crossed his legs.

What a messed-up attitude, I thought as I sat up slumped over, hands on each side of my face, holding up my head. "Where did that come from?"

The movie had evidently gone to his head, or was it the money that had changed him? I could see it in his body language. All of sudden he had gotten cocky. Where was that coming from? "Rubin," I said, angry and amazed.

He tapped his foot to the R&B song that was playing. "Yes?"

"I don't like who you are right now," I said, looking over at him.

He barked, "*What?*"

"You're different. I don't like the man I'm seeing."

"That's because I'm not the man I was."

I sat back on the couch. "*What?* Come *on*, Rube. Now, what does that mean?"

I said, "I'm not the man I was."

"Well, that's obvious. You've completely changed, even from the last time we were together. Matter of fact, I like the man I met in 1976 with the bald head."

"I'm not that man either anymore, nor am I the one I was a year ago." He uncrossed his legs, and then spread them apart. "Yeah, I'm different than then."

Chills ran down my spine. "You got that right."

He gawked at me coldly, said, ". . .Hm," then became quiet.

I was shocked by his arrogance and coldness. Where was it coming from? And he planned to stay a week with me in that position. Suddenly, I saw what his plan was—to use me as usual, get me to go pick up Charles and take them to the airport. This trip wasn't really about me or us.

I reflected back on the week before Rubin arrived, when he called with energy and happiness in his voice. "Hi, baby."

"What's up, Rube?" I'd responded.

"I want you to do something for me."

"What's that?"

"Go to Linden over by Charles."

"I'll have to go during the week," I'd said, realizing he'd bring every-one up to visit but me. I'd felt hurt but refused to reveal it to him. Nor was I excited about going back to that rat hole either, but I'd do it for him. I felt as though I always sacrificed myself as usual and did what Rubin asked of me.

I worked in Berkley Heights at the time, and drove down to Linden on my lunch hour. I knocked on Charles's door; he opened it a crack and peeked out. "Hi," I said as I stood back.

He was startled. "Oh! Hi, Jan. What are you doing here?"

"Rubin asked me to come because he needs to talk with you. Is there a phone close by so you can call him?" I glimpsed around to see if I could spot a pay phone, but couldn't.

He said, "There's one in the store down the street. Give me a minute. I have to put something on."

"Okay," I said, hoping he wouldn't invite me in.

"I'll be right back," he said, leaving the door closed, which was fine with me. I went back to the car and leaned against it as the sun beat down on my head. It was extremely hot out. Within seconds, he'd returned, and we walked down to the bodega a block away.

"I ran down here on my lunch hour, hoping I would catch you at home."

"Oh, you're on lunch?"

"Yes."

"Yeah, this is a good time to have caught me." Charles pointed down the street. "The store's right over there."

The streets were empty; it was high noon, ninety-nine degrees, and a weekday. When we approached the store door, it was wide open—I guess it was to let the warm breeze flow through, because there wasn't any air conditioning in sight. At the counter, two middle-aged men sat on stools, wearing white tee shirts and jeans. A man behind it, who looked like the owner, placed a drink in front of each one of them. The men gave me the impression they frequented the place daily. I slyly took a glance around, noticing how clean the place was kept. It was more like a small coffee shop then the variety store the sign advertised.

Charles waved to the man behind the counter. "Hey, man, how are you doing today?" Then he nodded over at the others as we passed.

One replied in a Spanish accent, "Fine, and yourself?"

We walked over to the wall behind them, where the pay phone hung. Using my calling card, I dialed Rubin, and Win answered, "Hello?"

I said softly, "Hello, may I speak to Rubin?"

"I'm sorry, but he's busy right now and can't come to the phone."

"Would you tell him I'm on the phone, please?" I knew she knew it was me. "He's expecting my call."

"Janet?" she asked.

"Yes."

"Hold on," she said, and put me on hold.

My ear began to perspire from the heat. I heard the men chatting in the background while Charles stood along side me, listening. Rubin got on. "Hi, Jan."

"Hi, Rube. I have Charles here with me."

"Oh you were able to get a hold of him. . . . Good."

I'd been holding on to a tissue and began to wipe the sweat from the ear piece. "Yeah."

"Put him on, baby."

"Okay." I handed Charles the sweaty receiver.

"Hey, Rube." Charles said with excitement then got silent. "Um-Hm. You're coming to pick me up? Alright. That sounds good. In a couple of weeks. I sure will. Yes, I'll be ready." He paused for seconds. "Okay, man. I'll see you then." He handed me back the phone.

"Yeah, Rube?" I'd expected him to tell me what they had just discussed, especially the part about him coming for Charles in two weeks but he never said a word.

"Thank you Jan, for doing that," he said. "I'm a little busy right now, but I will talk to you later."

THE WEEK WENT BY QUICKLY with tension between us. Later that weekend, Rubin lay across the love seat with his back turned to me. He'd had his legs dangling over the edge. "Jan?" he said.

I shook my head. "What, Rubin?"

He turned his head and looked my way, then turned away. "Don't try getting into my head."

Lying on my back, on the other side of the room, I frowned at him. "What are you talking about, Rubin?"

He mumbled, "Don't think you can get into my head."

"I'm not trying to get into your head. What makes you think that?"

With his head against his arms, he said, "Stop trying to use that psychology shit on me. Psychiatrists have tried for years and couldn't. What makes you think you can? You sure can't."

What bizarre behavior, I thought. "I'm *not* trying to do that!" I shouted. "You're crazy, Rubin. The only one doing that is you to me."

He stretched his head back around and stressed, "Yes, you are."

My head fell back against the seat. "No, I'm not. Don't tell me what

I'm trying to do, either. I've never tried to do that, and you know it."

"You are, but that's not going to happen."

". . .Rubin, what's this about?"

"You want to figure me out."

I began to get upset. "Oh, now I'm trying to figure you out!" I screamed, and a tear ran down my face. I couldn't understand what was going on with him; there was no reason for his behavior. It was as if he'd flipped on me.

He turned, fixed his eyes on the television, and muttered, "I know what you're doing."

"You *think* you do. The bottom line is you've changed, Rubin."

"Jan, bullshit. I know about a woman's scorn."

"*A woman's scorn?* What are you talking about *now?* What, you and Win are at it again? Or is it another woman? Who's *scorning* you, Rubin? *I'm* sure not. Who are you talking about?"

I marched into the bedroom, threw myself on the bed, threw my arm over my forehead, and cried. I jumped up, leaned against the living room doorway, and pleaded, "Rube, what's this *about?*" I waited for a response but he didn't answer. I shouted, "Do you think you're *better* than me?"

Still no response. I went back to the bedroom and cried. He shouted, "Now, that's something you've manifested in your own mind, that mumbo-jumbo bullshit. Get the hell out of here with that!"

I hung around for another fifteen minutes then grabbed my jacket and purse and told him I was running out to Shop Rite, which was just a few miles away. Actually, I had sneaked off to see Lee. I knew he'd be a comfort and would treat me with respect as a person. First, I stopped at the store, picked up several items, and headed to Union. My intention was to sit and talk for thirty minutes. But my visit turned into two hours, because I stayed and made love to him.

We lay naked across Downy-smelling, queen-size, blue-striped sheets; I stared up at the whirling blades on the ceiling fan. "Lee, I'm so upset with Rubin. It's absolutely over between us. I told you it was coming to that. Especially, after I chose to start seeing you. That was something I'd never done before."

Speaking calmly as always, he said, "What happened?"

"He seemed to have just changed overnight. Yesterday he was himself, so I thought. He had passion and was romantic. Today, he's being mean and cold to me. I hadn't said or done anything to him that warranted that type of behavior towards me."

"Why's that? Are you sure you didn't say or do something to him, even *unconsciously*, that made him behave like that towards you?"

"No. I thought about that, too. We were just chillin'." I grabbed Lee's hand. "I haven't done a thing. He started talking some crap about a woman's scorn. I had no idea what he was getting at with that."

He reached down the side of the bed and picked his boxers up from the floor. I was holding onto his hand. He rose slowly. "Maybe it's another woman."

Letting his hand go, I said, "Another woman?"

Of course, I didn't want to hear that, but it was a possibility, especially with Rubin's history with me. Not wanting to believe Lee, I quickly dismissed that idea from my mind and looked at him as if he'd said it because he was jealous, maybe.

He slid his medium-built frame into his boxers, pressed his left elbow into a pillow, and rested his head—styled like Billy Dee Williams's—on his hand. "Maybe. I don't know."

". . .If he is, I'm not going to see him again for sure. I'm tired of it and the way he's treating me."

Lee's light-brown eyes settled amorously on me. "Well, you have to make that decision."

"I know I do, and I'm getting there. It's not as easy as you say. We've been trying to get it together for twenty-five long years now—a soul mate, who appeared out of no where, at least three to four times, in my life time. Maybe we're just not meant to be with each other, Lee."

He rose, walked over to the desk, took a seat, and looked my way. "You might be right about that," he said as he turned on the electric piano.

"I don't know. And I wouldn't be surprised."

He ran his fingers back and forth over the keys. "If Rubin is seeing someone, it'll come out eventually. It always does."

I shook my head. "He's such an asshole, Lee. I'm getting the feeling he thinks he's better than me all of a sudden." I rolled up on the edge of the bed. "I don't like that at all."

Lee pounded on the electric piano. "It's because of the movie. It's getting to his head." He hummed to a song he had written.

"Yeah, Rubin isn't the same. He's turned, and I'm finding out he's a big-ass liar, too. Boy, do I despise a liar. He makes me wonder about him."

A soft jazz melody poured through the speakers. "Hm," Lee said, humming the song.

I glanced up at the clock. "I better shower and get dressed to go. I've been gone awhile. . . . Oh, wow, it's going on two hours. I can't say I went to the Shop Rite out by me. It doesn't take that long. I'll make up something."

He replied, "Tell him you went to several stores and browsed around."

"That's a good idea. Gotta go. I'll call you when he leaves."

"Okay. I'm here if you need me."

"Thanks for the talk and making me relax." I chuckled. "It's over between him and me. I'm really sick of his bullshit. I don't care who the hell he is." I grabbed my clothes, headed to the bathroom, and showered.

When I got home and laid the bags on the kitchen counter, I peeked at Rubin, who was still stretched across the couch. He said, "It took you a long time to go to the store. It's only around the corner."

I hung my purse on the back of a chair, stepped into the kitchen, and begun putting the groceries away. "Yeah. I stopped at the supermarket then went to browse around in some stores." I glanced in at him when I finished; he had fallen asleep, where he chose to sleep for the rest of that week on the couch. He'd been to the room with me twice—the first night, and the night before we went to Trenton. He had been invited to dinner and took me along, to the house of a guard he knew from prison who was portrayed in the movie. Thursday night we had dinner in Trenton, at the guard's house. Rubin was pleasant to me that evening—pretending we were a couple. He still needed me to take him to Linden to pick up Charles and drop them both at the airport.

I'd come to realize Rubin and I discussed nothing. Yes, we were soul mates; that was a fact. Passion was all we had had between us, though, and what I'd come to know, which had distorted my vision of love. Rubin, being a big romantic, combined with that gentle touch of charisma, had made me feel as though he was the nicest man I'd ever known. Our relationship had been based on that for years— damn, *decades*—besides the fact I had been eighteen years younger. I'd truly believed that Rubin 'Hurricane' Carter really loved me.

For eight years we'd spent most holidays together, building our own family unit, separate from the rest; but it had turned out that Rubin was a master of deception, knowing exactly what he was doing the entire time. Rubin, whom I considered my man, had kept me hidden all those years, holding back a big part of himself, and not revealing his true self, to me.

THE FOLLOWING WEEKEND QUICKLY rolled up on us. My car had been giving me problems overheating, leaking antifreeze, and I hadn't had the chance to fix it, so I kept a container of antifreeze in the trunk, adding it whenever the radiator began to steam up.

Rubin and Charles were leaving Friday morning around ten o'clock. That Thursday night, he came to the bedroom and slept with me, then somehow ended up on the couch. That morning, we left for Elizabeth, picked up Charles, and shot over to the airport.

I pulled in front of Air Canada's drop-off area and let them out. Hurricane was dressed in business attire on that day. He leaned over and kissed me on the cheek. "I'll be right back, my love."

"Okay." I hopped out and opened the trunk for them. They grabbed their luggage and scurried inside. I went back in the car and waited with the engine running for Rubin to return. I thought he'd be back quickly, but through the large window, I watched them walk up to the check-in line, and Rubin walked away, leaving Charles in line. I thought he was heading out to the car and studied the automatic sliding doors, but he wasn't anywhere in sight.

Then I glanced at the thermostat gauge. The needle was heading towards the red zone, and I immediately turned the car off, but it was too late. The radiator had already begun to smoke. I sat there, feeling embarrassed, though I didn't know why.

I tried hard to find Charles on the line, to see if Rubin had come back, but he was still standing in the same spot there, alone. Smoke had begun to pour from under the hood, and antifreeze dripped onto the road. I looked again; Rubin, meanwhile, was back, standing next to Charles on the line. He had to have seen the car smoking, and I wondered why he hadn't come out to help. The white smoke continued to rise into the air until it fizzled out. I knew I had to add antifreeze, but I didn't want to do it there, because it was so embarrassing to me. Once again, I glanced toward the window; Rubin had disappeared and wasn't coming out of the doors, either. Where was he? I asked myself. I didn't see him anywhere.

Charles was still near the end of the line—it was moving slowly—and he wouldn't reach the counter anytime soon. I figured by the time he got up there, I could pull out of the airport onto a side street in Elizabeth, add the antifreeze, and get back, hopefully before Rubin noticed I wasn't there.

I hurried out of the airport to find a secluded street, jumped out, snatched the antifreeze from the trunk, added it, and rushed back to the airport. I was able to get the same car spot and looked through the window carefully to see if Charles had moved up. All of a sudden, Rubin popped up out of nowhere. I had hoped he hadn't come outside. He turned and looked my way, turned away, and took off again. I sat for ten minutes more and then left, because it was so hot out, sweat was pouring off me. I couldn't wait to get home and into the air conditioning.

When I got home, I expected to see the answering machine light flashing, but it wasn't. Several hours passed, and the phone didn't ring. I knew he should've boarded the plane and been home by then. Why hadn't he called? I was furious—he hadn't had the decency to call me. I dialed his private line first, but there was no answer; his voice mail came on. Next, I dialed the business line, knowing Winifred would pick it up. "Hello?" she said.

"Hi, Win. May I speak with Rubin?"

She said with a smug voice, "Oh, he's not in yet."

I replied, pretending nothing was wrong because I sure didn't want her to know, "Alright."

"He called and told me his plane was delayed."

"Oh, okay, I'll call him back later. Thank you."

That made matters worse. Why hadn't he called *me* and told me that? Later that evening, I placed another call to Hurricane because he still hadn't called me back. He answered with enthusiasm. "Hello?"

I said coldly, "Hi, Rube."

"Hi, Jan," he said as the happiness disappeared from his voice.

"How come you didn't call me?"

"Call you for what?" he said coldly.

"To tell me your flight was delayed?"

"My calling card didn't work." He was lying; he didn't know I'd called and had spoken to Win.

"Your card wouldn't work? That's what you're telling me?"

"Yes."

"You could've called me collect. You have in the past. Why didn't you do that?"

"I didn't have time to do that. I had to take the shuttle over to the other side of the airport to get the Continental flight. You know how I get, girl."

"Continental on the other side?" He didn't respond. What he was talking about, I thought to myself. I knew you don't catch planes on the other side unless it's a private jet. "You told me you were coming back out to the car and didn't."

He became silent, and his tone changed. "I said I had to get over to the other side. Listen, I'm just getting in. I'll call you later." He hung up.

What a liar, I thought. I didn't want anything else to do with the man; that was it. Keeping me around for his own selfish reasons—now that he was getting the fame back, walking around in tailor-made suits, he thought he was too good for me. I made my decision: I no longer wanted to walk in Rubin's shadow.

In December 1999, several weeks before Christmas, Rubin called, waking me up as usual. I wasn't sure if I even wanted to pick up the phone, especially after what he had done.

"Jan, I'm leaving for California next week."

"Okay. When will you get back?"

"Hold on. Let me look at my schedule." I could hear him rattling papers around. "On December 21."

"Can you come spend Christmas with me?"

He hesitated. ". . .Yeah, baby, I should be able to do that."

I said, as I stretched. "You know what, Rube?"

"What, my love?"

"I had a strange dream about us last night."

"Oh? You did? What was it about?"

I looked up at the ceiling and noticed how dusty the floodlights were. "The dream caused me to wake up moaning."

"Really? It had to've been a nightmare. My ugly face must have scared you," he said, busting out in laughter.

"Nah. We were in Canada somewhere. I'd found out you had gotten married. You rode past me in a car with a woman in the passenger seat."

"Another woman was with me?"

"Yes. It was your wife. The woman I had been told you married. I started chasing after the car, trying to catch up to you. You seemed to be heading towards your house."

"I was married?"

"Uh-hmm. That was a strange dream. I wonder what that all means, Rube. You know how I am about dreams. It means something is going to happen soon. I'll know within the next week. It'll be revealed to me."

"Yes, I do know that about you. You're spooky like that, Jan. . . . Well, my love I have to get off this phone. When I get back, I'll call you."

The new millennium was approaching; I'd been reminded daily of Rubin's social success and contributions, his face thrust all over the television. Commercials sounded like trumpets advertising his recent biography, and the portrayal of him by Denzel Washington. He was out in

California at the opening with his mother—so I had been told by him.

A week later, I was lying in bed, watching television, when the phone rang. It was my best friend, Irene. "Hey, Neenah. What are you doing? Have you been watching the news?" she asked anxiously.

"No, I'm watching a movie," I said, slowly because I had been concentrating and focused on it and not her. "Hold on for a minute—the best part's coming up."

"Okay." A few seconds passed.

"Alright, it's over."

I asked as I rolled over on my back, "Now, what were you saying about the news?"

"Rubin was on the news."

I replied with one leg folded over the other, "Yeah, for the movie."

"Yep. But guess what—he wasn't alone."

"I know," I said.

She asked in an agitated voice, "You know? What are you, crazy?"

"Yeah, he's with his mother."

"With his *mother?* Well, I have news for you."

"What?" I was wondering what she could be talking about.

"He was walking down the red carpet with a woman, but it sure wasn't his mother."

". . .Are you sure?"

"Well, does his mama look like she's in her late thirties?"

I said, with a chuckle, "Hell, no."

"A women in her late thirties was walking arm and arm with him up the red carpet, and the newspeople called her his wife."

"His. . . . *What?* His *wife?* He told me he was taking his *mother* to the premiere." My heart dropped into my stomach.

"He lied to you, girlfriend, because she definitely wasn't his mother. She's a dark-skinned girl with braids who wasn't as pretty as you are, that's for sure. Do you know her?"

"No. I have no idea who she is." I sat straight up in bed and leaned my head back up against the wall. "Irene, you're not going to believe this, but last week I had a dream he got married. I told him about it, too, before he left for California."

"You did? What did he say?"

"He didn't say a word." I sat there in disbelief.

"He said nothing? What an asshole."

"Do you think he got married and just didn't say anything to me?"

"Evidently. Don't get depressed over this, do you hear me?"

"I won't. . . . That's probably why he was acting the way he was when he was here last. Remember? I told you about it."

"Yeah, he was probably married then. That's his reason for sleeping on the couch all week."

"Yeah, and he must have been feeling guilty about what he was doing there with me."

"Are you okay? . . . Well, he's getting his cake and eating it, too."

"I'm fine, but I'm calling that motherfucker when he gets back. Irene, remember the part about the ring, which had to have been all an act—he knew it then, also. I asked him if he'd come see me when he gets back next week for Christmas week. And do you know what he said."

"What?"

"He told me, 'Oh, I could do that.' What a fuckin' liar he is."

"Yep, it makes sense now. All these years he'd been telling you he was going to marry you. Wow. He's a big-ass liar."

"He's deceitful, and I don't like that. Matter of fact, he's a professional at it. I'm never going to talk to him again after I curse his ass out, Irene."

"Good for you. I wouldn't. Cut that motherfucker loose."

"I am. Telling me he was coming for the holidays. He can't help himself from lying, evidently. I'm going to ask him if he's married."

"He's going to deny it, so expect that."

"I know. Oh, I'm cursing his ass out. I can't wait until he gets back. He better never try to speak to me again in my life."

"Take it easy, and call me after you speak with him. Let me know what he says. I wish I could be here for you, but you know, we're getting ready to leave for Florida tomorrow."

"I know. I'll be fine. Thanks for calling and letting me know. He's hurt me before, but this is it for me. All I feel is numbness at the moment. I don't think I can cry, because that would be feeling sorry for myself. I can't believe I've sat around waiting for him all this time, because he'd promised we'd get married. I believed him. No more for me, Irene. He can forget it. Have a good trip, and trust me, I'll be fine."

ON DECEMBER 21, 1999, I HURRIED home from work around 5:30 PM. I walked in, threw my long wool navy coat, and my bag, on the couch, snatched the cordless from its receiver, and dialed Rubin's number, hoping he was home to pick up. His voice came on. "Hello."

I said tranquilly, "Hi, Rube."

"Hey, there, baby. How are you?"

My right leg was shaking furiously on its own as I stood there, wanting to crawl through the phone and kick his ass. "I'm fine. And you?"

"I'm just great," he said jovially, as though nothing was wrong.

"Really. Tell me something, Rube."

I felt his smile beam through the phone. "What's that, my love?"

"Is it true what the reporters are saying? Are you married? *Are* you, Rubin?" I shouted.

There was complete silence. ". . .Yes, I am."

"It's true you are, really are? How long have you been married, and when were you going to tell me that, Rubin? Huh? Were you married when you were here last month?"

He didn't answer that question. "I married my angel."

"Your *angel!*" I shouted angrily.

"Yes," he said. All of sudden, a strange feeling came across me that he wasn't married at all. Rubin was bullshitting me again. Maybe it was all a publicity stunt, because he was talking to me as if I was a reporter he'd prepared a speech for. I knew him too well.

"Well, you'd better hope it's your angel. Who the hell do you think you are? How could you do that to me? You told me you were taking your mother. You lied to me as usual."

"What do you mean, 'as usual'?"

"Rubin, you *promised* me. You've told me *we* were getting married *all this time!*" I stared out at the big leafless oak tree in the middle of the court.

He screamed back, "Why can't you let me *live my life?* You've lived yours."

"What? What are you *talking* about? What has this to do with anything I'm saying? And, mind you, my life has been centered—most of it—around yours and the promises you've made to me. We discussed it over and over for *decades*, Rube."

"I *was* going to marry you," he had the nerve to say.

"You *were?* What the hell are you *saying?*" I knew then it was a publicity stunt. "Rubin, you're nothing but a fuckin' liar. I hope you have a nice life with your third wife. I have to go."

"Jan, don't hang up. Merry Christmas?"

He thinks he's funny now, I thought. "Same to you," I added.

"Jan, I know you won't believe this, but I do love you."

"You *love* me? How can you *say* that, Rubin?"

"But. . .I do. I really do."

"You *can't* love me. You married someone *else.*"

I began wondering, How could he have married anyone when he hadn't divorced Lisa? Now I knew he was lying to me. "Bye, Rube."

He said sadly. "Take care of yourself."

When I hung up, I had a vision of our souls letting each other's hand go, and my soul walked away from his and didn't turn back. I was so angry at him, I've never cried over it; besides I'd reached a place where I no longer wanted to spend life with him either.

WEEKS LATER, RUBIN APPEARED ON all the top talk shows: Oprah, Larry King, the works, but his so-called wife, Teresa, was never by his side or mentioned. I thought that was quite strange. They appeared together in *Jet* magazine, posing at the movie's opening party, with no mention of her being his wife.

A few days later, Elaine called. She told me she'd called Rubin's house to congratulate him on the movie. "Some woman answered the phone."

I told her the story; boy, was she shocked. "Oh, that's his wife," I said.

"His *wife?* What the hell are you talking about? *You're* supposed to be his wife."

"That's what I thought, too. I called him and asked if it was true."

"What did he tell you? Did he say yes?"

"Actually, he didn't answer the question. He said something about he'd married his angel, though."

"What, is he drinking again?"

"Who knows?"

"You know, Opera believes in angels."

"No, I didn't know that. Now I understand his presence on Oprah's show."

My friend Irene called and told me the news reporters had said he was with some woman at the premiere, they were calling his wife. The newspeople were calling her his wife. And he said yes. How's that? He's been telling you, all of us, he was going to marry you, for years."

"I know. Did she say she was his wife when she answered?"

"No, she didn't."

"That's strange."

"I can't believe this shit. I don't and can't believe he's married at all, Janetta. I did ask her who I was speaking with, and she said, 'This is Teresa'."

"She didn't add, 'I'm his wife'?"

"Nope. You'd think she would, huh?"

"Yeah, as a newlywed. I'm convinced he's not married, Elaine."

"I bet you're right. They do that publicity shit in Hollywood, you know, for images." After she said that I became more and more convinced he wasn't married at all.

WHEN THE MOVIE HIT THE THEATERS in January 2000, I chose purposely not to watch it. The story had been embedded in my head for too long, and I'd been nothing but a shadow at his side.

I didn't, in any case, want to speak or see Rubin Carter—he'd taken twenty-five years of my life and wasted them on broken promises. He may have been my soul mate, but I knew we weren't going to spend our lives together any more. What the hell? I kept the relationship with Lee going for a few years before I let him go.

Our family's destinies or interventions (and not blood-related) were really the only reason my great-aunt had met his uncle. It truly was always about us, Rubin and me, what God had planned for our destiny as soul mates. Neither events in our life that we couldn't understand, nor a connection we had no control over, nor sovereignty (free will) had much to do with what had been going on between Rubin and me. We had been brought together to be soul mates. . .and nothing more.

I O

THE CALM AFTER THE STORM

ONE AUTUMN DAY TWO AND a half years later, I was sitting in a park, wearing jeans and a heavy, multi-colored shirt. The leaves shimmered with orange and red under a clear blue sky that the sun was glimmering through. I'd been playing with the buttons on my cell phone when I accidentally dialed Rubin's number. A phone rang as I lifted it to my ear, and heard his message come on. It was the same one it'd always been: *If you got this far, then you know what to do.* It was still his voice, not a woman's, but I immediately hung up when I realized it was him.

That weekend I stopped by Dee's house, another one of my friends. She asked, "Have you heard from Rubin?"

"No, but strange you asked that. A couple of days ago, I was playing around with my cell and accidentally dialed his number."

Dee tilted her head, and her brown-and-blonde-streaked hair swung across her face. "Did you leave a message?"

I frowned. "No. Why would I do that? I'm finished with that man. You know how I am. After I heard his message, I hung up."

"Why'd you do that?" she said. "Call him back."

"No way," I said, swiveling in the kitchen chair toward the three windows that the sun was beaming through. "I don't want to hear from him."

"Have you cried yet?"

"Cried?"

"Yes, over what happened between the two of you."

"Nope. I don't know why I haven't, either."

She grabbed her purse off the cluttered counter and the keys that hung on a hook near the door. "How long has it been since you last spoke to Rubin, Jan?"

"About two years now. I haven't spoken to him since December of 1999. He'd just got back from California."

"Two *years?*"

"Yep. He told me he was married, married to 'his angel.' What do I need to talk to him for?"

We left and got into her car. Dee tried hard for an hour, as we drove over to Passaic, to get me to call him back, but I refused. When we arrived, we grabbed something to eat at a Spanish take-out restaurant there she knew of. We parked across the street from the place, got out, went over and ordered take-out.

We went back to the car, and Dee slid into the driver's seat, smiling as she opened her styrofoam container and began to eat. We sat in that-clean blue Camry with a fresh pine scent. I was holding my cell in my left hand. Suddenly, she snatched it and searched through my numbers until she found Rubin's, and dialed him. As the phone rang, she shoved it against my ear and said, "Leave him a message."

I shook my head back and forth, said, "No," then grabbed it. "If his voice message comes on, I'm hanging up again."

With a mouth full of food she shouted, "*No!* Leave a message."

As soon as I held the phone to my ear, a voice said, "Hello?" It was Rubin.

In shock, I didn't know what to do. ". . .Hi, Rube, how are you?" I said, looking over at her, and whispered, "I'm going to kill you." She smiled and continued eating.

He replied. "I'm fine, and yourself? Who's this, Ruthie?"

I became pissed because he didn't recognize my voice. It hadn't been that long. "No, it's not Ruthie. This is Janet."

Dee placed her hand over her mouth and whispered, "Ruthie," then finished chewing. I nodded with disgust written all over my face.

"Jan? Oh, *Jan*," he said.

I glanced down at my container of food that sat on the floor under my legs, wanting to open it up and start eating, too, especially while it was hot. "Yes, it's me."

"Oh, girl, how have you been? I thought I'd never hear from you again."

"I'm good. How are you doing?" I looked over at Dee and smiled as I said, "Well actually, my cell accidentally dialed your number."

"That was good. Wasn't it? It made you talk to me. I'm great, doing great. . . . It's been a long time, Jan. I haven't heard from you since you cursed me out."

"I didn't curse you out, but I should've. I told you off, you mean." All I could do was smell the wonderful aroma of Spanish chicken and rice that made me feel famished.

"I'm in shock, Jan," he said with a sigh. "I don't know what to say."

"Personally, I didn't think you had the same number."

He laughed. "Surprise, surprise. It's me."

"I'm not going to keep you, Rube. I'm sure you're busy."

"It's sure good to hear from you, Jan. I'd sure. . .like to see you, if you want me to."

"You want to *see* me?" Dee was stuffing her face with food, raised her eyebrows, and smiled the entire time. "For *what?*" I added, taken back.

"I miss you, that's why. And yes, I want to. Call me and let me know if that's possible. Will you?

". . .I might."

"You can come here, or I'll come to you. Hear, Jan? Call me back."

"Okay," I said but had doubts that it would happen. "Aren't you married?"

"Call me, and I'll explain everything."

WEEKS WENT BY. I GREW weak to his offer and gave into my heart, which led me back to Rubin Carter. I agreed to meet him in September 2002, in New Jersey. He said he'd come to the States to see me. For a second, I wondered why he hadn't asked me to meet him in Canada, at his house, but I let it go—as usual.

Rubin called and gave me details for his arrival. "Hi, there, my love," he said.

"Hi, Rube," I said as a spark of love lit my heart, making me feel as if I loved him the same, hearing his voice. It was amazing, but I was going to move with caution this time around.

"Jan, I'm going to be in Princeton the weekend of September 13."

"Okay. That's where you want me to meet you?"

"Well, I was hoping you'd say that. I've missed you, Jan, believe it or not."

"Really."

"Yes. Really." He replied.

"Before I agree to do that, I need for you to be honest with me about something, Rube. Tell me the truth—are you married?"

"No! No, I'm not married. I'm not married to anyone but myself."

"What? You're not?" I said. "You're really not married, Rubin?"

"No, my love, I'm not."

"You're *sure?*" I said, carefully listening to his voice.

"I'm not married. Nor do I live with a woman."

"Alright." There were many other questions I wanted to ask, but I figured I'd wait until we were face to face.

He said, "I can't wait to see you, girl. Are you still working out?"

"Yep, I sure am."

"This is nice."

"What's nice?"

"I'm going to see my baby. It's been a long time."

"It sure has. Two years, to be exact, Rube."

He was surprised. "It's been that long, Jan?"

"Yep, it has," I said, and retained my reservations about him.

He said sincerely, and even appeared to have come back down to Earth, "Well, it's time."

A FEW WEEKS LATER, ONE FRIDAY evening, my phone rang shortly after I'd come in from work. "Hey, Jan, I'm here in Princeton." It was Rubin.

"Good, I just walked in the door from work. I'll head down when the traffic dies some. I should get there around eight. Is that alright?"

"That'll be perfect. You're going to stay the entire weekend with me, right?"

"Yes, I planned on it." I was excited about seeing him, too, but nervous. I'd wanted to be honest and tell him I had begun writing a story about our long off-and-on relationship of twenty-five-years.

"You're going to be moving around with me to all the weekend activities," he said.

I panicked. "There are *activities?*" I knew I had to find dress clothes.

"Saturday there's a picnic and a function on Sunday. We're going to church Sunday."

"Church? You're going to church on Sunday with *me?*"

"Yeah, that'll be fine. Won't it?" He laughed. "It's going to be good, baby. I love you, girl."

I wasn't sure weather to respond to that or not, but did anyway. ". . .I love you, too, Rube." After I said it, I wasn't sure if I should've.

I scurried around, packing and freshened up before leaving. I was familiar with the Princeton area, because I'd traveled there for job training courses.

I left when planned, and when I neared the Hyatt Regency Hotel, I called Rubin from my cell. "Hey, there, Rube. I'm getting ready to pull into the parking lot."

"You *are?*" he shouted. "My baby is here! Can't wait to see you, girl."

I focused on a few oncoming cars as I made the turn. "What's your room number?"

"Pull up to the entrance. I'll meet you down in the front. We'll park the car together. I'll be right down."

"Okay." I hung up. For some strange reason, I'd begun to sweat even with the air conditioner on—and not because it was hot and muggy out that September night. The sky was clear; I was wearing a short sky-blue skirt with a white blouse, because I knew Rubin loved me in clothes like that.

When I pulled up to the entrance, Hurricane wasn't there yet. I quickly freshened up, but when I turned towards the door—there he was. He didn't recognize me at first, and stood until I rolled the window down and said, "Rube."

He did a double-take and bent down to see who'd been calling his name. "Jan?"

"Yes. It's me." He approached the car, looked in again before he opened the door, and stood staring at me for several seconds in a pinkish twill suit jacket, then hopped in with a wide grin on his face.

He studied me up and down before closing the door. "Look at you."

All I could do was smile back, blush, and say, "What?"

"You look good, Jan."

I replied. "So do you, Rube." He was an expert charmer.

He closed the door and said, "Not as good as you look. You brought yourself a new car."

"Yeah, didn't want to, but I was forced. The other one died on me."

"That's why I didn't recognize you."

I slid the automatic shift into drive. "I know," I said, pulling into a large parking area full of cars with no spaces in sight.

He adjusted his jacket. We both scooted around. "We'll find a spot. It's full over here," he said. "Drive towards the back, my love."

I pulled around to the rear of the lot. "There's one," he said, pointing to my left. I parked and unlocked the doors. Rubin opened his, reached to the back, and snatched my overnight bag from the back seat. We strolled slowly towards the main entrance.

He stepped behind me. "Wow, girl, you look damn good in that skirt."

I spun around. "Thanks, Rube."

He moved to my side once again and reached out. "I touched you, now," he said. "What are you going to do?"

"Nothing. What did you think I would do, Rube?"

"You didn't want me to touch you at all. I can tell." We both broke out laughing.

"I didn't say you couldn't touch me."

He said with a devilish grin, "No, you didn't, but your body language sure did."

We reached the main entrance, entered, and headed directly for the elevator doors. When we reached the floor, we walked arm in arm down the corridor toward the room. Rubin said, "Here we are again, Jan."

I looked up at him. "Yep, here we are again." I said. We kissed and marched leisurely along.

After we settled in the room, John Artis, along with some people from Mohammad Ali's circle, came to Hurricane's room. Everyone was scattered throughout the room, talking about people and topics I had no association with, for about an hour. I stayed seated on the edge of the bed near the wall, listening and smiling on the entire time. Finally, they left, and only Artis remained behind for another fifteen minutes.

It was the beginning of a non-stop weekend. I moved over to the right side of the bed. John and Rubin sat on opposites sides of the table near the window.

SATURDAY MORNING, WE AWOKE EARLY to go to the picnic being held by the Centurion Ministries organization. The organization was honoring men and women from all over the country who had been released after having been wrongly imprisoned.

We lay in bed with our legs entwined. ". . .Rube?" I said, feeling panicky inside.

He tilted his head toward me. "Yes, my love?"

"Do you remember me telling you once how I've always wanted to write a book since high school. That I'd love to write one day, like you?"

Wrinkles began to form and then appeared across his forehead. "Uh-huh," he said. I fidgeted around next to him. "Well, I have something to tell you."

His eyes opened wide. "You do? What could that be?"

I looked him straight on. "I'm writing a book about our relationship."

He calmly said, "No one writes books about me but me," and reached over for his pack of cigarettes on the end table next to the bed.

I wanted to die when he said that, although I didn't think he was upset. I moved in closer. "Actually, the book's *my* story. You just happen to be *in* it. You know, you've played a large part in my life. Not just that, but you've occupied it, Rube. You know what I'm saying."

He propped himself up. "Oh," he said, and lit the cigarette.

"I already have an editor who line-edits as I go along."

He sat back against the headboard. "You do?" he said, surprised. "I want to see it first. Make a copy and send it to me."

I leaned up on my elbow. "Why would you want to see it? I'm not finished yet."

"I want to see it in case you put stuff in there that needs to be taken out."

"Taken out? Oh, alright, I'll do that." But I thought, *I'm not sending him a copy; he'll try to discourage me.* He thinks I don't know what he wants to do. "I'll mail you a copy," I said.

He seemed calm. "Good. Make sure you do that." He laid the cigarette in the ashtray. "We have to get up now and start getting ready, Jan."

It was hot that September, and heavy sweaters or jackets weren't required. We showered and dressed casually. Artis called to tell Rubin where to meet him at downstairs. We hurried with what we had to do, and got down to the lobby and out to John in his silver CRV.

When we reached the park, he had to park in a lot that was a distance from the entrance to the tents of the celebration ceremonies. As we strolled over, Rubin reminisced with John about the first time we'd all met in 1976. John remembered seeing me in Valisburg, Newark. We

approached the check-in point and all signed in, spending the day surrounded with people who continually asked "The Hurricane" for pictures
and autographs, and questions about his life.

Sunday we attended a 9:15 church service at the Nassau Presbyterian
in Princeton, where the director of the ministries attended each Sunday.
That afternoon, we parted, and I knew I was never going to see him again
after that weekend and day.

Our final knockout, a month later, was on a brutally cold and windy
Friday in Manhattan, after a major Nor'easter in January of 2003. I'd
met Rubin at La Guardia Airport before noon that day. It was a rushed
day for me because I hadn't planned well and had been messing around
with washing clothes all morning. Not realizing, I'd placed some pieces
in a broken dryer that I wanted to take with me. I tried but couldn't get
them to dry before leaving. So, rushed—leaving later than I was supposed to—I folded them and placed the damp clothes in the back seat
of the car. I rushed out to La Guardia, crossed the Tri-Borough Bridge,
and called Rubin, letting him know I was running late but was in New
York close by. When I reached the airport and Air Canada, he was standing outside in the cold, wearing a long tan wool coat, smoking a cigarette.

I pulled up and rolled down the window. "I'm sorry for being late,
Rube. I was doing the wash and had a problem with a drier that had no
heat. The stuff on the back seat is still damp."

He glanced back. "That's okay, baby."

"I hope you weren't waiting long outside. It's cold out there?"

"No, baby, I wasn't out there long. Matter of fact, I had just walked
out before you pulled out."

He put his bag in the back, next to the clothes, and hopped in the
front seat. We drove into Manhattan, to the Mark on Madison and Sev-
enty-seventh. I pulled up in front of the hotel; the doorman, dressed in
a dark-gray uniform and hat, quickly approached, opened the back door,
and removed our bags from the back seat. Embarrassed about having
the damp clothes lying in the back, I jumped out and snatched them up
before he could reach them, and glanced at Rubin to see his reaction.
The doorman handed Rubin the parking stub as I approached the curb.

Rubin asked, "Where do you park the cars?"

"In the lot around the corner."

"Okay."

The doorman hopped in the car and went to park it. Snow was high and everywhere. Rubin grabbed hold of me as wind and snow whirled around the building, smacking us. It was hitting me in the head, giving my brain freezer burn.

We entered the hotel, and walked up to the front desk, which was tucked in a corner down to our left of the door. I noted the traditional English style each step of the way, elegant and restrained. A snobby old white couple passed with a look of wonderment, especially with me carrying those damp clothes. I became even more embarrassed. I knew I should have just left them home, but they were heavy sweaters I needed to wear. When Rubin was done at the desk, we went directly to the small elevator, which we shared with two other people who got off before us.

When we entered the room, it was smaller than he was accustomed to. He did his traditional inspection of it and decided it was fine, though. We put everything down. I'd carried my laptop and speakers of course, for music while we were stuck there for the next five days because of the weather. Rubin was leaving the following Tuesday, but we'd have the chance to spend Saturday and Sunday together, alone.

Saturday was another brutally cold day, so we hung around in the room without much of a view in that place. I could look out the window and see other high-rise buildings, and if I got up close, I'd see cars passing in the street down below or the doormen parking cars. We spent the day talking. I sat at the rectangular table, mostly on the laptop, watching Rubin walk from the bathroom to the bed.

I turned around in the chair to face him. "Rube, what happened with us? We should've been married by now."

"I know, Jan." He stopped, looked at me, and said, "We'll definitely do that. If there's anyone I would marry, Jan, it would be you."

Why would he say that? What a strange remark, I thought. I wondered about that statement, *If there's anyone I'd marry, it would be you.* "When will that happen, Rubin? You've been telling me that for years." I reached over, shoved another CD into the player, and turned the volume down some to give us a little ambiance.

"We can do that, but I still have to get divorced from Lisa."

I looked at him in surprise. "I thought that had been taken care of by now." He rose from the bed. "You still have to get divorced? I thought you said you weren't married."

"I haven't married *again*. I'm still married to that woman."

"*What* woman, Rube?" I watched him closely now.

"Lisa," he said, moving near the television, to grab the remote. He plopped back down on the bed near me in a thick long white terricloth robe, picked up the remote, and surfed channels.

I had thought he'd divorced her by now. Two years had gone by; why hadn't he done that? Or was he lying to me again? "Oh," I said. How many times had I heard that come from his mouth before? Don't tell me he was taking me there again, I thought.

"So, Rube, will you buy me that ring I wanted?"

"Yes. Matter a fact, I'm going to Europe next month for awhile, and while I'm there I'll pick it up."

I smiled. "You're serious, Rube?"

"Yes."

"You promise this time? Don't play with my emotions, Rubin."

He gazed over at me. "I'll do that, my love. I promise you."

He sounded sincere. I turned back and began to draw the design of the ring on a sheet of hotel-pad paper—a non-traditional, 18-caret, size 8 ring with an emerald stone surrounded by diamonds. I got up and handed him a sheet of paper. "Here, Rube, this is what I want."

He looked it over. "Okay, I'm putting this right here in my wallet." He picked it up off the table and slipped the sheet in.

I scooted back and played another game of spider solitaire on the laptop. "Remember, Rube, I'm allergic to 14-caret and have to have 18-caret. I wrote that on the paper." Was he back on track with the promise? I couldn't tell. Distance still existed between us and was an issue, even though we'd been together twice since Princeton and had talked to each other as we used to.

"Okay," he said, eyes fixed on the television.

Sunday evening, Rubin waited until the sun went down, amid whirling winds and with temperatures that dropped down in the single digits, to go out. "Jan, do you want to take a ride up to Harlem? I'm looking for some special videos I was told I could find there."

"You want to go walking around in Harlem at this time? The stores are going to close in about an hour."

"Yeah, we won't be out long."

"Okay." I got up and dressed in layers even though I knew we'd be in the car most of the time.

It was brutally cold, the wind gusts outrageous. The doorman brought the car around. We literally ran in and out of stores, looking for the tapes, to no avail; he wasn't lucky and ended up empty-handed, so we hurried back to the hotel.

Monday afternoon we were supposed to have had a brunch with his attorneys and their wives, but I had developed flu symptoms from going out to Harlem on Sunday. "I'm sorry, I can't make it, Rubin. I'm feeling quite sick. I was looking forward to going to brunch with you today. It came on me out of nowhere. I have a fever, too. I rarely get sick. It must be from going out last night, walking around in the cold," I concluded, hugged up under the blankets with a long white velour robe on.

"That's fine, baby. Besides, you don't look too good. Jan, I'm going to have to go to Beldock's office afterward for a meeting."

"I thought it was just brunch."

"Yes, it is, but we were planning on going to his office afterwards. We have to go over my case."

"What case?" I said as I shivered under the blankets.

"This woman is suing me for promises she says I made to her years ago when I was in prison. She's like all the other woman I know."

I turned in his direction. "You're being sued by a *lot* of different women?" I asked.

"Mae Thelma—she too just took a large amount of money from me because of this paper I signed when I was in prison."

"Oh." Everybody was taking his money, everybody but me. Doesn't he see that? I thought.

While Rubin was out, I lay in the bed with a fever, feeling and looking like crap. I had to call my job and notify them I'd be out sick a few days, too. The mini-trip with him worked out to my benefit. I'd actually gotten sick and could call in and not have to take both days as vacation or personal ones. I felt hungry and called room service for breakfast.

Rubin surprised me and returned earlier than I had expected that day. When he came through the door, I had been on my cell phone with a colleague. The cart from breakfast was still in the room, up against the wall near the door. He was probably standing at the door, listening to my conversation. He saw the cart, me on the phone, and he gave me the strangest look. I hurried my colleague off and hung up. From that point on, I'd noticed a difference in him—and the man I'd pulled myself away from for the past two years emerged again. For the rest of that day we were distant and hardly spoke, but then I hadn't felt well to begin with.

Before the five days were up, his arrogance slowly resurfaced, and the bullshit floated to the top. I'd caught on quickly this time. Tuesday morning we gathered our belongings and packed to leave. Around 11:30 AM, Rubin grinned and asked. "Are you ready, Jan?"

I lifted my laptop from the chair but felt weak, though not as feverish as the day before either. "Yep, I'm ready to go."

"Let's do it." He picked up our bags. I just carried the laptop and moved slowly.

We left the room and went down to the lobby, so Rubin could check out. Before he went up to the desk, he handed the bellman near the door the parking ticket. "Sit down over there on the bench while I check out, Jan."

I plopped down on the cushioned bench near the front entrance and waited. Rubin returned, sat next to me, and both of us sat silently, waiting for the car.

Hurricane sat in the passenger's seat with a pleasant look on his face as I drove him back to the La Guardia. We rolled up to the airport; I pulled over to the drop-off area and parked. The airport traffic was light because it was a weekday. "Sorry I got sick on you, Rube," I said as I pushed the button and popped the trunk open.

"That's alright, baby. At least we had a chance to spend five beautiful days together." He opened the door and put on his coat . The cold air slammed inside.

I said weakly, "Yeah, but it could've been better."

He smiled. "I had a chance to rest up. You know, the best way I do that is when I'm around you."

"Uh-hm," I said, reaching to the backseat to grab my jacket. We both got out and moved to the rear of the car. I lifted the trunk, and Rubin snatched his bag, then kissed me on the cheek and hugged me tightly.

"I have that piece of paper for your ring right here in my wallet," he said, patting it.

"Alright. I'd better get back in the car."

He kissed me again. "Bye, my love. I'll be talking to you when I get in. Take care of yourself."

"I will," I said, scurrying back out of the cold. I took my coat off, laid it on the passenger's seat, and glanced out at Rubin, who was standing near the entrance lighting a cigarette, smiling to himself. I wondered for a moment if he was stalling, pretending he was having a smoke but actually waiting on someone. I beeped the horn, waved, and drove away.

AFTER THAT TRIP WE SPOKE frequently for the rest of that month. Then Rubin flipped, slipping back to his old habits—not returning calls and seeming vague and mysterious. I had had enough of him and the way he had treated me after my lifetime relationship with him. I didn't deserve what he had dished out to me at all. The last time I called to talk with him, he didn't answer. I left a message, but he never called back.

I realized finally I didn't want to deal with his nonsense any longer; I called back for the last time and left Hurricane a voice message: *Hi, Rube. Listen, I've been calling you for days as usual, but you've refused to return my calls. I'm sick and tired of the way you're treating me. Not just that but all the lies you keep telling me, too. Hope you have a nice life.*

We never spoke again.

My lifetime devotion to Rubin Carter gave me much insight. One important lesson I learned from all of it was not to ever trust or believe in him again, and I didn't, nor did I ever want to live in his shadow again.

www.ingramcontent.com/pod-product-compliance
Lightning Source LLC
Chambersburg PA
CBHW022120080426
42734CB00006B/193